REVISION WORKBOOK

Family Law

Second Edition

CONSULTANT EDITOR: LORD TEMPLEMAN
EDITOR: MALCOLM DODDS
BA, LLM, Barrister,
Area Director of Legal Services, North Kent Magistrates' Court

OLD BAILEY PRESS

OLD BAILEY PRESS
200 Greyhound Road, London W14 9RY

First published 1997
Second edition 1999
Reprinted 2000
Reprinted 2001

ISBN 1 85836 343 8

British Library Cataloguing-in-Publication.

A CIP Catalogue record for this book is available from the British Library.

Printed and bound in Great Britain.

Contents

Acknowledgement

Some questions used are taken or adapted from past University of London LLB (External) Degree examination papers and our thanks are extended to the University of London for their kind permission to use and publish the questions.

Caveat

The LLB answers given are not approved or sanctioned by the University of London and are entirely our responsibility.

They are not intended as 'Model Answers', but rather as Suggested Solutions.

The answers have two fundamental purposes, namely:

a) To provide a detailed example of a suggested solution to an examination question, and

b) To assist students with their research into the subject and to further their understanding and appreciation of the subject of Law.

Introduction

This Revision WorkBook is aimed to be of help to those studying family law. Its coverage is not restricted to any one syllabus but embraces all the core topics which can be found in university and college examinations.

Students will hopefully find it useful not only at examination time but also as a helpful summary of and introduction to the subject when studying it for the first time.

The WorkBook has been designed specifically to address common problems suffered by students when studying any legal subject. All examination based courses consist of four main processes, all of which may cause problems for some students. The WorkBook can be of help with each of these processes.

a) *Acquisition of knowledge*

This is achieved by individual work – attending lectures and reading the relevant textbooks and source materials such as cases and articles. The WorkBook is not intended to be a textbook and is in no way a substitute for one. However, the 'key points' and 'recent cases and statutes' sections will help students to direct their study to the important areas within each topic.

b) *Understanding*

Whilst difficulties in understanding a topic or particular point are best solved by a teacher's explanation, the WorkBook offers a summary of the essential points together with cases. This is the key to understanding for many students.

c) *Learning*

The process of learning is also a highly individual one. As a rule, however, students find it much easier to learn within a clear structure. The WorkBook will be an aid to those who find learning a problem.

d) *Applying the knowledge to the question*

This is, perhaps, the most common problem of all. The WorkBook includes examination questions and answers covering possible question variations within each topic. All such suggested solutions are of a length which a student could reasonably be expected to produce under the time restraints of an examination.

The final chapter contains the complete June 1997 University of London LLB (External) Family Law question paper, followed by suggested solutions to each question. The student has the opportunity to review a recent examination paper in its entirety, and can, if desired, use this chapter as a mock examination – referring to the suggested solutions only after first attempting the questions.

How to Study Family Law

The importance of statute

While family law is a heavy case law subject all the major areas are covered by legislation; eg the Matrimonial Causes Act 1973 covers the whole of the basic law on divorce, nullity and ancillary relief, three major examination areas. Accordingly students must be able to paraphrase (examiners would not expect precise repetition) the major provisions of the statutes as highlighted in this book.

The use of cases

The doctrine of precedent is not applicable to family law – per Ormrod LJ in *Sharpe* v *Sharpe* (1981) 11 Fam Law 121. While, therefore, you will come across a large number of cases these should be used to illustrate how the judiciary approach Family Law matters and how, by analogy, the problem in any particular question can be resolved both in practice and in the resolution of academic problems. When writing an answer to a problem question, it is seldom necessary to refer to large numbers of cases nor to refer to the facts of cases in any depth. The cases should be used to show principles upon which the particular problem will be resolved.

Approach to the examination

It is artificial in family law to advise a wife, for example, that she can divorce and not then go on to consider the implications of the divorce as regards maintenance, property adjustment and children. It is increasingly common for examiners to require the student to demonstrate a wide general knowledge of family law. The University of London LLB (external) examiners do this by asking questions which include up to three discrete areas whereas other examiners sometimes set a compulsory question that can include almost any of the areas studied. In short, it is dangerous to question spot in the sense of choosing to revise a limited number of topics. Whilst minor topics (eg jurisdiction and guardianship) may be superficially dealt with you must know in depth the major overlap areas, ie the law relating to divorce, ancillary relief, ouster orders and disputes concerning children.

Dealing with essay questions

Examiners favour problem questions. Consequently there will rarely be more than three essay questions on an examination paper.

No essay question will be asking you to write everything you know about a particular topic even though that tends to be the common approach of students to such questions. The examiner will be seeking to see whether you are able to adapt your general knowledge of the area in question to a particular slant. The skill, therefore, is to identify the particular slant of the question and ensure that each paragraph you write is relevant to that slant. If you do this you will achieve high marks whereas if you simply write everything you know, you will achieve no more than a bare pass.

Because family law is a topical subject it is quite likely that essay questions will require comment on current proposals for reform or current issues eg the debate surrounding surrogacy.

Dealing with problem questions

Problem questions are often lengthy. Whatever the length, it is important to read the issues you are being asked to advise on at the end of the question before reading the facts. In this way you are more likely to identify the relevance of the facts. Be clear who you are asked to advise, be concise and relevant, support your answer with evidence and if you are asked to advise X be sure that you do.

Revision and Examination Technique

(A) REVISION TECHNIQUE

Planning a revision timetable

In planning your revision timetable make sure you don't finish the syllabus too early. You should avoid leaving revision so late that you have to 'cram' – but constant revision of the same topic leads to stagnation.

Plan ahead, however, and try to make your plans increasingly detailed as you approach the examination date.

Allocate enough time for each topic to be studied. But note that it is better to devise a realistic timetable, to which you have a reasonable chance of keeping, rather than a wildly optimistic schedule which you will probably abandon at the first opportunity!

The syllabus and its topics

One of your first tasks when you began your course was to ensure that you thoroughly understood your **syllabus**. Check now to see if you can write down the **topics** it comprises from memory. You will see that the chapters of this WorkBook are each devoted to a topic. This will help you decide which are the key chapters relative to your revision programme. Though you should allow some time for glancing through the other chapters.

The topic and its key points

Again working from memory, analyse what you consider to be the key points of any topic that you have selected for particular revision. Seeing what you can recall, unaided, will help you to understand and firmly memorise the concepts involved.

Using the WorkBook

Relevant questions are provided for each topic in this book. Naturally, as typical examples of examination questions, they do not normally relate to one topic only. But the questions in each chapter *will* relate to the subject matter of the chapter to a degree. You can choose your method of consulting the questions and solutions, but here are some suggestions (strategies 1–3). Each of them pre-supposes that you have read through the notes on key points and question analysis, and any other preliminary matter, at the beginning of the chapter. Once again, you now need to practise working from *memory*, for that is the challenge you are preparing yourself for. As a rule of procedure constantly test yourself once revision starts, both orally and in writing.

Strategy 1

Strategy 1 is planned for the purpose of *quick revision*. First read your chosen question carefully and then jot down in abbreviated notes what you consider to be the main points at issue. Similarly, note the cases and statutes that occur to you as being relevant for citation purposes. Allow yourself sufficient time to cover what you feel to be relevant. Then study the *skeleton solution* and skim-read the *suggested solution* to see how they compare with your notes. When comparing consider carefully what the author has included (and concluded) and see whether that agrees with what you have written. Consider the points of variation also. Have you recognised the key issues? How relevant have you been? It is possible, of course, that you have referred to a recent case that *is* relevant, but which had not been reported when the WorkBook was prepared.

Strategy 2

Strategy 2 requires a nucleus of *three hours* in which to practise writing a set of examination answers in a limited time-span.

Select a number of questions (as many as are normally set in the examination you are studying for), each from a different chapter in the WorkBook, without consulting the solutions. Find a place to write where you will not be disturbed and try to arrange not to be interrupted for three hours. Write your solutions in the time allowed, noting any time needed to make up if you *are* interrupted.

After a rest, compare your answers with the *suggested solutions* in the WorkBook. There will be considerable variation in style, of course, but the bare facts should not be too dissimilar. Evaluate your answer critically. Be 'searching', but develop a positive approach to deciding how you would tackle each question on another occasion.

Strategy 3

You are unlikely to be able to do more than one three hour examination, but occasionally set yourself a single question. Vary the 'time allowed' by imagining it to be one of the questions that you must answer in three hours and allow yourself a limited preparation and writing time. Try one question that you feel to be difficult and an easier question on another occasion, for example.

Mis-use of suggested solutions

Don't try to learn by rote. In particular, don't try to reproduce the *suggested solutions* by heart. Learn to express the basic concepts in your own words.

Keeping up-to-date

Keep up-to-date. While examiners do not require familiarity with changes in the law during the three months prior to the examination, it obviously creates a good impression if you show that you know about recent changes. Try to check the cumulative indices to law reports, such as the *All England Law Reports* or *Weekly Law Reports* or *Family Law Reports* or the daily reports in *The Times*. Another helpful source is the specialist journal, eg *Family Law*.

(B) EXAMINATION SKILLS

Examiners are human too!

The process of answering an examination question involves a *communication* between you and the person who set it. If you were speaking face to face with the person, you would choose your verbal points and arguments carefully in your reply. When writing, it is all too easy to forget *the human being who is awaiting the reply* and simply write out what one knows in the area of the subject! Bear in mind it is a person whose question you are responding to, throughout your essay. This will help you to avoid being irrelevant or long-winded.

The essay question

Candidates are sometimes tempted to choose to answer essay questions because they 'seem' easier. But the examiner is looking for thoughtful work and will not give good marks for superficial answers.

The essay-type of question may be either purely factual, in asking you to *explain the meaning* of a certain doctrine or principle, or it may ask you to *discuss* a certain proposition, usually derived from a quotation. In either case, the approach to the answer is the same. A clear programme must be devised to give the examiner the meaning or significance of the doctrine, principle or proposition and its origin in common law, equity or statute, and cases which illustrate its application to the branch of law concerned.

The problem question

The problem-type question requires a different approach. You may well be asked to advise a client or merely discuss the problems raised in the question. In either case, the most important factor is to take great care in reading the question. By its nature, the question will be longer than the essay-type question and you will have a number of facts to digest. Time spent in analysing the question may well save time later, when you are endeavouring to impress on the examiner the considerable extent of your basic legal knowledge. The quantity of knowledge is itself a trap and you must always keep within the boundaries of the question in hand. It is very tempting to show the examiner the extent of your knowledge of your subject, but if this is outside the question, it is time lost and no marks earned. It is inevitable that some areas which you have studied and revised will not be the subject of questions, but under no circumstances attempt to adapt a question to a stronger area of knowledge at the expense of relevance.

When you are satisfied that you have grasped the full significance of the problem-type question, set out the fundamental principles involved. You may well be asked to advise one party, but there is no reason why you should not introduce your answer by:

'I would advise A on the following matters ...'

and then continue the answer in a normal impersonal form. This is a much better technique than answering the question as an imaginary conversation.

You will then go on to identify the fundamental problem, or problems posed by the question. This should be followed by a consideration of the law which is relevant to the problem. The source of the law, together with the cases which will be of assistance in solving the problem, must then be considered in detail.

Very good problem questions are quite likely to have alternative answers, and in advising A you should be aware that alternative arguments may be available. Each stage of your answer, in this case, will be based on the argument or arguments considered in the previous stage, forming a conditional sequence.

If, however, you only identify one fundamental problem, do not waste time worrying that you cannot think of an alternative – there may very well be only that one answer.

The examiner will then wish to see how you use your legal knowledge to formulate a case and how you apply that formula to the problem which is the subject of the question. It is this positive approach which can make answering a problem question a high mark earner for the student who has fully understood the question and clearly argued his case on the established law.

Examination checklist

1   Read the instructions at the head of the examination carefully. While last-minute changes are unlikely – such as the introduction of a *compulsory question* or *an increase in the number of questions asked* – it has been known to happen.

2   Read the questions carefully. Analyse problem questions – work out what the examiner wants.

3   Plan your answer *before* you start to write. You can divide your time as follows:

   (a) working out the question (5 per cent of time)

   (b) working out how to answer the question (5 to 10 per cent of time)

   (c) writing your answer

   Do not overlook (a) and (b)

4   Check that you understand the rubric *before* you start to write. Do not 'discuss', for example, if you are specifically asked to 'compare and contrast'.

5   Answer the correct number of questions. If you fail to answer one out of four questions set you lose 25 per cent of your marks!

Style and structure

Try to be clear and concise. Basically this amounts to using paragraphs to denote the sections of your essay, and writing simple, straightforward sentences as much as possible. The sentence you have just read has 22 words – when a sentence reaches 50 words it becomes difficult for a reader to follow.

Do not be inhibited by the word 'structure' (traditionally defined as giving an essay a beginning, a middle and an end). A good structure will be the natural consequence of setting out your arguments and the supporting evidence in a logical order. Set the scene briefly in your opening paragraph. Provide a clear conclusion in your final paragraph.

Table of Cases

Table of Statutes

1   Family Law and Society

As society changes so too the law must change to reflect prevailing social norms, and this is particularly the case in the study of the law that relates to the social group defined as the family. The history of family law reflects changes that have occurred in society's attitude towards divorce, to the significant changes that have occurred in the status of women, to the recognition of the separate status of children and to the acknowledgement that the state has a role to play in protecting members of a family who are 'at risk', in the sense that they are the victims of sexual abuse or violent attack.

Since the mid-1850s social reform in both public and private law which has had an impact on the regulation of family life has gained momentum. In private law, the establishment of a coherent secular divorce law, together with the development of the separate legal status of the wife within marriage, has now reached a point where a divorce petition is based on the 'irretrievable breakdown' of the marriage and husbands and wives enjoy equal rights and obligations within marriage. In public law, legislation which started by regulating child employment and introduced compulsory education has now reached a point at which the state can remove children from a family if it is established that they are 'at risk' through physical and sexual abuse.

Social change has been significant during the last 25 years. The changing role of women, a massive increase in reported child abuse, the very rapid increase in the divorce rate and the large numbers of couples who choose to cohabit rather than marry are social phenomena which have posed and continue to pose problems for family law. Accordingly, there have been a number of reforms during that period - for example reforms which seek to give protection to the battered wife, and others which seek to remove the stigma associated with illegitimacy. The Children Act 1989 is a comprehensive measure which has introduced radical changes in both public and private law.

At the time of this latest revision Parts I (principles underlying reform of divorce law) and IV (occupation of the family home and domestic violence) of the Family Law Act 1996 had been brought into force. Parts II and III (the reform of the law on divorce and separation) had not been brought into force. As a result questions on divorce and separation have been dealt with according to the current law and not as stated in Parts II and III of the Family Law Act 1996.

It can be argued that welfare, housing, taxation and education law relate to the family. For examination purposes family law focuses on the more traditional questions of marriage and how to resolve family disputes about property or children.

1

2 Nullity of Marriage

2.1 Introduction

2.2 Key points

2.3 Recent cases

2.4 Analysis of questions

2.5 Questions

2.1 Introduction

A marriage may be terminated in two ways: either a petition for divorce or a petition for nullity. Insofar as there are nearly 160,000 divorce decrees and only 1,000 nullity decrees each year the practical importance of the law relating to nullity of marriage is put into its proper perspective. A person would only seek a decree of nullity if he or she was not willing to petition for divorce (eg because of religious objection to divorce). However, despite its relative lack of practical importance it remains a regular examination topic.

2.2 Key points

a) *The difference between a void and voidable marriage*

Section 11 of the Matrimonial Causes Act 1973 lists grounds of nullity which make the marriage void; s12 those that make the marriage voidable only. The s11 grounds result in such a fundamentally flawed marriage that the law considers there to have been no marriage at all – technically a party to a void marriage can go ahead and contract another marriage without having the first marriage declared void by a court.

The s12 grounds are of less fundamental effect and the law recognises a marriage which is affected by one of the s12 grounds as valid until such time as one party petitions the court that it should be deemed void. However, a party to such a potentially void marriage cannot delay too long. Section 13 of the Matrimonial Causes Act generally bars an application to make a voidable marriage void unless the application is brought within three years of the date that the applicant knew that he/she could rely on one of the s12 grounds. It should be emphasised that s13 does not apply to s11 at all, nor does it apply to s12(a) or 12(b) – the non-consummation grounds.

b) *The s11 grounds*

i) Failure to comply with Marriages Acts 1949–70

- within prohibited degrees of relationship
- either party under 16

This only applies to a marriage (wherever in the world it is contracted) if at least one of the parties is domiciled in England at the time of the marriage.

Compare *Pugh* v *Pugh* [1951] 2 All ER 680 with *Mohamed* v *Knott* [1968] 2 All ER 563.

2

- failure to comply with the formalities of marriage

  The purpose behind reading the banns is that publicity is given as to who is getting married, therefore the banns must be published in the name one is commonly known by even if that is not one's real name: *Dancer* v *Dancer* [1948] 2 All ER 731.

  Note: The Marriage Act 1994 removed many of the restrictions on where civil marriages could take place. Local authorities can licence various places (eg hotels) to carry out wedding ceremonies. The restrictions on religious marriages remain (eg *Gereis* v *Yagoub* [1997] 1 FLR 854 in which a marriage was void because it took place in an unlicensed church and without due notice having been given).

ii) That at the time of marriage either party was already married – ie bigamous marriages

iii) That the parties are not respectively male and female

  English law only recognises marriages between parties of the opposite sex.

  Difficulties arise if a person changes his or her sex. The leading case in English law is *Corbett* v *Corbett* [1970] 2 All ER 33 which held that a person's sex is fixed at birth and cannot subsequently be changed for the purposes of marriage. This decision has been reaffirmed in *Re P and G (transsexuals)* [1996] 2 FLR 90. The English legal position has been upheld in the European Court of Human Rights in *Rees* v *UK* [1987] Fam Law 157, *Cossey* v *UK* [1991] Fam Law 362, *X, Y and Z* v *UK* [1997] 2 FLR 892 and *Sheffield and Horsham* v *UK* [1998] 2 FLR 928. However, the student must be aware that the law in this area is under review. The European Court is moving towards recognising the rights of transsexuals but is awaiting more of a consensus to emerge.

iv) Actual or potentially polygamous marriages

  A marriage is not polygamous if at its inception neither spouse has any additional spouse (see s11 MCA 1973 as amended by the Private International Law (Miscellaneous Provisions) Act PIL(MP)A 1996).

  As a result s11(d) only applies if a marriage is actually polygamous. If a marriage is potentially polygamous, but neither spouse has an additional spouse, then s11(d) will not make the marriage void. See also s5 PIL(MP)A 1976 which confirms that a marriage entered into outside England and Wales is not void on the ground that it is entered into under a law which permits polygamy and that either party is domiciled in England and Wales (provided neither party is not already married).

c) *The s12 grounds*

i) Non-consummation through incapacity – s12(a)

  Note:

  The degree of consummation necessary: *W* v *W* [1967] 3 All ER 178.

  A petitioner can rely on his own impotency: *Pettit* v *Pettit* [1962] 3 All ER 37.

  Refusal to undergo a simple operation without danger to health which would cure the physical incapacity may amount to wilful refusal under s12(b): *D* v *D* [1979] 3 All ER 337.

ii) Non-consummation through wilful refusal – s12(b)

Note:

The definition of wilful refusal – must be more than a temporary unwillingness due to shyness but rather a fixed and steadfast refusal come to without just excuse: *Horton* v *Horton* [1947] 2 All ER 871.

Therefore there will not be wilful refusal where:

- The marriage was between elderly persons 'for companionship only': *Morgan* v *Morgan* [1959] 1 All ER 539; but probably not companionship marriage between those of child bearing age: see *Brodie* v *Brodie* [1917] P 271.
- The validity of the marriage was dependent as far as the parties were concerned on a religious ceremony which has not taken place: *Jodla* v *Jodla* [1960] 1 All ER 625; *Kaur* v *Singh* [1972] 1 All ER 292; *A* v *J* *(nullity)* [1989] 1 FLR 110.

iii) Lack of consent through duress, mistake, unsoundness of mind or otherwise – s12(c)

- Duress

This is a very popular examination area – look for a scenario where one party is coerced into marrying another.

A useful framework for an answer is provided by the three requirements suggested by Scarman J in *Buckland* v *Buckland* [1967] 2 All ER 300, namely:

– a sufficient degree of fear to vitiate consent;
– that the fear be reasonably entertained;
– that the fear arose from some external factor which the petitioner had not brought upon himself.

'Sufficient degree of fear'

This was usefully defined in *Szechter* v *Szechter* [1970] 3 All ER 905 as requiring a threat to 'life limb or liberty'.

More recently in *Hirani* v *Hirani* (1983) 4 FLR 232 Ormrod LJ adopted the phrase 'such a coercion of the will so as to vitiate consent' to indicate the degree of pressure required.

Examples of such pressure are found in both *Szechter* v *Szechter* and *Buckland* v *Buckland* [1967] 2 All ER 300 namely consenting to marriage to escape unjust imprisonment.

'Fear to be reasonably entertained'

The debate here has been whether the test should be subjective or objective ie is it sufficient that the petitioner was frightened or must it be shown that a reasonable person in her position would have been frightened as well.

Initially the test was purely subjective: *Scott* v *Sebright* (1886) 12 PD 21. However, cases such as *Buckland* v *Buckland* and *Szechter* v *Szechter* strongly favoured an objective approach.

The question of whether the test should be objective or subjective is of great importance in the area of arranged marriages where someone marries out of respect for his/her parents' wishes. If an objective test applies, then such marriages cannot be annulled due to duress. This was so in the case of *Singh* v *Singh* [1971] 2 All ER 828 which followed an objective approach. However, in *Hirani* v *Hirani* the Court of Appeal reverted to the subjective approach and allowed a decree in such an arranged marriage.

After *Hirani* it is generally accepted that the test is now purely subjective: was the petitioner in fact sufficiently frightened so as to give his/her consent to marriage?

'Not brought on himself'

For example if, in *Buckland* v *Buckland*, the petitioner had in fact had sexual relations with the Maltese girl he would not have succeeded.

- Mistake

  It must be a mistake as to the nature of the ceremony not as to its effect.

  Compare *Mehta* v *Mehta* [1945] 2 All ER 690 with *Way* v *Way* [1949] 2 All ER 959 and *Vervaeke* v *Smith* [1982] 2 All ER 144. In *Militante* v *Ojunwomaju* [1993] FCR 355 the distinction made seems difficult to justify.

- Unsoundness of mind

  One does not have to be very sane to understand the nature and effect of marriage: *In the Estate of Park* [1953] 2 All ER 1411.

- Or otherwise

  There have been no cases on this – it probably covers the situation where someone consents to marriage while under the influence of alcohol or drugs.

iv) Mental disorder within meaning of Mental Health Act 1983 – s12(d)

Virtually any mental illness is covered by Act. If you do not understand the nature and effect of marriage you can annul it under s12(c); if you do understand the nature and effect but are incapable of carrying out the normal marital duties because of a mental illness then the marriage may be annulled under s12(d): *Bennett* v *Bennett* [1969] 1 All ER 539

v) Suffering from venereal disease – s12(e)

vi) Pregnancy by another – s12(f)

Section 12(e) and s12(f) only apply if the petitioner was ignorant of the facts at the time of marriage.

The s13 requirement to petition within three years of marriage only applies to s12(c) to s12(f).

d) *The s13 Bar*

Remember this section can only bar s12 petitions; it does not apply to s11 grounds.

One needs to show:

i) Conduct by the petitioner (after he/she became aware that a petition for nullity was available to them) which leads the respondent to believe the marriage will not be annulled eg adopting children: *D* v *D* [1979] 3 All ER 337; and

ii) That it would be unjust to grant the decree.

Note that where the marriage is an empty shell it would seldom be just not to grant the decree: *D* v *D* [1979] 3 All ER 337.

As regards the three year time limit remember this only applies to the grounds in s12(c) to s12(f) and while time generally runs from the date of the marriage this is not so when, during that period, the petitioner has suffered from a mental illness within the meaning of the Mental Health Act 1983.

2.3 Recent cases

Re P and G (transsexuals) [1996] 2 FLR 90

Sheffield and Horsham v *UK* [1998] 2 FLR 928

2.4 Analysis of questions

Problem questions normally concentrate on the voidable grounds contained in s12 of the Matrimonial Causes Act in particular s12(a) and s12(b) – the non-consummation grounds – and/or s12(c) lack of consent due to duress. An answer to a problem question involving the s12 grounds is never complete without the candidate going on to consider whether the action may be barred by reason of the matters in s13. It should also be noted that it is sometimes the case that a nullity problem question is combined with another aspect of family law eg financial/property provision or matrimonial injunctions.

Essay questions fall into two types; either requiring a critical discussion of a particular ground (the most common being s11(c) and the effect thereon of the decision in *Corbett* v *Corbett* [1970] 2 All ER 33 and s12(c) the law relating to lack of consent due to duress) or a more general question requiring the candidate to consider whether or not there is a continuing need for a law of nullity in its existing form ie can it be abolished altogether or should it be modified so that only s11 – the void grounds – are retained? The Family Law Act 1996 will end fault-based divorce and this raises the question whether fault (eg wilful refusal to consummate) should remain as a basis for nullity. At present there are no proposals for any change in the law of nullity.

2.5 Questions

QUESTION ONE

Anthea and Bob, aged 16 and 19 respectively, went through a ceremony of marriage at the head office of the 'Peace and Purity Church'. No formalities were required by the church, which is located on the thirtieth floor of an office block in Manchester. Anthea had not told her parents that she was getting married.

After the ceremony, the couple spent a weekend in a hotel. There were repeated attempts to consummate the marriage, but Bob was nervous because the bed creaked and the hotel walls were thin and he failed to penetrate Anthea for more than two seconds. His confidence was damaged and he has refused to attempt to consummate again until he receives counselling.

Clarissa, Bob's counsellor, advised him to undergo a course of sex therapy with her, during which they fell in love and began a sexual relationship. Anthea, who became suspicious and believed Bob was cured, asked Bob to attempt to consummate the marriage. Bob found he was unable to have intercourse with her and asked her to wait until he has further therapy.

Anthea, who is still in love with Bob, but depressed, wants to know whether the marriage can be annulled.

University of London LLB Examination
(for External Students) Family Law June 1991 Q1

General Comment

This is an unusual question in that it concerns nullity alone and it was thought that this type of question, testing one area of the syllabus only, was a thing of the past. The question raises an issue on formalities with regard to the void grounds of nullity which has not been examined in recent years. However, the remainder of the question relates to non-consummation, a tried and tested examination topic, and so should hold no surprises for the well prepared student.

Skeleton Solution

- Consider void marriages – s11(a) MCA 1973 – failure to comply with formalities. Query whether the civil preliminaries have been complied with; thereafter discuss whether the place of celebration is a 'registered building'.
- Anthea's age must be discussed and following on from that the question of whether her parents' lack of consent would also make the marriage void.
- Deal with the voidable grounds – s12(a) and (b) MCA 1973. Consider if the marriage has been consummated.
- On the basis that it has not, consider incapacity – define and discuss psychological defects. Also consider if the incapacity must be in existence at the time of the celebration of the marriage.
- Next consider wilful refusal to consummate – define and consider whether Bob is in fact refusing to consummate – refer to the attempts to consummate during the honeymoon and subsequently. Query his motives for asking Anthea to delay any further attempt to consummate until he received further therapy.

Suggested Solution

For a marriage celebrated after 31 July 1971 to be annulled, one of the grounds set out in s11 or s12 Matrimonial Causes Act 1973 (hereinafter MCA 1973), which deal with void and voidable marriages respectively, must be made out. A void marriage is deemed never to have existed and any decree is merely declaratory. A voidable marriage is in all respects a valid marriage until a decree of nullity is pronounced.

Under s11(a) MCA 1973 a marriage will be void if the parties have failed to comply with the requirements as to the formation of the marriage. All marriages, other than those conducted in the Church of England, must be preceded by preliminary formalities which are designed to give notice of the intended marriage and therefore to allow objections to be made. The usual procedure, which includes giving notice to the Superintendent Registrar of the registration district(s) where the parties have resided for the previous seven days, and thereafter the notice of the intended marriage being displayed in the Superintendent Registrar's office for 21 days, leads to the issue of the Superintendent Registrar's certificate, which authorises the solemnisation of the marriage within three months from the day when notice was entered in the marriage notice book.

We are told that the church required no formalities to be fulfilled prior to the marriage ceremony. If this means that Anthea and Bob did not fulfil the civil preliminaries required under the Marriage Acts 1949–1986 and therefore that they did not obtain a Superintendent Registrar's certificate or other licence, then the marriage will be void for lack of formality. See *Gereis* v *Yagoub* (1997).

There are two other problems with regard to formalities to be discussed on these facts. The certificate, if obtained, will state where the marriage is to take place. Normally this must be a registered building in the district where one of the parties resides. A registered building must be a 'separate building' which is a 'place of meeting for religious worship' (s41(1) Marriage Act 1949). In *R* v *Registrar-General, ex parte Segerdal* (1970) Lord Denning stated that religious worship involved reverence or veneration of God or a supreme being and that the 'place of meeting' meant a place where people came as a congregation to do reverence to a deity.

Anthea and Bob marry at the church's head office which is sited in an office block. It may be therefore that it is not to be construed as a place of meeting for religious worship and it may not be a registered building under the Marriage Acts. Although it is possible for a marriage to be authorised outside a register office, Anglican church or registered place of worship under a Registrar General's licence, such a licence is only available where there is evidence that one of the persons to be married is seriously ill and is not expected to recover and that he/she cannot be moved to a place where the marriage could be solemnised under the Marriage Act 1949.

This exemption will not apply to Anthea and Bob and therefore if the church's head office is not a registered building under the Marriage Act 1949 the marriage will be void for want of formality on this basis also.

The second problem referred to relates to Anthea's age and the obvious lack of parental consent to her marriage. Being 16 Anthea is of the legal age to get married. However, between the ages of 16 and 18 a party to the marriage requires the consent of his/her parents to the marriage. This defect will not render the marriage void if it was conducted pursuant to a common licence or a Superintendent Registrar's certificate (s48(1) Marriage Act 1949). So if the other problems referred to above do not apply, the lack of parental consent is unlikely to render the marriage void on its own. It seems however that Anthea and Bob's marriage is void for lack of formality in that the civil preliminaries were not complied with, the ceremony took place in a place which is not a designated registered building, and the required parental consent is absent.

Consideration must also be given to whether the marriage is voidable under s12(a) or (b) MCA 1973 on the basis that it has not been consummated, due to either the incapacity of either party to consummate it (s12(a)), or the wilful refusal of the respondent (s12(b)). A marriage is consummated as soon as the parties have sexual intercourse that is 'ordinary and complete and not partial and imperfect' (*D* v *A* (1845)) after the marriage. We are told that Bob was unable to penetrate Anthea for more than two seconds on the occasions that sexual intercourse was attempted on the honeymoon, since which time it has been attempted, unsuccessfully only once it seems. To fulfil the requirements of consummation there must be an erection and penetration for a reasonable length of time (*R* v *R* (1952)), although it is not necessary for either party to have an orgasm. It is submitted therefore that the attempted sexual intercourse on the honeymoon will not amount to consummation.

The next question to consider is whether the non-consummation is due to incapacity on the part of Bob, or his wilful refusal. To satisfy the requirements of the incapacity, it must be shown that Bob's problem is permanent and incurable which has been held to mean not only that it is incapable of remedy, but also that it can be cured only by an operation which is dangerous, or which has little likelihood of success or where the respondent refuses to undergo the treatment (*S* v *S* (1956)). The incapacity does not have to relate to a physical defect; a psychological impotence may also suffice. Further, incapacity can be made out in a situation where the party suffering from the incapacity is capable of having intercourse with other partners but not with his or her spouse (*G* v *M* (1885)); (*G* v *G* (1924)).

It is not clear whether Bob's problem can be classified as permanent and incurable and Anthea would be advised that the courts have shown a willingness to await the outcome of treatment to decide whether the defect complained of should be so viewed (*S* v *S* (1963)).

A further consideration with regard to incapacity relates to the point whether the incapacity must be in existence at the time of the marriage, or whether a supervening incapacity as appears to apply in Bob's case where the problem seemingly arose during the honeymoon, will suffice. It was a requirement of the common law, on which the current law of nullity is based, that the incapacity exist at the time of the celebration of the marriage. The codification of the law was not intended to effect any change. However the wording of the statute makes no reference to the fact that the incapacity must be in existence at the time of the marriage. It may be therefore that a supervening incapacity will suffice, but the point is unclear.

Turning now to wilful refusal to consummate the marriage, this is defined as 'a settled and definite decision ... without just excuse' (*Horton* v *Horton* (1947)), not to consummate. It is submitted that this ground cannot be made out on these facts because Bob has attempted to have sexual intercourse with Anthea on several occasions. Although the last occasion occurred after he had been able to have sexual relations with Clarissa, there is no evidence that when Bob attempted to have intercourse with Anthea he deliberately failed in the attempt. He has asked her to wait until he has further therapy before they attempt to consummate the marriage. Certainly if this is a genuine request on his part then the ground under s12(b) will fail because essentially Bob is prepared to consummate the marriage when his problem is resolved. If however, his request to wait is a ploy to allow him to continue his relationship with Clarissa then it is possible that this ground will now apply as it may be evidence that he has no intention to pursue a married life after all (*Ford* v *Ford* (1987)).

In conclusion it seems that the marriage is void under s11 MCA 1973 for lack of formality in relation to an apparent failure to comply with civil preliminaries and the question whether the church's head office is a registered building where marriages can take place within the law. The lack of consent on the part of Anthea's parents is unlikely to render the marriage void on its own although if the civil preliminaries have not been complied with, this also will be a problem.

With regard to voidable grounds the application of s12(a) and (b) MCA 1973 is questionable on these facts.

QUESTION TWO

Hector, aged 22, and Andromache, aged 27, who are both members of a small religious community, the Trojans, resident in southern England, were married in December 1989. Although they had had a casual sexual relationship prior to their marriage, they did not really wish to marry each other, but did so because it is customary for Trojans to marry and because the community elders threatened to ostracise them socially and financially if they did not marry.

The wedding took place in the customary place of worship of the community and was celebrated by a Trojan prelate. Andromache, however, refuses to have sexual relations with Hector because he has still not arranged the wedding breakfast that all Trojan grooms must provide before the community will consider the wedding ceremony to be complete.

Advise Andromache who would like to bring her marriage to an end, but who has told you that Trojans disapprove of divorce.

University of London LLB Examination
(for External Students) Family Law June 1992 Q4

General Comment

The question requires consideration of the rules relating to termination of marriage by nullity and not by divorce because we are told that Trojans do not approve of divorce.

Skeleton Solution

- Deal with s11 MCA 1973.
- Consider s12(a) and disregard s12(b).
- Next consider s12(c) – lack of consent.
- Bars under s13 MCA 1973.

Suggested Solution

Andromache says that Trojans, the religious community of which she is a part, do not approve of divorce, so we will not advise her on ending her marriage by divorcing Hector. Instead we must decide whether the marriage between Andromache and Hector can be annulled.

For a marriage celebrated after 31 July 1971, annulment can only occur if a ground under s11 or s12 of the Matrimonial Causes Act (MCA) 1973 can be made out. Section 11 deals with void marriages and s12 with voidable marriages.

Under s11(a)(iii) MCA 1973 the marriage may be void on the ground that the parties have intermarried in disregard of the formal requirements.

Because the marriage was not a Church of England marriage, it will not be void on the grounds of non-publication of banns etc but instead it must comply with the requirements laid down by the Marriage Act 1949 for celebration of non-Anglican marriages. It must have been celebrated pursuant to a superintendent registrar's certificate with a licence and in a registered building.

The marriage took place in the customary place of worship of the community and was celebrated by a Trojan prelate. The Marriage Act 1949 states that the marriage must take place at a building registered by the Registrar General as a place of meeting for religious worship and be conducted by a minister of religion concerned, namely a person authorised to carry out marriages, in public and in the presence of two or more witnesses. Therefore, provided that the above requirements have been complied with, the marriage will not be void. And in any event the Marriage Act 1949 specifically enacts that a marriage shall not be rendered void if the registered building in which the parties were married had not been certified as a place of worship.

Next consideration should be given to s12 MCA 1973 which sets out the grounds upon which a marriage may be deemed voidable. Under s12(a) the marriage may be voidable on the ground 'that the marriage has not been consummated owing to the incapacity of either party to consummate it'. Under s12(b) a marriage may be voidable owing to the wilful refusal of the respondent to consummate it. A marriage is consummated as soon as the parties have sexual intercourse that is ordinary and complete (*D* v *A* (1845)) after the marriage.

Andromache and Hector had sexual relations before the marriage but this does not amount to consummation; there must be intercourse after the marriage: *Dredge* v *Dredge* (1947).

Section 12(a) does not appear to be relevant here because it is not due to the incapacity of either party that the marriage has not been consummated but instead due to Andromache's wilful refusal to consummate.

A person may not, however, petition on his/her own refusal to consummate, therefore in this instance Andromache may not rely on this ground in respect of her own refusal to consummate the marriage. However she may be able to argue that Hector has wilfully refused to consummate the marriage.

Wilful refusal connotes 'a settled and definite decision come to without just cause' and the whole history of the marriage may be looked at (per Lord Jowitt LC in *Horton* v *Horton* (1947)).

Following the decision in *Kaur* v *Singh* (1972) Hector's refusal without just excuse to make arrangements for the wedding breakfast could amount to wilful refusal to consummate the marriage.

Alternatively, it may be possible for Andromache to argue that she had not given proper consent to the marriage and it is provided that if either party to the marriage did not validly consent to it in consequence of duress, mistake, unsoundness of mind or otherwise, the marriage will be voidable: s12(c).

In this case there is evidence that both Andromache and Hector did not validly consent due to duress arising out of the fact that the community elders threatened to ostracise them socially and financially if they did not marry.

To decide whether the threats amounted to duress the following points should be considered. In the case of *Szechter* v *Szechter* (1970) Sir Jocelyn Simon P stated that 'It must ... be proved that the will of one of the parties thereto has been overborne by genuine and reasonably held fear caused by threat of immediate danger (for which the party himself is not responsible) to life, limb or liberty so that the constraint destroyed the reality of consent'.

Whether there is a sufficient degree of fear to vitiate consent is a question of fact in each case and if a party is more susceptible to pressure brought to bear on him than another person might be, the marriage may still be voidable: *Scott* v *Sebright* (1886). The court will not necessarily apply the test of threat to life, limb or liberty too literally as stated in *Hirani* v *Hirani* (1982) Ormrod J thought that in his test Sir Jocelyn Simon P was merely contrasting a disagreeable situation with one that constituted a real threat and he stated that 'the crucial question in these cases is whether the threats, pressure or whatever, is such as to destroy the reality of consent and overbears the will of the individual. In *Hirani* v *Hirani* a threat to turn a girl who was wholly dependent on her parents out of her home unless she married the man of her choice was sufficient to vitiate her consent and the marriage, making it voidable.

In this case there is no literal threat to life, limb or liberty, but it may be argued that the threat to ostracise them socially and financially was enough to override their true will because the threat of financial and social ruin may work as strongly as the threat of physical violence in some minds.

In these circumstances this seems to be satisfied and the marriage could be annulled.

Next we must consider whether Andromache can be barred from relying on this. Section 13(2) MCA 1973 states that proceedings for nullity under s12(c), (d), (e) or (f) must be instituted within three years of the marriage. Andromache and Hector were married in December 1989 and it is now June 1992 therefore Andromache must petition for nullity before December 1992 as there does not appear to be a ground on these facts to warrant an application for leave to institute proceedings after the three year period.

QUESTION THREE

'It is crucial to retain the concept of the voidable marriage to provide relief for those groups who are unable to countenance divorce.'

Discuss.

University of London LLB Examination
(for External Students) Family Law June 1994 Q5

General Comment

There are relatively few nullity petitions each year, particularly compared with divorce petitions. The law needs to retain the concept of void marriages, namely marriages which contravene such basic rules as to be void ab initio. However, does the law need to retain the concept of voidable marriages whereby the defect in the marriage is not so fundamental? The question requires that voidable marriages be defined and the need for them explored, particularly in relation to those groups who for religious or other reasons choose not to use divorce as a way of ending marriage.

Skeleton Solution

• The distinction between void and voidable marriages.
• Voidable marriages:
  – non-consummation due to incapacity;
  – non-consummation due to wilful refusal;
  – lack of consent;
  – mental disorder;
  – venereal disease;
  – pregnancy by some other person.
• Groups who are unable to countenance divorce.
• The need for the concept of voidable marriages.

Suggested Solution

The number of petitions presented for nullity of marriage is very small, particularly compared with the many thousands of petitions presented for divorce. This calls into question the need for the concept of nullity and in particular the need for the concept of voidable marriages.

Petitions for nullity can be divided into two categories – those where it is alleged that the marriage is void and those where it is alleged that the marriage is voidable. Void marriages

12

are those which are so defective on social and public policy grounds that the purported marriage cannot be said to have ever existed. Strictly speaking there is no need for a decree since a void marriage does not exist, but either party or indeed a third party may apply for a decree to confirm the status of the marriage and, in the case of the parties to the void marriage, to enable them to apply for ancillary relief. Examples of a void marriage include:

a) a marriage within the prohibited degrees of relationship (eg between father and daughter – s11(a)(i) of the Matrimonial Causes Act (MCA) 1973);

b) a marriage where one of the parties is under the age of 16 (see s11(a)(ii) MCA 1973);

c) a marriage where the parties have disregarded certain essential procedural requirements (eg in a Church of England marriage the banns have been deliberately published in false names – see s11(a)(iii) MCA 1973 and s25(b) of the Marriage Act 1949);

d) a marriage where one or both of the parties are already lawfully married (see s11(b) MCA 1973);

e) a marriage where the parties are not respectively male and female (see s11(c) MCA 1973);

f) certain polygamous marriages (see s11(d) MCA 1973).

In such cases the marriage is deemed to be so fundamentally wrong that it is void and is as if it had never taken place.

A voidable marriage is defective but not in such a fundamental way. The marriage is treated as remaining valid until either party obtains a decree that the marriage be annulled (see *De Reneville* v *De Reneville* (1948)). Only the parties can petition – a third party cannot intervene in the same way as with a void marriage. Since the marriage is treated as valid until a decree is obtained the consequences of the marriage may remain. For example, children of a voidable marriage will be treated as the children of married parents both before and after decree, whereas children of a void marriage will always be treated as children of unmarried parents. A voidable marriage will be treated as having revoked a pre-existing will even after the marriage has been annulled (see *Re Roberts* (1978)). Another difference between void and voidable marriages is that once a marriage is declared to be voidable there are special defences which can prevent the grant of a decree (see s13 MCA 1973). There can be no such defences once a marriage has been found to be void.

On what grounds can a marriage be said to be voidable? The first two grounds relate to the failure to consummate the marriage, either because either party is incapable of consummating the marriage or because the respondent has wilfully refused to consummate the marriage (see s12(a) and (b) MCA 1973). A marriage is deemed to have been consummated as soon as the parties have sexual intercourse after the celebration of the marriage. The sexual intercourse must be ordinary and complete and cannot be partial or imperfect (see *D* v *A* (1845)). The sterility of either party is not relevant as long as there is full penetration. Where a party lacks the capacity to consummate the marriage the defect must be incurable or curable but only by treatment which involves danger to that party (see *S* v *S* (1962)). A party cannot petition on his or her own wilful refusal to consummate. He or she can petition on the other party's wilful refusal where the respondent has come to a settled and definite decision without just excuse (see *Horton* v *Horton* (1947)). Refusal can include situations where religious belief requires that there be both a civil wedding (as required by English law) and a religious wedding (as required by the religious beliefs and customs of either or both parties). If one party fails or refuses to arrange or participate in the religious wedding he or she can be said to be indirectly wilfully refusing to consummate the marriage. Examples of cases where the courts have annulled a marriage in these circumstances include *Jodla* v *Jodla* (1960) where the husband refused to take part in the Roman Catholic wedding service and *Kaur* v *Singh* (1972) where the husband refused to arrange a Sikh wedding.

A marriage can also be voidable where either party to the marriage did not validly consent to it, whether in consequence of duress, mistake, unsoundness of mind or otherwise (see s12(c) MCA 1973). Examples of cases involving such marriages include *Mehta* v *Mehta* (1945) (where one of the parties thought that the marriage ceremony was in fact a conversion to the Hindu religion), *Szechter* v *Szechter* (1971) (marriage in order to escape from imprisonment in a foreign country which threatened the life of the wife) and *Buckland* v *Buckland* (1967) (marriage to a prosecution witness to avoid almost certain imprisonment for an alleged sexual offence). A marriage can also be voidable because either party was suffering from a mental disorder which rendered him or her unfit for marriage or at the time of the marriage the respondent was suffering from a communicable form of venereal disease or was pregnant by some other person (see s12(d),(e) and (f) MCA 1973).

Even if one of these grounds is satisfied there may be a defence available to the respondent (see s13 MCA 1973). For example, if the petitioner, knowing that it was open to him or her to have the marriage avoided, so conducted him or herself so as to lead the respondent to reasonably believe that the petitioner would not do so and that it would be unjust to the respondent to grant the decree then the court cannot grant the decree (see s13(1) MCA 1973). This was the case in *Pettit* v *Pettit* (1962) where the husband was impotent. His wife had a child by him through artificial insemination and kept house for him for twenty years. He then petitioned on his incapacity to consummate the marriage. His petition failed.

Criticisms have been levelled against the concept of the voidable marriage. The Law Commission examined this question when the whole law of nullity was reviewed in 1970. One proposal was that the grounds for annulling a voidable marriage should be incorporated into those for divorce and included in the facts needed to satisfy the court as to irretrievable breakdown. These proposals were rejected for a number of reasons which still exist today. Firstly, the Christian faith places some importance on the distinction between nullity of marriage and divorce. While divorce can result in restrictions in future religious life (eg on remarriage in church) an annulled marriage may not have these consequences. Non-Christian faiths may also find the concept of the voidable marriage more acceptable than that of divorce. This may be particularly true of English citizens who are obliged to marry under English civil law but who then confirm their marriage with their own religious ceremony. The failure of either party to co-operate in this second and important ceremony can be a ground for avoiding the marriage which does not involve the same stigma as divorce. Secondly, divorce still has a moral, religious and social stigma for certain people. A marriage may be voidable on medical or mental health grounds which do not carry the kind of stigma which the grounds for divorce may have (eg adultery, desertion or behaviour). This may be particularly true for older couples who have married but who have such problems. Their view of the stigma of divorce may be quite different to the younger generation who have been brought up in a world more accepting of divorce. The courts can deal with such cases of voidable marriages in a more appropriate and, where medical details are involved, in a more confidential manner than divorce cases. Thirdly, there is a bar to petitioning for divorce within the first year of marriage (see s3(1) MCA 1973). This does not apply to petitions for nullity.

In conclusion, the concept of the voidable marriage is necessary. It is not only necessary for those groups who are unable to countenance divorce but is also necessary for the other reasons outlined above. It should be retained even though it is only used in a small number of cases.

QUESTION FOUR

a) Aziza, who is now 20, reluctantly married Bourhan, a 50-year-old wealthy businessman, in December 1992. Aziza's parents had arranged the marriage with Bourhan and told Aziza, who was then still at school, that if she did not marry Bourhan, she would disgrace her family, who would then disown and disinherit her. In 1993, Aziza was informed by a specialist that she would never be able to have any children and in 1994, she and Bourhan adopted twin boys. Aziza, who has never been happy with Bourhan, has now met Conrad, whom she wishes to marry.

Advise Aziza whether she can successfully petition for a decree of nullity.

b) Deborah and Edward, aged 17 and 21 respectively, married at a register office in June 1994. Deborah had not told her parents that she was getting married. The marriage was not consummated because Deborah was afraid of intercourse. In November 1994, Deborah began seeing a psychiatrist so as to resolve this difficulty. Edward, who has repeatedly urged Deborah to consummate the marriage, has discovered that she is having a sexual relationship with her psychiatrist.

Advise Edward whether he can successfully petition for a decree of nullity.

University of London LLB Examination
(for External Students) Family Law June 1995 Q1

General Comment

The two parts of the question both ask about how to petition for nullity. The first part deals with a possible lack of consent to marriage on the basis of duress, but then raises a possible defence of approbation through agreeing to an adoption. The second part deals with non-consummation of a marriage and requires discussion of both refusal to consummate and the inability to consummate.

Skeleton Solution

a) • Whether Aziza did not validly consent to the marriage in consequence of duress (s12(c) MCA 1973).
   • Defence of approbation (s13(1)(a) MCA 1973).

b) • That the marriage has not been consummated due to the incapacity of Deborah (s12(a) MCA 1973).
   • That the marriage has not been consummated due to Deborah's wilful refusal (s12(b) MCA 1973).

Suggested Solution

a) Aziza asks for advice as to whether she can successfully petition for a decree of nullity with respect to her marriage to Bourhan. Aziza can be advised that a petition for nullity can be brought either on the basis that her marriage with Bourhan is void or that it is voidable. Her marriage with Bourhan would be void if it was fundamentally defective, namely, one or more the grounds outlined in s11 of the Matrimonial Causes Act 1973 (hereinafter

15

referred to as the MCA 1973) applied. None of those grounds appear to apply in Aziza's case. There is no suggestion that there was any defect in the marriage formalities or that she and her husband are within the prohibited degrees of relationship or are under age or that either party was already lawfully married. There is no suggestion that they are not respectively male or female. There is also no suggestion that the marriage was entered into outside England and Wales and was a polygamous marriage and contravened s11(d) MCA 1973.

Her marriage with Bourhan would be voidable if one or more of the grounds in s12 MCA 1973 applied. There is no suggestion that the marriage has not been consummated so it appears that s12(a) and (b) MCA 1973 cannot apply. Of the remaining grounds only one could apply in Aziza's case, namely that she did not validly consent to the marriage in consequence of duress (see s12(c) MCA 1973). For these purposes 'duress' means fear which is so overbearing that it destroys any free consent to the marriage. Aziza would have to show that her will was so overborne by a genuine and reasonably held fear caused by a threat or immediate fear (for which she is not responsible) to life, limb or liberty, so that the restraint destroys the reality of consent (see *Szechter* v *Szechter* (1971)). Duress does not have to be a threat to physically harm or imprison Aziza. She can be advised that a threat from her family to disown and disinherit her may be sufficient to destroy the reality of consent and overbear her will (see *Hirani* v *Hirani* (1983)). However, a mere dislike of her husband and going through with the marriage out of respect for her parents and the traditions of the family would not constitute duress (see *Singh* v *Singh* (1971)). In Aziza's case it appears that her circumstances are more similar to those in *Hirani* than those in *Singh* because her family threatened to disown and disinherit her. She therefore appears to have a claim to petition for nullity on the basis of lack of consent.

However Aziza should be advised that should her husband oppose the petition he can raise a defence. That defence would be that Aziza, with knowledge that it was open to her to have the marriage avoided, so conducted herself in relation to her husband as to lead him to reasonably believe that she would not seek to petition for nullity and that it would be unjust to him to grant the decree of nullity (see s13(1) MCA 1973). He could argue that by Aziza agreeing to adopt the twins she has acted in such a manner. Aziza should be advised that there is conflicting authority dealing with this point. In *W* v *W* (1952) it was held that an adoption application involved a representation to the court that the joint adopters were husband and wife so that it would be contrary to public policy to allow either to claim that the marriage was a nullity. By contrast, in *D* v *D* (1979) it was held that public policy was irrelevant and that s13(1) related wholly to conduct between the parties. In that case a petition for nullity succeeded. Aziza can be advised that *D* v *D* is more likely to be followed so that the adoption would not be an absolute bar to a petition for nullity. If she did not know of her right to petition for nullity for lack of consent when the adoption took place then the s13(1) defence could not apply. Equally if the court was not satisfied that there would be any injustice to Bourhan by the granting of the decree then again such a defence would not succeed. Given the difference in age between them, the circumstances of the marriage and Bourhan's wealth it may be difficult for Bourhan to argue that it would be unjust for a decree to be granted.

Aziza should be advised that she must bring any petition within three years of the marriage otherwise the court could not grant her decree (see s13(2) MCA 1973). It is possible to consider a decree under s12(c) outside this period, but for reasons which do not appear to apply in Aziza's case. She must therefore not delay in bringing a petition should she wish to do so.

b) Now turning to Edward, he can be advised that the first ground which needs to be considered would be that Deborah married at the age of 17 without parental consent. The marriage would not be void on the basis of her age since the minimum age for marriage is 16 (see s11(a)(ii) MCA 1973). A person aged between 16 and under 18 should obtain the consent of those with parental responsibility for her (normally both her parents if they are married) (s3 Marriage Act 1949). However, the lack of consent from Deborah's parents would not make the marriage void (see s48(1)(b) MCA 1949) unless either parent has lodged a caveat with the superintendent registrar (see ss29 and 30 Marriage Act 1949). Since her parents did not seem to be aware of the marriage no caveat is likely to have been lodged. None of the other grounds under s11 MCA 1973 making a marriage void appear to apply.

The marriage may be voidable because it appears not to have been consummated. Edward is able to petition for nullity on the basis either that the marriage has not been consummated because of Deborah's incapacity to consummate it or that she is wilfully refusing to consummate the marriage (see s12(a) or (b) MCA 1973). An incapacity to consummate is normally a physical incapacity but may be a psychological one. A psychological incapacity must amount to an invincible repugnance to the act of intercourse. A mere dislike or aversion to Edward would not be sufficient (see *Singh* v *Singh*). In order for Edward to succeed on the basis of Deborah's incapacity he must be able to show that this is incurable or could only be cured by an operation which is attended by danger or which is unlikely to succeed or where Deborah refuses to undergo treatment (see *S* v *S* (1962)). None of these features appear to apply. If Deborah is having a sexual relationship (which it is assumed involves sexual intercourse) with her psychiatrist it will be difficult to maintain that her incapacity is incurable. She has consented to treatment which appears to be working albeit in a most unfortunate manner. Therefore Edward is more likely to succeed if he petitions on the basis of her wilful refusal to consummate the marriage. In order to show wilful refusal he would have to show that Deborah has come to a settled and definite decision without just excuse (see *Horton* v *Horton* (1947)). If Deborah started out with an inability to consummate, but this has been cured by virtue of her relationship with her psychiatrist, then any refusal to consummate her marriage with Edward is likely to amount to wilful refusal. She is unlikely to be able to persuade a court that she has a just excuse for not consummating the marriage if she is having sexual intercourse with another. In these circumstances Edward is likely to succeed in a petition for nullity. None of the defences available against a petition where a marriage is voidable appear to apply.

3 Divorce

3.1 Introduction

The first modern law relating to divorce dates from 1937. The grounds for divorce were fault based eg adultery, cruelty and desertion and had to be proved beyond reasonable doubt – the criminal standard of proof. The term 'matrimonial offence' characterised divorce grounds as being quasi-criminal in nature. By the late sixties the need for reform had become apparent. It was argued that the divorce laws did not accord with social reality and the quasi-criminal nature of the proceedings resulting in unnecessary bitterness between the divorcing couple. Two reports published at this time, *Putting Asunder* (presented by a group appointed by the Archbishop of Canterbury) and *Reform of the Grounds of Divorce The Field of Choice* (Law Commission Report No 6 (1966), Cmnd 3123), paved the way for reform. The objectives of the reforms were twofold:

a) To buttress rather than to undermine the stability of marriage;

b) To enable the empty shell of marriage to be destroyed with the minimum of bitterness, distress and humiliation.

The Divorce Reform Act of 1969 made irretrievable breakdown of marriage the sole ground for divorce. The breakdown had to be established by one of five 'facts' which included two years living apart with consent and five years living apart without consent. These are the no fault grounds. However adultery, desertion and behaviour were retained as evidence of irretrievable breakdown alongside the no fault grounds and it remains possible to obtain a divorce on proof of, for example, behaviour which the petitioner cannot reasonably be expected to tolerate. The law is now contained in the Matrimonial Causes Act of 1973.

In 1977 procedural changes were introduced. Undefended divorces are now dealt with by the District Judge. The District Judge examines the petition and a supporting affidavit and, if satisfied that the contents are proved, will issue and file a certificate to that effect. The decree nisi is then issued in open court at a later date. The result has been that the 'ability of the court to carry out its statutory duty to enquire into the facts alleged is greatly circumscribed' (see the Booth Report – Report of the Matrimonial Causes Procedure Committee 1985) and District Judges do little more than rubber stamp petitions. In some respects this is tantamount to divorce on demand. Alongside these procedural changes, parties are increasingly encouraged to resolve disputes over the residence of children and over maintenance and property themselves. This process, referred to as conciliation, has as its objective the establishment of a settlement which involves both parties and which will therefore result in less future hostility between them.

18

The Family Law Act 1996 has now been enacted but has yet to be brought into force. When in force it will make radical changes to the process of obtaining divorce (see chapter 4: *Divorce law reform*).

3.2 Key points

a) *One year ban*

Under the Matrimonial Causes Act (MCA) 1973 a petition could not be presented within three years of the marriage unless the petitioner suffered 'exceptional hardship' or where the respondent was 'exceptionally depraved'. Section 1 Matrimonial and Family Proceedings Act 1984 replaced s3 of the MCA 1973, putting an absolute bar on the presentation of a petition within one year of the celebration of marriage.

This is strictly enforced. In *Butler* v *Butler* [1990] 1 FLR 114 eleven months after her marriage the petitioner wife presented a petition for judicial separation which was later amended to become a petition for divorce, which was granted. The divorce was set aside on the ground that the petition had been presented one month too early. There was no discretion to ignore the one year bar.

Note: (i) that although a petitioner has to wait 12 month before issuing a petition, he/she may rely in that petition on matters that occurred in those first 12 months; and (ii) the one year bar will be retained when the law of divorce is radically altered in line with the Government's White Paper, *Facing the Future*, April 1995. See chapter 4 – *Divorce law reform*.

b) *The ground for divorce*

A petition for divorce may be presented by either party to a marriage on the ground that the marriage has broken down irretrievably – s1(1) MCA 1973. The petitioner must satisfy the court of one of five facts set out in s1(2). It is important to emphasise that there is no causal connection between s1(1) and s1(2). In other words the petitioner has to prove two things: firstly that the marriage has irretrievably broken down and secondly that one of the facts in s1(2) is satisfied. The petitioner does not have to prove that the marriage has broken down because of one of the facts in s1(2). (See *Buffery* v *Buffery* [1988] 2 FLR 365.) Note that the ability of the court to inquire into the facts alleged is very limited in undefended cases. This is especially so as regards a petition based upon the respondent's adultery. Since October 1991 the petitioner does not have to cite the co-respondent (the person with whom it is alleged the respondent has committed adultery) even if she knows the identity of the co-respondent. It suffices for the petitioner to state that the identity of the person with whom the respondent is known to the petitioner but the petitioner prefers not to cite that person as co-respondent.

c) *The 'five facts' – s1(2) Matrimonial Causes Act 1973*

i) Section 1(2)(a): That the respondent has committed adultery and the petitioner finds it intolerable to live with the respondent.

- The adultery must be voluntary. This clearly excludes rape.
- Sexual intercourse is the penetration by the male of the female genitalia: *Dennis* v *Dennis* [1955] 2 All ER 51.
- The definition of adultery presupposes a sexual relationship with a person of the

opposite sex. The respondent's homosexuality may be sufficient for a petition based on s1(2)(b).

- The standard of proof is high: *Serio* v *Serio* (1983) 4 FLR 756. This will by and large only be an issue in defended cases.

- The Act is not clear on whether the intolerability must arise from the act of adultery or whether it can be independent of it. The Court of Appeal took the latter view in *Cleary* v *Cleary* [1974] 1 WLR 73 and although some doubts were cast on this interpretation in *Carr* v *Carr* [1974] 1 WLR 1534 this is now the established position.

- The petitioner will not be permitted to rely on this ground where the parties have lived together for a period or periods exceeding six months following disclosure to the petitioner of the adultery. The disregard of a shorter period is intended to allow the parties to attempt reconciliation: s2 MCA 1973; *Biggs* v *Biggs* [1977] 1 All ER 20.

ii) Section 1(2)(b): That the respondent has behaved in such a way that the petitioner cannot reasonably be expected to live with the respondent.

- The test is whether a right thinking person would come to the conclusion that this husband has behaved in such a way that this wife cannot reasonably be expected to live with him taking account the whole of the circumstances and the characters and personalities of the parties.

There exists therefore both a subjective and objective element: *Livingstone-Stallard* v *Livingstone-Stallard* [1974] 2 All ER 776; *Buffery* v *Buffery* [1988] 2 FLR 365.

- A wide range of behaviour is included

Financial responsibility: *Carter-Fea* v *Carter-Fea* [1987] Fam Law 131.

Physical violence: *Bergin* v *Bergin* [1983] 1 All ER 905.

Alcoholism coupled with violence: *Ash* v *Ash* [1972] 1 All ER 582.

Acts which trivial in themselves were 'a constant atmosphere of criticism, disapproval and boorish behaviour': *Livingstone-Stallard* v *Livingstone-Stallard* (above); *O'Neill* v *O'Neill* [1975] 3 All ER 289.

- Some forms of behaviour will fail. It must depend on all the circumstances: *Birch* v *Birch* [1992] 1 FLR 564.

Mere lack of affection: *Pheasant* v *Pheasant* [1972] 1 All ER 587.

Extreme moodiness: *Richards* v *Richards* [1972] 3 All ER 695.

Mere drifting apart: *Buffery* v *Buffery* [1988] 2 FLR 365.

Unsatisfactory sexual performance: *Dowden* v *Dowden* (1977) 8 Fam Law 106.

- Involuntary behaviour. It is not necessary to prove intention and the fact that the respondent is suffering from some illness is not necessarily a bar to a decree.

Manic depressive illness: *Katz* v *Katz* [1972] 3 All ER 219.

Epilepsy: *Thurlow* v *Thurlow* [1976] Fam 32.

It is a question of fact and degree in each case: *Richards* v *Richards* [1972] 3 All ER 695.

- Any period of less than six months cohabitation after the last incident relied upon in the petition shall be disregarded for establishing the reasonableness of continued cohabitation: s2(3) MCA 1973.

A longer period will be disregarded if the petition had no alternative but to remain with the respondent.

iii) Section 1(2)(c): That the respondent has deserted the petitioner for a period of at least two years immediately preceding the presentation of the petition.

- It is only necessary to rely on this ground where the respondent will not consent to a petition based on two years separation, there are no other grounds for divorce and the petitioner does not want to wait for the expiry of the five year period under s1(2)(e).

- The fact of separation. There must be a complete withdrawal from cohabitation.

  Desertion is a withdrawal from a state of affairs rather than a place: *Milligan* v *Milligan* [1941] 2 All ER 62.

  Separation can be complete under the same roof: *Naylor* v *Naylor* [1961] 2 All ER 129; *Hopes* v *Hopes* [1948] 2 All ER 920.

- Intention to desert. Usually inferred from the fact of departure. An involuntary desertion can constitute desertion once the intention is formed and communicated: *Beeken* v *Beeken* [1948] P 302; *Nutley* v *Nutley* [1970] 1 All ER 410.

  Desertion will continue through involuntary separation if the intention had been formed beforehand.

  Where the respondent suffers from mental illness the question is whether he is capable of forming the necessary intention to desert.

- Petitioner does not consent.

  Consent can be expressed – a separation agreement – or implied, but relief at departure is not consent: *Harriman* v *Harriman* [1909] P 123.

  Consent after the de facto separation can bring desertion to an end: *Pizey* v *Pizey* [1961] P 101.

  Consent to separation can be for a limited period in which case desertion will begin at the end of the period: *Shaw* v *Shaw* [1939] P 269.

  The refusal of a reasonable offer of reconciliation can result in desertion beginning: *Gallagher* v *Gallagher* [1965] 2 All ER 967.

- No just cause to leave.

  There are few recent authorities on this point but it is logical to assume that it must be lined to behaviour in s1(2)(b).

  Where the petitioner's conduct is relied upon it must be 'grave and weighty' and not merely the wear and tear of married life: *Quoraishi* v *Quoraishi* [1985] FLR 780.

- No period of six months cohabitation shall break the continuity of separation for the two year period but any period of cohabitation shall not count towards that two year period.

- The termination of desertion. Factors include an agreement to live apart, a decree of judicial separation, the resumption of cohabitation for a prolonged period and by the deserting spouse making a genuine offer to resume cohabitation.

- Constructive desertion. This is conduct by one spouse which has the effect of driving the other spouse out. Such behaviour would almost always give rise to a petition based on s1(2)(b).

iv) Section 1(2)(d): That the parties to the marriage have lived apart for a continuous period of at least two years immediately preceding the presentation of the petition and the respondent consents to a decree being granted.

- Living apart. Section 1(6) states that the parties will not be living apart if they are living in the same household. The term household is not defined.

  There must be recognition by at least one of the parties that the marriage is at an end but oddly this need not be communicated to the other: *Santos* v *Santos* [1972] 2 All ER 246.

  The parties can live apart in the same household: *Mouncer* v *Mouncer* [1972] 1 All ER 289; *Fuller* v *Fuller* [1973] 2 All ER 650.

- Consent. Consent must be freely given and may be withdrawn at any time up to the decree nisi. There must be capacity to give consent.

- No account will be taken of any period or periods not exceeding six months during which the parties resumed living together.

- The day of separation is excluded for the purpose of calculating the two year period.

v) Section 1(2)(e): That the parties to the marriage have lived apart for a continuous period of at least five years immediately preceding the presentation of the petition.

- Interpretations of living apart are the same as considered above.

vi) Financial protection to petitions based on s1(2)(d) and s1(2)(e).

- Under s10 the courts have powers to consider on application the respondent's financial position on divorce and to delay the decree absolute unless satisfied that the financial provision is fair and reasonable or the best that can be made in the circumstances.

- Section 10(3) directs the court to consider all the circumstances including the age, health, conduct, earning capacity, financial resources and financial obligations of each of the parties and includes regard to the financial position of the respondent after the death of the petitioner: *Lombardi* v *Lombardi* [1973] 3 All ER 625.

- The sole purpose is to delay the decree absolute until a financial settlement is reached. The court can refuse the application if there are circumstances which make the granting of the decree desirable and has obtained an undertaking that satisfactory provision will be made: *Grigson* v *Grigson* [1974] 1 All ER 478.

- In *Garcia* v *Garcia* [1992] 1 FLR 256 the Court of Appeal held that s10 could be properly invoked to remedy the fact that the petitioner husband and father had failed to make maintenance payments for his child contrary to a previous agreement. This may be a useful authority for those mothers faced with child care costs prior to the Child Support Agency making an assessment.

vii) Refusal of a decree after five years separation.

- Under s5 of the Act the respondent can oppose the grant of the petition on the grounds that dissolution of the marriage would result in grave financial or other hardship and that it would be wrong in all the circumstances to dissolve the marriage.

- Cases on financial hardship have focused almost exclusively on the loss of pension rights particularly where the parties are approaching retirement and the marriage has lasted many years: *Le Marchant* v *Le Marchant* [1977] 1 WLR 559.

- Other forms of hardship alleged have relied on the social stigma attached to divorce within certain cultures. None have been successful: *Banik* v *Banik* [1973] 3 All ER 45; *Parghi* v *Parghi* (1973) 117 SJ 582.

- Grave in this context has its ordinary meaning. Accordingly young petitioners will find it hard to establish grave financial hardship. *Mathias* v *Mathias* [1972] 3 WLR 201.

- The likely refusal of the petition can result in an improved offer of a financial settlement to offset any loss: *Le Marchant* v *Le Marchant* [1977] 1 WLR 559.

The compensation must however offset the loss: *Julian* v *Julian* (1972) 116 SJ 763.

In *Jackson* v *Jackson* [1993] 2 FLR 851 the 71-year-old husband petitioned under s1(2)(e) and his 62-year-old wife put in a s5 defence arguing that the loss of a British Rail widow's pension of £15.00 per week would cause her grave financial hardship. Her income comprised £28.00 per week state pension and £25.00 per week board and lodgings from her son. The defence failed and the Court of Appeal dismissed her appeal. Although the loss of £15.00 per week to a £60.00 per week income person might be considered a grave loss, the fact that such receipt would pro rata reduce her state provision meant that, in reality, there was no loss.

- The court will consider the conduct of the parties, the interests of the parties and any children or other persons concerned in deciding whether it would be wrong to dissolve the marriage.

Note that the hardship defence is retained in the Family Law Act 1996 (see chapter 4 – *Divorce law reform*).

3.3 Recent cases

Butterworth v *Butterworth* [1998] 1 FCR 159

K v *K (financial provision)* [1996] 3 FCR 158 on defence of grave hardship under s5 MCA 1973 (loss of pension rights).

Wickler v *Wickler* [1998] 2 FLR 326

3.4 Analysis of questions

Problem questions are fairly standard, requiring students to analyse a given situation and advise on the applicability of the 'five facts' to establish irretrievable breakdown. Care should be taken to apply the law on divorce relevantly and avoiding the temptation to simply provide the examiner with a simple summary of the five facts. Questions invariably require a detailed analysis of one or two of the facts in support of irretrievable breakdown.

Students will often be expected to advise not only on the divorce implications but also on maintenance, either during marriage or on divorce.

Occasionally examiners may ask a fairly straightforward essay question which requires students to review the law on divorce and comment critically on whether it has achieved its original objective.

3.5 Questions

QUESTION ONE

Mary and John, who have two children aged 6 and 7, were married in 1980. Since the beginning of the marriage, John has been an active human rights campaigner. In 1985, John's activities began to take up a considerable amount of time and Mary complained that if he did not devote more attention to the family, she would consider leaving him. John promised that he would spend more time with the family, but he did not really do so. At the end of 1986, Mary therefore decided to move into the spare room.

In January 1988, John went to Burma to study the human rights situation there. Unfortunately, he was taken hostage by a terrorist group, and while it is clear that he is still alive, he has not yet returned to England. Advise Mary, who would like to divorce John.

University of London LLB Examination
(for External Students) Family Law June 1991 Q3

General Comment

This is an awkward question on divorce which requires detailed consideration of the facts in s1(2)(b), (c) and (e) Matrimonial Causes Act 1973. Whereas the separation for five years fact is relatively straightforward, the question of whether behaviour or desertion applies is more complex and care must be taken to point to the difficulties arising on the facts of the problem.

Skeleton Solution

- Consider the one ground for divorce – s1(1) MCA 1973. Discount adultery.
- Discuss a behaviour petition – s1(2)(b). Identify possible behaviour. Discuss subjective and objective elements of the test and s2(3) MCA 1973. Is such a petition appropriate on these facts?
- Desertion – s1(2)(c) – discuss when separation begins. Does John have an intention to desert? Does Mary consent?
- Separation – discount s1(2)(d) – lack of consent to decree
- Consider s1(2)(e) – have the parties been separated for the required period? *Santos* point to be considered.

Suggested Solution

There is one ground for divorce, namely that the marriage has broken down irretrievably (s1(1) Matrimonial Causes Act 1973, hereinafter MCA 1973) and Mary must prove this by relying on one or more of the facts set out in s1(2) MCA 1973. In the absence of proof of one of these facts no divorce will be granted even if it is clear that the marriage has broken down irretrievably (*Richards* v *Richards* (1972); *Buffery* v *Buffery* (1988)).

There is no evidence of adultery in this case so a petition under s1(2)(a) MCA 1973 is not appropriate. Similarly a petition under s1(2)(b) MCA 1973 may be inappropriate on these facts. Under s1(2)(b) a petition is available where the respondent has behaved in such a way that the petitioner cannot reasonably be expected to live with the respondent. This involves establishing behaviour against John and whereas it might be alleged on the basis of his lack of attention to the family in the past, it would seem inappropriate to rely on it at this time. Certainly simple desertion, if his leaving the home to visit Burma in 1988 can be construed as such, will not be accepted as evidence of behaviour (*Stringfellow* v *Stringfellow* (1976)).

If John's failure to give proper attention to the family can be regarded as behaviour, it is for the court to decide if Mary can reasonably be expected to live with him taking into account the behaviour of both parties, their characters and personalities, their faults and other attributes good and bad, and the whole history of the marriage (*Ash* v *Ash* (1972); *Pheasant* v *Pheasant* (1972); *Livingstone-Stallard* v *Livingstone-Stallard* (1974)).

A factor which may work against Mary relates to the reconciliation provisions in s2 MCA 1973. By virtue of s2(3) MCA 1973, the court must disregard any period of cohabitation after the last act of behaviour complained of, if it is less than six months, when deciding if it is reasonable to expect the petitioner to continue living with the respondent. If, as discussed below, it is deemed that when Mary moved into the spare room this did not terminate cohabitation, then the parties continued to live together. It could be argued that John's behaviour continued throughout the cohabitation up to and including his decision to go to Burma since which time the parties have of course been living separately. If so the parties have not lived together for more than six months since the last act complained of and therefore this will not be a factor to be considered when deciding if Mary can be expected to continue to live with John. However, the fact that Mary continued to cohabit with John and the fact that the alleged behaviour took place so long ago may indicate that a s1(2)(b) petition is not appropriate at this time.

To establish a petition under s1(2)(c) MCA 1973 it must be proved that the respondent has deserted the petitioner for a continuous period of at least two years. 'Desertion is not a withdrawal from a place, but from a state of things' (*Pulford* v *Pulford* (1923)) so it is necessary to establish that John has withdrawn from the marriage. Further it must be shown that he has the intention 'to bring the matrimonial union permanently to an end' (*Lang* v *Lang* (1955)). As a matter of fact we know that John and Mary have been separated since, at the latest, January 1988 and the fact that John has been captured by terrorists and has been unable to return home since then would not necessarily interfere with a desertion petition if his intention to desert before his capture could be established. However, unless it could be argued that his continued attention to the human rights campaigns, despite Mary's warnings should he fail to give attention to the family, could be construed as evidence of an intention to bring the marriage to an end, it is unlikely that an intention to desert can be made out against him.

There may be another problem in proving desertion in that it is necessary to establish that the petitioner does not give consent to the separation. In view of Mary's behaviour in moving into the spare room it may be difficult to establish such lack of consent on her part although it is doubtful anyway whether such action establishes separation in its own right. It could be argued that John's behaviour drove Mary to separate herself from him and so constructive desertion may arise. However, as indicated above, the intention to desert on John's part may be difficult to establish.

This leaves the separation facts under s1(2)(d) and (e) MCA 1973. Under s1(2)(d) it has to be established that the parties have lived apart for a continuous period of at least two years immediately preceding the petition and that the respondent consents to the decree being granted. However, although the fact of separation for the required period can be established together with the mental element required, Mary will be unable to obtain John's consent to the decree and without this a petition under s1(2)(d) will fail. Mary would have to provide positive evidence that John freely gave his consent to the decree with full understanding of the nature and consequences of what he was doing (*Mason v Mason* (1972)). Clearly, as it seems that Mary has had no contact with John since he was taken hostage, no such consent will be forthcoming at this time.

To establish a petition under s1(2)(e) MCA 1973 Mary must prove that the parties have lived apart for a continuous period of five years immediately preceding the presentation of the petition. If such separation can be made out together with the required mental element, there is nothing further to be proved by Mary and the divorce would be granted.

Living apart involves living apart in a physical and a mental sense. To establish physical separation Mary must prove that the parties have lived in separate households for the relevant period although this does not necessarily involve living in separate houses. In other words there must be a rejection of all the obligations of marriage, a cessation of cohabitation. The test to be applied is whether there has been any sharing of a domestic life and whether one spouse has been providing matrimonial services for the other (*Mouncer v Mouncer* (1972); *Fuller v Fuller* (1973)). In *Mouncer* the parties were held to be living together where they shared their meals and living accommodation even though they slept in separate bedrooms, no longer had sexual relations and largely led separate lives. Similarly in *Hopes v Hopes* (1949) the wife did no mending or washing for her husband and never cooked separate meals for him although he had most meals with the rest of the family and when he was not in his bedroom he shared the rest of the house with the family. There was deemed to be no living apart in that case. Conversely in *Fuller* there was deemed to be a separation where the wife, having left her husband to live with another man, subsequently took the husband in as a lodger because he had nowhere else to live. The nature of the relationship between the parties had changed and it could not be said that the wife was performing matrimonial services for the husband whom she treated as a lodger and who paid for the services provided.

Therefore it will be a question of fact and degree whether Mary and John have been living apart for a continuous period of five years. Certainly when John left in January 1988 physical separation can be established from that time. However it is questionable whether separation can be established earlier than that date. We are told that at the end of 1986 Mary moved into the spare room suggesting that she no longer shared a bedroom with John and that there was no further sexual relationship between them. However we are given no information as to the other household arrangements, that is whether Mary cooked meals for John or did cleaning for him or whether he shared the house with the rest of the family etc. It seems that he probably did share the house with the family and probably ate his meals with them when he was at home. If so, the mere fact that some part of the matrimonial life has come to an end, (in this case the sexual relationship) does not mean that the parties are living separate and apart. It seems therefore that separation cannot be established in 1986, but that it started only in January 1988 when John left for Burma. If this is the case no petition under s1(2)(e) can be presented until January 1993.

Once physical separation is established the mental element must also be shown. In *Santos v Santos* (1972) it was held that the parties would not be treated as living apart unless consortium had come to an end and so long as both spouses intend to share a matrimonial home when circumstances permit, consortium is regarded as continuing. Therefore to establish living apart it is also necessary to show that one party at least regards the marriage as at an end for the whole of the relevant period, although it is not necessary for that party to communicate this fact to the other. In this case it could be argued that Mary treated the marriage as at an end from the end of 1986 when she moved into the separate room. If so, the mental element of the fact is established and when the physical separation can be made out for the relevant period she will be able to obtain a divorce under s1(2)(e).

QUESTION TWO

John and Susan married in 1984. They have twin boys, Damien and Derrick, who are now aged six. At the time she married John, Susan was aware that he suffered intermittently from depression, but she believed she could cure him. In late 1987 John, who concluded without foundation that Susan was having an affair, moved into the spare room and refused to speak to her. He communicated with her by leaving messages on his personal computer. They continued to eat meals together in silence and both looked after the twins, who started to exhibit signs that they were upset by their father's behaviour to their mother.

In June 1990 Susan decided that she could no longer go on living with John, particularly in view of the fact that his behaviour was affecting the twins. Accordingly, after leaving a message on the computer indicating that she believed the marriage was over, she left, with the twins, to live with her parents.

Can either John or Susan obtain a divorce? In the event that either wishes to resist the other's petition, what avenues are available to them?

University of London LLB Examination
(for External Students) Family Law June 1992 Q5

General Comment

A general question regarding divorce.

Skeleton Solution

MCA s1(1) – and consideration of the facts to show application of s1(1) – discounting those that are irrelevant.

Suggested Solution

Under the Matrimonial Causes Act (MCA) 1973, there is only one ground for divorce, namely that the marriage has broken down irretrievably s1(1). This can be shown by establishing one of the five facts in s1(2).

a) *Whether John can obtain a divorce*

John may try to rely on s1(2)(a) – 'That the respondent has committed adultery and the petitioner finds it intolerable to live with the respondent'. However, there is no evidence of adultery at all, in fact we are told that John's belief is without foundation, therefore John will not be able to rely on this fact.

Next we will consider if John may obtain a divorce by establishing any of the other facts.

Firstly, s1(2)(e): 'That the parties have lived apart for a continuous period of at least five years immediately preceding the presentation of the petition'.

'Living apart' – under s2(6) of the MCA 1973 the parties to the marriage are to be treated as living apart unless they are living in the same household. The meaning of the phrase 'living in the same household' has to be determined and is a question of fact to be decided by the court. In this case John and Susan ate their meals together and assumed joint responsibility for looking after their children and following the decision in *Mouncer* v *Mouncer* (1972) it probably cannot be said they were living apart. A rejection of the normal relationship between husband and wife coupled with the absence of normal affection was not sufficient to constitute living apart. So John will not be able to rely on s1(2)(e), as he cannot show a period of five years separation from his wife despite the lack of communication between them.

Secondly, consider s1(2)(d):

'That the parties have lived apart for a continuous period of at least two years immediately preceding the presentation of the petition and the respondent consents to a decree being granted.'

Living apart means more than the physical separation of the parties. There must be a recognition by at least one of the parties that the marriage is at an end.

Susan moved out of the house in June 1990 and it is now June 1992, so that the requirement that the parties live apart for a continuous period of two years prior to the presentation of the petition will be satisfied either immediately or in the near future depending upon the exact date on which Susan moved out. To satisfy the requirement that there must be recognition by at least one of the parties that the marriage is at an end, the computer message left by Susan may be referred to. Therefore unless Susan refuses consent to the divorce for some reason, a petition based on s1(2)(d) will be successful.

Finally, John may be able to rely on s1(2)(c) 'That the respondent had deserted the petitioner for a continuous period of at least two years immediately preceding the presentation of the petition' – this section is not used very often.

To rely on it he will have to establish four things:

1. the de facto separation of the spouses;

2. the intention on Susan's part to remain separated;

3. the absence of his consent;

4. the absence of any reasonable cause for his wife's departure.

The first factor should cause no problems since Susan has left the matrimonial home. The same should be true of the second requirement, since Susan, by way of the computer, told John she believed the marriage was over. The third requirement of consent is a question of fact. It may be expressly given but it may also be implied from the conduct of the deserted spouse. It may be the case that John has implied consent to his wife leaving by his conduct, ie his unswerving belief in her adultery and his refusal to communicate other than by leaving messages on his personal computer may suffice to demonstrate his consent to the parties living apart. If this were so, he could not assert that his wife was in desertion. However, it is clear that there must be an agreement to live apart – it is not enough that one party is simply glad to see the other go – and it is submitted that, on the facts, there is not enough evidence to prove the requisite consent on John's part such that he could still rely on s1(2)(c).

Lastly, it must be shown that there was no reasonable cause for his wife to leave otherwise there will be no unjustifiable separation and thus no desertion on her part. John's behaviour is obviously relevant here, for it may be such that Susan was justified in leaving. It has been said that the conduct of the petition must amount to 'such a grave and weighty matter as renders the continuance of the matrimonial cohabitation virtually impossible': *Young* v *Young* (1984).

Looking at the facts of this case, John refused to speak to Susan, ate his meals in silence and only communicated by leaving messages on his personal computer. It may be that, provided Susan left because of John's behaviour, she cannot be held to be in desertion.

b) *Whether Susan can obtain a divorce*

The same factors relating to s1(2)(d) and (e) above are relevant here, but Susan will probably rely on s1(2)(b) – 'That the respondent has behaved in such a way that the petitioner cannot reasonably be expected to live with him'.

The test to be applied is an objective one but the court must have regard to the people actually before it: *Livingstone-Stallard* v *Livingstone-Stallard* (1974); *Ash* v *Ash* (1972); *Buffery* v *Buffery* (1988).

It is not really clear what sort of behaviour will satisfy s1(2)(b). However, in *O'Neill* v *O'Neill* (1975) allegations by the husband that the children of the family were not his were sufficient to satisfy the section. By analogy, it is possible that repeated accusations of an adulterous relationship which are untrue may well suffice. As a result of *Thurlow* v *Thurlow* (1976), the court has to take into consideration all the obligations relating to marriage, including that of caring for a spouse who is unwell. The fact that Susan knew of John's mental illness when she married him may operate against her establishing his behaviour. However, regard should be had to the principle in *Katz* v *Katz* (1972) where it was held that while a spouse may reasonably be required to care for a partner who is unwell and to tolerate a certain degree of abnormal behaviour, there may come a time when that partner's condition becomes such that the spouse can no longer reasonably be expected to continue living with the other party. This is particularly relevant here, where the children, Damien and Derrick were also becoming upset by their father's behaviour. Negative behaviour can also be taken into consideration but it should be intentional behaviour which John's does appear to be.

Susan could also seek to rely on s1(2)(c) to show that John was in constructive desertion of her. The court will have to determine whether the four criteria referred to in relation to John's divorce (above) are satisfied in this situation. In particular, it will have regard to John's conduct to determine whether he made living together for any further period of time impossible. It may well find that he behaved in such a way as to drive his wife away, for example by persisting in the unsubstantiated belief that Susan was committing adultery and refusing to communicate with her other than by leaving messages on his computer. Also his conduct was having an adverse effect on his children's health.

With regard to the other criteria, Susan can obviously prove that she and her husband are separated. She can also show that there was no reasonable cause for John's desertion since she was not in fact committing adultery. A reasonable but mistaken belief in her adultery would have justified his desertion but not John's persistent and unreasonable belief. Since he continues to insist that she is having an affair, he remains in desertion, and this fact would seem to show in intention on his part to remain separated permanently from his wife. Therefore Susan can probably have a divorce on this ground.

QUESTION THREE

Antonia married Benjamin in 1975. Their marriage was an extremely happy one until early 1988 when Benjamin started having an affair with Clarissa, the owner of a local health club. Benjamin chose not to leave the matrimonial home, but moved out of the bedroom he shared with Antonia and into the spare room in June 1988. Antonia continued to do Benjamin's laundry for him and he ate at least four meals a week with her. In late 1991, however, Benjamin decided to move in with Clarissa.

Benjamin now wishes to divorce Antonia and marry Clarissa. Antonia does not want to be divorced as she believes that she and her husband can be reconciled. She is, further, very worried about her position with respect to the private pension plan that Benjamin has been investing in since their marriage.

Advise Antonia.

University of London LLB Examination
(for External Students) Family Law June 1993 Q2

General Comment

This question invites discussion as to whether Benjamin can satisfy one or more of the facts which establish irretrievable breakdown and so enable him to petition successfully for divorce. Particular attention has to be paid to the living apart facts, particularly the fact of five years living apart. Advice has to be given as to whether such a fact can be satisfied and, if it can, the special defences open to Antonia in ss5 and 10 Matrimonial Causes Act 1973 and how they might safeguard the position as regards her widow's pension.

Skeleton Solution

• The ground of irretrievable breakdown for divorce.
• Which of the five facts in s1(2) MCA 1973 could Benjamin seek to satisfy?
• The fact of living apart for five years – in particular 'living apart' in the same household.
• The defence in s5 MCA 1973 of grave financial hardship and unjust to grant a divorce, with reference to Antonia and the widow's pension.
• The safeguard in s10 MCA 1973 with regard to the widow's pension.

Suggested Solution

Antonia should be advised that there is only one ground for divorce, namely that the marriage has 'broken down irretrievably' (s1(1) Matrimonial Causes Act (MCA) 1973). Benjamin would have to satisfy the court that this was the case and also establish one or more of five facts before he could successfully petition for divorce (s1(2) MCA 1973, *Buffery* v *Buffery* (1988)). Before discussing whether Benjamin could establish one or more of those facts Antonia should be advised that if Benjamin does petition for divorce any solicitor acting for him has to discuss the possibility of a reconciliation with him (see s6(1) MCA 1973). It is assumed that Benjamin does not wish to be reconciled with Antonia notwithstanding her wish to be reconciled with him.

Benjamin cannot petition on the fact of his own adultery (see s1(2)(a) MCA 1973). There is no indication of adultery on Antonia's part. There is no indication that Antonia has behaved in such a way that Benjamin cannot reasonably be expected to live with her as is required to satisfy the second fact (see s1(2)(b) MCA 1973). There is no indication that Antonia has deserted Benjamin or has so behaved as to drive him out in a manner amounting to constructive desertion (see the fact in s1(2)(c) MCA 1973). Antonia has made it clear that she does not want a divorce so she would not give consent as is required to satisfy the fourth fact, that of living apart for two years and the respondent consenting to the decree (see s1(2)(d) MCA 1973).

This leaves one remaining fact upon which Benjamin might seek to rely, that of living apart for five years (see s1(2)(e) MCA 1973). The facts in this case suggest that in June 1988 Benjamin moved out of the matrimonial bedroom and moved into the spare room. However, he did not move out of the matrimonial home until late 1991. If Benjamin wishes to petition for divorce immediately using the fact of living apart for five years he must show that he and Antonia were living apart within the same household from June 1988 to the time he actually left the household. It will not be easy for Benjamin to satisfy a court in this respect. Firstly a court will look to the statutory interpretation of 'living apart' whereby a husband and wife shall be treated as living apart 'unless they are living with each other in the same household' (see s2(6) MCA 1973). Benjamin may seek to argue that he and Antonia were no longer 'living with each other' from June 1988 even though he remained in the same house. He may also seek to argue that there was no 'household' from June 1988. It is important to note that Antonia continued to do Benjamin's laundry and that he continued to share at least four meals a week with her. This suggests that there was still a common household even though they did not share the same bedroom. In *Mouncer* v *Mouncer* (1972) there were similar facts. The husband and wife slept in separate bedrooms but ate their meals together and with the children. The wife prepared the meals. They shared the cleaning though the wife in that case did not do the husband's laundry. It was held that the spouses had not been living apart. They still shared the same household. The rejection of the normal physical relationship between husband and wife and the absence of normal affection was not sufficient to constitute living apart. On the basis of that authority it would appear that Benjamin would be unsuccessful in petitioning on the basis of five years living apart.

There is another authority, *Fuller* v *Fuller* (1973), where spouses living in the same house were held to be living apart. That case had special facts and involved a gravely ill husband going to live in the house where the wife lived with another man. The wife prepared the husband's meals which he ate with the rest of the household. She did his laundry. However both spouses clearly regarded the marriage as at an end since the wife lived with another man. The husband was no different to a lodger. That case can be distinguished from that of Antonia. Antonia did not regard the marriage as at an end during the relevant period. She and Benjamin continue to share the matrimonial household and apparently carry on as a household in terms of meals and laundry. In such circumstances it is unlikely that Benjamin could successfully petition on the basis of five years living apart at this moment in time.

Antonia should be advised that 'living apart' only requires one party to recognise that the marriage is at an end. This need not be communicated to the other party at the time the 'living apart' is said to commence though the court must be able to identify some occurrence confirming the petitioner's recognition that the marriage was at an end (see *Santos* v *Santos* (1972)). In the unlikely event that Benjamin is able to establish living apart he can show the court that this began at the moment he started his affair with Clarissa even if Antonia was not aware of that at the time.

With regard to Antonia's pension position it is assumed that if there is no divorce her position will remain unaltered. If there is a divorce she could lose her right to a share in that pension after Benjamin has retired and, after his death, her right to the widow's pension. In this respect she could defend a petition brought under s1(2)(e) if she could show that the dissolution of the marriage would result in grave financial or other hardship and that it would in all the circumstances be wrong to dissolve the marriage (see s5 MCA 1973). The court would consider all the circumstances including the conduct of the parties. Hardship includes the chance of acquiring pension rights (including a widow's pension) (see s5(3) MCA 1973). A private pension plan, when compared with a state pension, is likely to be a substantial benefit to Antonia. Therefore the loss of the chance of acquiring such a pension could amount to 'grave financial hardship'. If Antonia is relatively young and able to go out to work and re-establish herself and the prospect of the pension is remote because Benjamin is also relatively young, then the loss of the pension rights may be too remote and so not grave (see *Mathias* v *Mathias* (1972)). If Antonia is older, has not worked during the marriage and so has little prospect of financial independence and the prospect of enjoying the pension rights is in the foreseeable future then the loss of those rights is more likely to be grave (see *Dorrell* v *Dorrell* (1972)). This could be the case given that Antonia has been married to Benjamin for some 18 years. If Antonia is able to satisfy the court that she would suffer grave financial hardship she must also satisfy the court that it would be wrong to dissolve the marriage. If Antonia has been blameless and is of such an age and situation as to have little financial independence (having depended on Benjamin financially) then the court may conclude that it is unjust to allow Benjamin to divorce her. Benjamin may argue that it would be just to dissolve the marriage so that he can marry Clarissa but such an argument is likely to fail if the court considers that he has treated Antonia badly. Benjamin can also seek to compensate Antonia for any loss that she would suffer if there was a divorce (see *Parker* v *Parker* (1972); *Le Marchant* v *Le Marchant* (1977)). Caselaw suggests that such compensation would have to be generous in order to safeguard Antonia's position (see *Parker* and *Julian* v *Julian* (1972)).

Antonia should also be advised that should Benjamin obtain a decree nisi of divorce under s1(2)(e) she could prevent the decree from being made absolute until Benjamin satisfies the court that he need make no financial provision for Antonia or that he has made reasonable financial provision for her or has put forward firm proposals for such provision (see s10 MCA 1973). This is likely to force Benjamin to provide for Antonia to make up for any loss in his private pension.

In conclusion Antonia can be advised that Benjamin is unlikely to be successful in petitioning for divorce at this point in time. The only fact upon which he could seek to rely is that of living apart for five years and that fact would be difficult to establish given that he remained in the same household as Antonia for most of the five years period. Even if he were successful Antonia's financial position would be safeguarded by firstly s5 and then by s10 of the Matrimonial Causes Act 1973. Benjamin will be able to bring a petition based on five years living apart in late 1996 but again Antonia's financial position is likely to be protected by ss5 and 10.

QUESTION FOUR

Albert married Bridget in 1987. In December 1989, Bridget, a professional skier, was involved in a skiing accident, as a result of which she incurred permanent brain damage, leaving her with severe mental and physical disabilities.

Following the accident, Bridget spent six months in hospital. On her release in June 1990, she returned to the matrimonial home where she has been cared for ever since by Albert and his mother.

Albert's initial reaction to Bridget's misfortune was that, given his view of marriage as a life-long commitment, he would stay with his wife, although he might have affairs from time to time. As the years have passed, however, and there has been no improvement in Bridget's condition, he has changed his mind. Albert would now like his marriage to be dissolved.

Advise Albert.

University of London LLB Examination
(for External Students) Family Law June 1994 Q1

General Comment

The question requires discussion of the grounds of divorce in the difficult circumstances of a spouse suffering brain damage after an accident. The question as to whether such a spouse has 'behaved' in such a way that the petitioning spouse can no longer reasonably be expected to live with her requires particular discussion. The living apart grounds should also be mentioned.

Skeleton Solution

- Single ground for divorce – irretrievable breakdown (s1(1) Matrimonial Causes Act 1973).
- Need to satisfy one or more of the five facts (s1(2) MCA 1973).
- Fact of behaviour (s1(2)(b) MCA 1973) and whether a brain damaged spouse could be said to have 'behaved' in such a way that Albert could not reasonably be expected to live with her.
- Whether Bridget has the capacity to consent in order to satisfy the living apart for two years with consent ground (s1(2)(d) MCA 1973).
- Living apart for five years (s1(2)(e) MCA 1973).
- Financial provision for Bridget (ss5 and 10 MCA 1973).

Suggested Solution

Albert should be advised that there is only one ground for divorce, namely that his marriage with Bridget has irretrievably broken down (see s1(1) of the Matrimonial Causes Act 1973 – hereinafter referred to as the MCA 1973). In addition, the court cannot hold the marriage to have broken down irretrievably unless he satisfies the court of one or more of five facts (see s1(2) MCA 1973). These are two separate requirements which must individually be satisfied (see *Buffery* v *Buffery* (1988)). Even if Albert is able to satisfy the court that the marriage has irretrievably broken down, a divorce cannot be granted to him unless one or more of the five facts is satisfied. Establishing one or more of the five facts is likely to be the main difficulty facing Albert when he tries to obtain a divorce from Bridget.

The first fact is based on adultery. There is no suggestion of any adultery on Bridget's part so this fact is not available to Albert. He could not rely on his own adultery. The second fact is that Bridget has behaved in such a way that Albert cannot reasonably be expected to live with her (s1(2)(b) MCA 1973). In order to satisfy this fact Albert must demonstrate that Bridget behaved in a particular way and that this behaviour had a particular impact on him. The court will then apply an objective test as to whether Albert can reasonably be expected to live with Bridget but taking into account the individual personalities, characteristics, disposition and behaviour of the parties (see *Ash* v *Ash* (1972)). Put in another way, the court would ask itself whether a right thinking person would come to the conclusion that Bridget has behaved in such a way that Albert cannot be reasonably expected to live with her taking into account the whole of the circumstances and the characteristics and personalities of the parties (see *Livingstone-Stallard* v *Livingstone-Stallard* (1974)).

33

The difficulty for Albert is that it may be difficult for him to satisfy a court that Bridget has 'behaved' in such a way that he cannot reasonably be expected to live with her. She has suffered an accident which incurred permanent brain damage leaving her with severe mental and physical disabilities. In *Katz* v *Katz* (4) the husband was mentally ill and behaved badly towards his wife. It was held that 'behaviour' was more than a mere state of affairs or a state of mind. It was action or conduct by one spouse which affected the other and which had some reference to the marriage. The court applied the test for s1(2)(b), after making allowances for the husband's disabilities, and granted a decree of divorce. It is important to note that in that case the mentally ill spouse was abusive towards his wife, so 'behaved' in an identifiable way. His wife was badly affected by his behaviour and attempted suicide. By contrast in *Richards* v *Richards* (1972) the mentally ill husband was moody and taciturn and did not sleep properly, which disturbed his wife. There was a minor incident of violence. The wife's petition was dismissed since the court made a value judgement about the husband's behaviour and the effect of that behaviour on the wife. Though the marriage had irretrievably broken down the wife had failed to satisfy s1(2)(b). In a third case, *Thurlow* v *Thurlow* (1975) a wife's behaviour gradually deteriorated due to a brain disorder. She became incontinent, was bad-tempered and threw objects about. She wandered the streets. Her behaviour caused her husband considerable distress. He tried to hold down a job, care for his wife and run the household. The strain made him ill. It was held that where 'behaviour' stemmed from misfortune which stemmed from accidental injury the court would take full account of all the obligations of being married. This included the normal duty to accept and to share the burden imposed on the marriage as a result of the physical or mental ill-health of one spouse. This had to be balanced against the capacity of the petitioner to withstand the stress imposed by the behaviour, the steps taken to cope with it, the length of time during which the petitioner had been called upon to bear it, and the actual or potential effect upon his health. Since the wife in that case required indefinite institutional care, and the strain on the husband was so great, a decree was granted. Whether Albert will succeed in satisfying s1(2)(b) will depend on how Bridget's condition manifests itself and the effect her condition has had on him. If her behaviour is similar to that of the wife and the effect on the husband as in *Thurlow* then a petition is likely to succeed. If the circumstances are more akin to that in *Richards* then a petition is likely to fail.

The next fact is based on desertion (see s1(2)(c) MCA 1973), but since there is no evidence of this it will not be discussed further. The next fact is based on Albert and Bridget having lived apart for a continuous period of two years and Bridget consenting to the petition (see s1(2)(d) MCA 1973). Albert does not appear to be living apart from Bridget at the moment. Indeed, he and his mother are caring for her in the matrimonial home. Should arrangements be made whereby he and Bridget live part then this ground may come to apply. However, Bridget may not have the mental capacity to give the required consent even if she wanted to. She must have the capacity to be able to understand what she is consenting to. This capacity is similar to that needed in order to consent to marriage (see *Mason* v *Mason* (1972)). If Bridget refuses to consent or does not have the capacity to consent then Albert may have to wait for five years and rely on the ground of five years of continuously living apart (when Bridget's consent would not be required) (see s1(2)(e) MCA 1973). Should Albert rely on either s1(2)(d) or (e) there are provisions which oblige him to make financial provision for Bridget (see ss5 and 10 MCA 1973). If he failed to make financial provision for her then she could defend or delay any petition he brought.

In conclusion, should Albert want an immediate divorce, the only fact he might be able to satisfy would be based on behaviour (see s1(2)(b) MCA 1973). This may be difficult to satisfy unless Bridget's condition is such that it causes her to act in a way that puts a considerable strain on Albert's health. If her condition is passive then a petition is likely to fail. Given the likely difficulties involved in obtaining any consent to a petition Albert would be left with the fact of living apart for a continuous period of five years.

QUESTION FIVE

Mary married Nicolas in 1980 and they have two children, now aged ten and eight respectively. When they married, Mary and Nicolas agreed that should Olive, Mary's schizophrenic sister, ever be in need of care or accommodation, she could come and live with them. The couple both knew that it would be very difficult if Olive ever did come to live with them, but nevertheless, in 1990, after she contracted pneumonia, Olive moved in with Mary and Nicolas. Olive's presence in the house resulted in domestic discord. Nicolas told Mary that the situation was impossible and that he would leave her if Olive remained. Mary told Nicolas that she would not abandon her sister.

In January 1992, Nicolas left the matrimonial home, telling Mary that although he still loved her and the children, he could not live in the same house as Olive. Nicolas returned in December 1992 for Christmas, but, as Olive was still there and the situation had not improved, he left again in early July 1993. Nicolas remained in touch with Mary both by telephone and letter and recently wrote to her asking to ensure that Olive would leave so that he and Mary could resume their marriage. Mary replied that she could never do this because she was afraid that Olive would commit suicide.

Nicolas has decided that his marriage is now over and wishes to divorce Mary.

Advise Nicolas.

University of London LLB Examination
(for External Students) Family Law June 1995 Q5

General Comment

The question invites discussion of various facts which must be shown in order to obtain a divorce. The fact of behaviour, whereby one party finds it unreasonable to live with the other, requires particular examination, especially in light of the unusual circumstances involving the mentally ill sister. There is also the fact of desertion. In this case it may be possible to show constructive desertion. Finally, there are the living apart facts. The fact of the parties living apart is complicated by the husband returning to the household. How this affects the period of living apart needs to be explained. Indeed, the reconciliation provisions in s2 of the Matrimonial Causes Act 1973 are a particular feature of the question in relation to all the available facts for divorce.

Skeleton Solution

• Need to establish irretrievable breakdown (see s1(1) Matrimonial Causes Act 1973).

• In addition need to establish one or more of five facts (s1(2) MCA 1973).

• Fact of wife behaving in such a way that not reasonable to expect husband to live with her (s1(2)(b) MCA 1973) – effect of wife's insistence that mentally ill sister live in family home – relevance of husband returning (s2(3) MCA 1973).

- Fact of desertion for a period of two years (s1(2)(c) MCA 1973) – can constructive desertion be shown and, if so, for what period? – relevance of husband returning (s2(4) MCA 1973).
- Fact of living apart for two years with consent (s1(2)(d) MCA 1973) – has two-year period been satisfied? – relevance of reconciliation provisions in s2(5) MCA 1973).
- Fact of living apart for five years (s1(2)(e) MCA 1973).

Suggested Solution

Nicolas should be advised that if he wishes to petition successfully for divorce he must satisfy the court that his marriage with Mary has irretrievably broken down (see s1(1) Matrimonial Causes Act 1973 – hereinafter referred to as the MCA 1973). Given the troubled state of the marriage and the differences between the parties Nicolas should be able to satisfy this requirement.

He should be further advised that in addition he must satisfy the court of one or more of five facts in order to obtain a divorce (see s1(2) MCA 1973). Both requirements are separate and each must be satisfied. If he establishes irretrievable breakdown, but not one or more of the facts, he will be unsuccessful in his petition (see *Buffery* v *Buffery* (1988)).

The first possible fact is that the respondent has committed adultery and that the petitioner finds it intolerable to live with her (see s1(2)(a) MCA 1973). Since there is no evidence of adultery on Mary's part Nicolas cannot make use of this fact. The second is that she has behaved in such a way that it is not reasonable to expect him to live with her (see s1(2)(b) MCA 1973). The court will ask whether any right-thinking person would come to the conclusion that Mary has behaved in such a way that Nicolas cannot reasonably be expected to live with her, taking into account the whole of the circumstances and the characteristics and personalities of the parties (see *Livingstone-Stallard* v *Livingstone-Stallard* (1974)). In other words can Nicolas, with his character and personality, with his faults and other attributes, good or bad and having regard to his behaviour during the marriage, be reasonably expected to live with Mary taking into account her character and personality and good and bad attributes? (See *Ash* v *Ash* (1972).) When they married in 1980 Nicolas and Mary agreed to allow Olive to come and live with them if the need arose. In 1990 they honoured that agreement. It is not clear what particular aspects of her behaviour then led Nicolas to change his mind, and to the domestic discord with his wife. If Olive's behaviour was obviously extreme and disturbed, and remains so, then Mary's insistence that Olive remain in the household is more likely to be considered unreasonable despite what was agreed in 1980 and then in 1990. If Nicolas and/or the children's physical or mental health has been adversely affected by Olive's behaviour then this would considerably strengthen Nicolas's case (see *Katz* v *Katz* (1972) and *Thurlow* v *Thurlow* (1975)). The court is unlikely to rule that the obligations of marriage include an obligation to keep and care for a seriously disturbed relative. If Olive's behaviour is no more than a nuisance and has not adversely affected Nicolas or the children then his claim would be weaker, since the court may take the view that he should honour what he agreed with his wife. Nicolas should be advised that the only decided cases in this area deal with mentally ill spouses and how far the obligations of the petitioning spouse go in terms of remaining married to the ill spouse. The circumstances in this case are different in that the cause of the dissension is an invited guest. Mary's obligations to her sister are likely to be considered less than her obligations to her husband and children. As a result Nicolas is more likely to succeed in establishing that Mary has behaved in such a way that s1(2)(b) is satisfied. Nicolas left in January 1992, then returned in December 1992 and stayed for what appears to a period of between six and seven months in 1993. This may weaken his claim that he cannot reasonably be expected to live with Mary since he in fact returned to live with Mary despite the incidents which persuaded him to leave in the first instance. If he had returned for a period of six months or less then the court would have disregarded this in deciding whether s1(2)(b) had been satisfied (see s2(3) MCA 1973). The fact that he appears to have returned to live with her for more than six months would be not be a bar to his case but may weaken it. If he returned because he was forced to (eg he had accommodation problems) this might persuade the court to ignore the time he stayed with Mary. If fresh incidents occurred during the December 1992 to July 1993 period he could use these in his petition, rather than rely on incidents prior to his return in December 1992.

The next fact is that Mary has deserted Nicolas for a continuous period of at least two years (see s1(2)(c) MCA 1973). Since Nicolas is the person who has left he could not rely on this fact unless he could establish constructive desertion, namely that Mary drove him out of the home by her behaviour in relation to Olive and that by virtue of expelling Nicolas she has constructively deserted him (see *Lang* v *Lang* (1954)). Whether Nicolas can establish this will depend on the nature of Olive's behaviour and its effect on Nicolas and the children. Since constructive desertion requires 'grave and weighty' behaviour on Mary's part this may be more difficult to establish than satisfying s1(2)(b). For this reason it may be better for him to rely on s1(2)(b) than s1(2)(c). The fact that Nicolas returned to live with Mary for over six months will have interrupted any continuous period of desertion (see s2(5) MCA 1973). This means that the two years would only have started again from July 1993 and the court would have ignored the early period of separation in calculating the two years. If Mary makes a reasonable offer of reconciliation to Nicolas this would end the desertion (see *Gallagher* v *Gallagher* (1965)). The court is unlikely to consider any offer from Mary reasonable if it involves Olive remaining in the household, assuming the court has found Mary's insistence that her sister live there had unreasonably driven Nicolas out in the first place.

Nicolas may also petition on the fact that he has lived apart from Mary for a continuous period of two years, and that Mary consents to a divorce (see s1(2)(d) MCA 1973). Mary would have to positively give her consent to the petition. If she is not willing to give her consent then no use can be made of this fact. Second, Nicolas would have to show that he has lived apart from Mary for a continuous period of at least two years. 'Living apart' means not living in the same household, and at least one of the parties being of the view that the marriage is over (see s2(6) MCA 1973 and *Santos* v *Santos* (1972)). Since they have lived apart since July, 1993 this appears to have been satisfied. The earlier period of living apart could not be counted since it was interrupted by Nicolas returning to live with Mary for a period of over six months (see s2(5) MCA 1973). The final fact Nicolas should consider is that of the parties having lived apart continuously for a period of five years (see s1(2)(e) MCA 1973). No consent from Mary is required. However, since Nicolas interrupted the period of living apart, which commenced in 1992, by returning to live with Mary for over six months, this means that the five-year period only commenced from July 1993 (see s2(5) MCA 1973). As a result, this fact is of no assistance to Nicolas should he want an immediate divorce.

In conclusion, Nicolas may be advised that he is most likely to succeed on the basis of irretrievable breakdown, coupled with the fact of two years living apart and Mary's consent or, failing that, the fact of behaviour under s1(2)(b). The fact of desertion under s1(2)(c) by way of constructive desertion is also available to him, but it is hard to see what advantages there are in using this fact when s1(2)(b) is available.

4   Divorce Law Reform

4.1   Introduction

4.2   Key points

4.3   Recent statutes

4.4   Analysis of questions

4.5   Questions

4.1 Introduction

Students are expected to be aware of current changes in family law. Currently the most radical change to family law is in the Family Law Act (FLA) 1996. Students will be expected to know of its provisions in relation to divorce law and the background to those changes.

In 1988 the Law Commission published a discussion paper concerning the possible reform of divorce law. This was followed in 1990 with its report *The Ground for Divorce* (Law Com No 192). In 1993 the Lord Chancellor published a Green Paper called *Facing the Future: Mediation and the Ground for Divorce*. This was followed by a White Paper in 1995 called *Looking to the Future: Mediation and the Ground for Divorce*. The White Paper drew much from the Law Commission's proposals, and was also based on responses to the Green Paper in addition to research commissioned by the Lord Chancellor's Department.

This action was taken against a background of public concern about divorce and the numbers of divorcing couples. Great Britain has the highest rate of divorce in Europe. Criticisms were made of the existing law. As has been seen most petitioners make use of the fault-based facts in order to obtain a divorce (since this enables them to obtain a speedier divorce). It was said that the present law encourages petitioners to make allegations (sometimes exaggerated) against their spouses in order to obtain a quick divorce. This could result in needless conflict, unfairness and a sense of injustice which does nothing to save marriages.

The Government therefore introduced proposals with the following objectives:

a) To support the institution of marriage.

b) To include practical steps to prevent the irretrievable breakdown of marriage.

c) To ensure that spouses understand the practical consequences of divorce before taking any irreversible decision.

d) Where divorce is unavoidable to minimise the bitterness and hostility between the parties and reduce the trauma for the children.

e) To keep to the minimum the cost to the parties and the taxpayer.

The proposals were that the single ground for divorce should remain that of the marriage having broken down irretrievably. After one or both parties have applied for a divorce this ground will be demonstrated by the passing of a period for reflection and consideration. During this period couples will be required to settle arrangements for their children, property and finances (unless the court dispenses with this requirement, for example, in the interests of the children). The spouse applying for the divorce will be obliged to attend an information-giving session which will inform him/her of the various options open to him/her (eg marriage guidance, counselling, family mediation and the legal consequences of divorce). The other spouse will be encouraged to attend. The Government proposed to limit legal aid to specific legal advice during this process so that it should no longer be necessary for parties to be legally represented to the extent they currently are now. The Government wished to make mediation available through the block funding of contracts for mediation services. Though mediation was not be made compulsory it is hoped that divorcing couples should keep control of their own affairs through mediation rather than be steered by lawyers.

The end result of this process of reform is the Family Law Act 1996 which was passed on 4 July 1996. Part I came into force on 21 March 1997. This lays down the general principles underlying Parts II and III (which deal with divorce and separation orders). The principles largely reflect the objectives already mentioned. Parts II and III are not due to come into force until 2000/2001. Pilot projects are underway to test various aspects of the new legislation (eg providing information to divorcing couples).

4.2 Key points

a) *The existing law – Matrimonial Causes Act 1973*

   i)   The sole ground – irretrievable breakdown: s1(1).

   ii) The only ways to prove it – the five facts: s1(2)(a)–(e).

        It is possible for a marriage to have irretrievably broken down but for no divorce to be possible because no fact can be established – is that fair or sensible?

   iii) Three 'facts' are based on fault – in order to obtain an immediate divorce have to rely on fault-based fact. 77 per cent of wife petitioners and 62 per cent of husband petitioners rely on fault-based facts.

        Therefore, there is still much bitterness associated with divorce which does nothing to assist continuing relationships between divorced parents and their children.

   iv) There are 158,000 divorce petitions a year – 40 per cent of marriages end in divorce – high cost to legal aid – high cost to spouses and children involved.

   v)   The existing 'special procedure' for divorce allows divorces to be dealt with by paperwork and does not oblige the parties to reflect on the process or on the consequences for any children.

b) *The Family Law Act 1996*

   The general principles of divorce (s1(a)–(c) FLA 1996)

   'The court and any persons in exercising functions under or in consequence of Parts II and III [of the FLA 1996], shall have regard to the following general principles –

   (a) that the institution of marriage is to be supported;

   (b) that the parties to a marriage which may have broken down are to be encouraged to take all practicable steps, whether by marriage counselling or otherwise, to save the marriage;

   (c) that a marriage which has irretrievably broken down and is being brought to an end should be brought to an end –

(i) with minimum distress to the parties and to the children affected;

(ii) with questions dealt with in a manner designed to promote as good a continuing relationship between the parties and any children affected as is possible in the circumstances; and

(iii) without costs being unreasonably incurred in connection with the procedures to be followed in bringing the marriage to an end.'

Divorce order (s2(1)(a) FLA 1996)

Application is made for a divorce order (which is what an order dissolving the marriage will be called).

A diagram provides a simplified illustration of the new provisions for divorce:

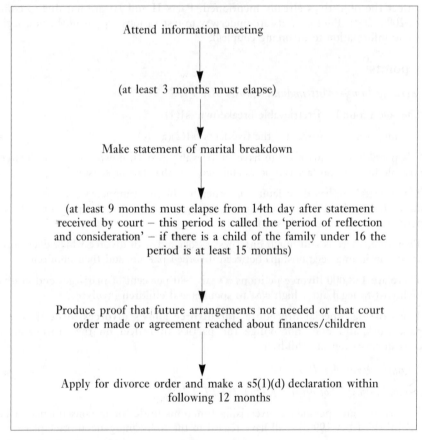

Attend information meeting

(at least 3 months must elapse)

Make statement of marital breakdown

(at least 9 months must elapse from 14th day after statement received by court – this period is called the 'period of reflection and consideration' – if there is a child of the family under 16 the period is at least 15 months)

Produce proof that future arrangements not needed or that court order made or agreement reached about finances/children

Apply for divorce order and make a s5(1)(d) declaration within following 12 months

Applying for the divorce order

Application cannot be made for the divorce order until:

i) the period for reflection and consideration fixed by s7 FLA 1996 has ended; and

ii) the application for a divorce order is accompanied by a declaration by the party making the application under s5(1) FLA 1996 that:

- having reflected on the breakdown of the marriage; and
- having considered the requirements of Part II FLA 1996 as to the parties' arrangements for the future

the applicant believes that the marriage cannot be saved.

The statement of marital breakdown and the application for a divorce order do not have to be made by the same party (s5(2) FLA 1996).

Arrangements for the future

Under s9(2) FLA 1996 a divorce order cannot be made unless one of the following is produced to the court:

i)   a court order (made by consent or otherwise) dealing with the financial arrangements; or

ii) a negotiated agreement as to their financial arrangements; or

iii) a declaration by both parties that they have made their financial arrangements; or

iv) a declaration by one of the parties (to which no objection has been notified to the court by that other party) that he/she has no significant assets and does not intend to make any application for financial provision; and he/she believes that the other party has no significant assets and does not intend to make an application for financial provision; and there are therefore no financial arrangements to be made.

Bar on application for divorce order within one year of the marriage

A statement as to marital breakdown made within the first year of the marriage is ineffective for the purposes of any application for a divorce order (see s7(6) FLA 1996).

Special defence to a divorce order (s10 FLA 1996)

If an application has been made by one party to the marriage the court may on the application of the other party order that the marriage is not to be dissolved. The court may only so order where it is satisfied that:

i)   the dissolution of the marriage would result in substantial financial or other hardship to the other party or to a child of the family; and

ii) it would be wrong in all the circumstances (including the conduct of the parties and the interests of any child of the family) for the marriage to be dissolved (see s10(1) and (2) FLA 1996).

For these purposes 'hardship' includes the loss of a chance to obtain a future benefit (as well as the loss of an existing benefit) (see s10(6) FLA 1996).

Welfare of children (s11 FLA 1996)

In any proceedings for a divorce order the court must consider whether there are any children of the family to whom s11 applies and, where there are such children, whether in the light of the arrangements which have been made or are proposed to be made for their upbringing and welfare it should exercise any of its powers under the Children Act 1989 with respect to any of them (see s11(1) FLA 1996).

Section 11 applies to any child of the family who has not reached the age of 16 at the date when the court considers the case in accordance with s11, and any child who has reached that age at that date and in relation to whom the court directs that s11 shall apply (see s11(5) FLA 1996).

Where it appears to the court that the circumstances require it or are likely to require it to exercise any of its powers under the Children Act 1989 with respect to any child and it is not in a position to exercise the power(s) without giving further consideration to the case and there are exceptional circumstances which make it desirable in the interests of the child that the court should give a direction, then the court may direct that the divorce order is not to be made until the court orders otherwise (see s11(2) FLA 1996).

The court must treat the welfare of the child as paramount in considering whether the circumstances of the case require the court or are likely to require it to exercise any of its powers under the Children Act 1989 with respect to that child (see s11(3) FLA 1996).

Under s11(4) FLA 1996, in making that decision the court must have particular regard on the evidence before it to:

i)   the wishes and feelings of the child considered in the light of his/her age and understanding and the circumstances in which those wishes were expressed;

ii) the conduct of the parties in relation to the upbringing of the child;

iii) the general principle that in the absence of evidence to the contrary the welfare of the child will be best served by his having regular contact with those who have parental responsibility for him and with other members of his/her family and the maintenance of as good a continuing relationship with his parents as is possible; and

iv) any risk to the child attributable to –

   • where the person with whom the child will reside is living or proposes or reside;
   • any person with whom that person is living or with whom he/she proposes to live; or
   • any other arrangements for his care and upbringing.

c) *Observations on the Family Law Act 1996*

Does the Family Law Act 1996 achieve the objectives its sets out for itself?

Does a year's period of consideration and reflection do anything to buttress a marriage that is capable of being saved? On the one hand the consequences of the divorce will be known to the spouses before a final decision is made. On the other the parties are required to make decisions as to their children and their finances at a time when they may feel most bitter about each other.

Do petitioning spouses need to 'blame' the other spouse by using a fault-based fact for therapeutic purposes ? Will a no fault-based divorce be acceptable?

Are the proposals really designed to save legal aid money by involving mediators more than lawyers ?

4.3 Recent statutes

Family Law Act 1996 (Part I which is in force and Parts II and III which are not yet in force)

4.4 Analysis of questions

Examination questions on the Family Law Act 1996 are likely to be of the essay type. They are likely to ask the student to describe the new law and to critically assess its provisions. In answering such questions the student will have to highlight criticisms of the current law and discuss how the new Act deals with those criticisms.

4.5 Questions

QUESTION ONE

'The current law of divorce is confusing and misleading, discriminatory and unjust, provokes unnecessary hostility and bitterness and does nothing to save the marriage.' Discuss. What reforms, if any, to the law of divorce do you consider appropriate?

University of London LLB Examination
(for External Students) Family Law June 1991 Q2

General Comment

This question requires a consideration of the Family Law Act (FLA) 1996 which derives from the Law Commission's report *The Ground for Divorce* (1990). Candidates should review the existing law and consider whether its aims have been met, and thereafter consider to what extent the FLA 1996 will fulfil these aims.

Skeleton Solution

• Discuss differing views relating to object of divorce law expressed by Archbishop of Canterbury's group in *Putting Asunder* and Law Commission.
• Outline current divorce law.
• Consider criticism of current law made by Law Commission in its report *The Ground for Divorce* (1990) and recommendation for reform accepted in the Government's White Paper *Looking to the Future* and enacted in the FLA 1996.
• Does reliance on fault facts add to the distress, bitterness and humiliation?
• Can divorce law save marriages?
• Is the current law confusing and misleading? Is it unjust and discriminatory?
• Consider the Law Commission's proposals and FLA 1996 reforms – one ground, but divorce to be granted only after a transitional period to allow for reflection and the making of arrangements for children and property.

Suggested Solution

The Divorce Reform Act 1969 which forms the basis of the current law on divorce was a compromise between two basic principles expounded by the Archbishop of Canterbury's Committee in its report *Putting Asunder* published in 1966, and the Law Commission.

The Archbishop of Canterbury's group favoured the substitution of 'breakdown' for the matrimonial offence as the basis of divorce law, taking the view that a divorce decree should be seen as a judicial recognition of a state of affairs with a consequent redefinition of status. The Committee favoured the view that the divorce court should carry out a detailed inquest into the alleged facts and causes of the breakdown of the marriage relationship in each case to avoid possible abuse of the law.

However, the Law Commission, which was appointed to investigate the reform of divorce law following the publication of *Putting Asunder*, did not agree that there should be such a detailed inquest, arguing that such a course would be impracticable. The Commission recommended that the grounds that existed already for divorce should be retained but that an additional ground as evidenced by a period of separation, which would be shorter if the respondent consented than if he or she did not, should be introduced. The Commission's aims were to preserve the stability of marriage but it recognised also the social function of divorce, that is to allow parties to enter new legal relationships if they so wished while giving any necessary protection to the children of the family and dealing with financial and property adjustment as required. Further, it believed that a machinery to allow for reconciliation should be provided if there was any possibility that a marriage could be preserved.

Under the Divorce Reform Act 1969 irretrievable breakdown of the marriage became the sole ground for divorce. However, it could only be inferred by proof of one or more of the specified facts which are akin to the old matrimonial offences, although they included two new facts based on separation.

This legislation has been described as an uneasy compromise between two inconsistent views on divorce policy. One view is that divorce should be available to either party to the marriage where it has irretrievably broken down and that the old matrimonial offences are mere symptoms of that breakdown. Another view, however, is that it would be fundamentally unjust to allow a party to petition for divorce on the basis of irretrievable breakdown alone as that could allow a party to rely on his or her own wrongdoing and to obtain a divorce even against the will of the innocent spouse.

Under the current law a divorce is obtainable only where there is evidence of irretrievable breakdown as evidenced by one of the 'facts' set out in s1(2) Matrimonial Causes Act 1973 and a divorce cannot be granted in the absence of one of these facts even where it is clear that the marriage has broken down irretrievably (*Richards* v *Richards* (1972)). This requirement of proof of one of the facts is to ensure that the innocent spouse cannot be divorced against his or her will, at least until five year separation is established and even then the respondent can prevent the divorce if grave financial or other hardship can be established along with injustice in granting the decree.

It is recognised that this reformed law has made it possible for virtually all broken marriages to be dissolved, even though in some cases it may only be after a period of delay. However, it is also recognised that the most commonly used 'facts' on which irretrievable breakdown is evidenced are the fault based ones and in particular adultery and behaviour. One of the objectives of the reformed law was to bury decently a dead marriage and enable the 'empty legal shell' of marriage to be destroyed with the maximum fairness and the minimum bitterness, distress and humiliation. It could be argued that reliance on the fault based facts would only add to the contention between the parties and this view was expressed by the Law Commission in its report *The Ground for Divorce* (1990) Law Com No 192. This would be particularly the case where serious allegations of behaviour were made. However, many practitioners also recognise that the fault facts are frequently used by their clients merely as a device on which to hang the decree nisi, and that any bitterness and hostility arise not really because of the divorce petition, but as a result of the consequences which flow from divorce, namely loneliness, a reduced standard of living and in some cases loss of close contact with one's children. It is argued that even if the basis for divorce was changed to allow a more civilised process, these consequences would still arise and the resultant bitterness would still be present (see Mears [1991] Fam Law 231).

The present law is also criticised by the Law Commission for failing to do anything to save marriage. However, it could be argued that because a petitioner is unable to obtain a divorce (except where the spouses have been separated for five years) without showing one of the fault facts is established or without the consent of the respondent, the law does go some way to saving marriages. In any event it is difficult to see how divorce law can save marriages except by making a divorce more difficult to obtain, and that may have the effect of adding to the tension and acrimony felt by the parties. It is recognised that it is pointless to try to keep any obviously dead marriage alive and by the time spouses seek legal advice on how to dissolve their marriage they have decided their marriage is dead. Therefore any counselling or mediation aimed at saving the marriage is futile at that stage. Divorce does not make a marriage break down. It is merely the mechanism by which the marriage is legally dissolved. The process should be as constructive as possible and the Law Commission stated in its report *The Ground for Divorce* that the aim of the law must be to promote the amicable resolution of practical problems in relation to finance and property and children, to minimise the harm suffered by children and to promote shared parental responsibility.

The Law Commission argued that the current law is confusing and misleading in that, for example, the facts relied upon to obtain a divorce may not really be the true reason for the marriage breakdown. This may be a valid point, for many spouses will seek to rely on a fact which will provide a speedy divorce and this may mean that the facts are used as a convenience rather than as a true reflection of the problems in the marriage. Some writers would question whether anyone is really confused or misled by the law, however, and argue that if the law worked well in practice, this would not be an important criticism.

The Law Commission also argued that the present law is unjust and discriminatory in that inter alia it is unfair that divorce is not readily available at the behest of one party and that the other party may use the requirement of his or her consent (where a petition under s1(2)(d) MCA 1973 only is relevant) as a basis for bargaining on other ancillary matters. However, given that the divorce may cause other adverse consequences such as a reduced standard of living or loss of home, it is questionable whether it is unfair to a petitioner that the respondent should seek to exact a price for his or her consent. Under the present law the 'innocent' spouse cannot be divorced without his or her consent (except where the parties have been separated for five years, subject to the s5 MCA 1973 defence). The Law Commission considered this to be unfair and favours the principle of divorce on demand (albeit after a period of reflection). But the divorce procedures cannot be looked at without also considering their consequences in relation to money, property and children, and given that these are the most important concerns of the parties it should be asked why an innocent spouse should have those consequences unilaterally imposed upon him or her.

The Law Commission's main proposals for reform of the divorce law was followed by the Government's White Paper *Looking to the Future – Mediation and the Ground for Divorce* (April 1995) which led to the Family Law Act (FLA) 1996. The Act is based on the principle that divorce should be available after a period of transition in which the parties are given the time to reflect on this step and to make necessary arrangements with regard to money, property and children.

The FLA 1996 provides for one ground for divorce, namely the irretrievable breakdown of the marriage. This would be established by a sworn statement by either or both parties. Statements giving details of any minor children of the family and the arrangements made for them, and where financial relief and property adjustment is sought, giving information relating to the financial positions of the parties, would also be filed in court.

The parties would be given information regarding the effects of divorce and counselling and conciliation services. These services could provide the forum in which the parties can air their grievances and resolve disputes with each other, a process which is recognised as essential to reduce future conflict and encourage co-operation between the parties.

On the expiration of a period for reflection and consideration either party will be entitled to apply for a divorce order. In their discussion paper *Facing the Future* (1988) Law Com No 170, the Law Commission suggested that a decree could be postponed where the issues in relation to the children had not been resolved or where proper financial or property arrangements had not yet been made. In *Principles of Family Law* (fifth edition) S M Cretney and J M Masson argue that if such postponements were allowed this would encourage hostile litigation to resolve these disputes. The objects of the period for reflection and consideration must include the opportunity to allow the parties to address the feelings of bitterness and hostility attendant on the marital breakup in an unpressured environment. These potential postponements could operate to exert further pressure on the parties.

It is argued that the FLA 1996 has much to recommend it if it means that the aims of the divorce process will be to provide support for families, particularly children, and to avoid conflict if possible. Any divorce process will involve pain and upheaval for the parties concerned and perhaps the most that can be expected of a divorce law is that it does not add to these problems. It must be remembered however that the real areas of conflict, namely financial and property matters and children, remain.

QUESTION TWO

'The retention of some notion of fault in the law of divorce is essential so as to maintain the sanctity of marriage.'

Discuss this statement in the light of the proposals for divorce law reform contained in the current Family Law Bill [now the Family Law Act 1996].

University of London LLB Examination
(for External Students) Family Law June 1996 Q5

General Comment

The Family Law Bill has had a troubled and controversial passage through Parliament. It has provoked much criticism, some of it misguided and misleading. This is not surprising given the strength of feeling about the rate of divorce in Great Britain and its consequences. The difficulty the critics of the Bill face is that the sanctity of marriage and the high divorce rate appear to be more a matter of social and historical forces rather than shaped by statute and the courts. The question invites a discussion behind the reasons for the Family Law Bill, particularly in relation to its proposals to eliminate the need to find fault as the basis for divorce.

Skeleton Solution

- Existing law of divorce – the ground of irretrievable breakdown and the need to satisfy the court of one or more of five facts (s1(1) and (2) MCA 1973).
- The extensive use of the fault facts of adultery and behaviour and consequences of this.
- Law Commission proposals for reform of divorce law.
- Government's approach to divorce law reform through the Family Law Bill – in particular the imposition of a period for reflection and to prepare for the consequences of the divorce – the use of mediation.
- Whether divorce law reform can maintain the sanctity of marriage – the wider social and historical forces which shape divorce.

Suggested Solution

The current divorce law reform contained in the Family Law Bill has provoked considerable controversy in its passage through Parliament. It seeks to remove the notion of fault in the law of divorce. The question asks whether this aim is a laudable one or whether the retention of some notion of fault in the law of divorce is essential to maintain the sanctity of marriage.

It should be remembered that divorce law went through a similar period of reform in the 1950s and 1960s. A Royal Commission (the Morton Commission) published a report on divorce law reform in 1956. This was followed by a report from the Church of England entitled *Putting Asunder* and a Law Commission report. The Law Commission report recommended that the aims of a good divorce law are to 'buttress, rather than undermine, the stability of marriage, and when, regrettably, a marriage has irretrievably broken down, to enable the empty legal shell to be destroyed with the maximum fairness and the minimum bitterness, distress and humiliation'. The consequence was the passing of the Divorce Reform Act 1969. The existing law is contained in the Matrimonial Causes Act 1973 (which replaced the Divorce Reform Act 1969). This law replaced the notion of the matrimonial offence as being the basis for divorce with the notion of irretrievable breakdown of the marriage: see s1(1) Matrimonial Causes Act 1973 – hereinafter referred to as MCA 1973. A petitioner has to establish that the marriage has broken down irretrievably. In addition, he or she must satisfy the court of one or more of five facts: see s1(2) MCA 1973. Three of these facts retain an element of fault. The first is that the respondent has committed adultery and that the petitioner finds it intolerable to live with the respondent: see s1(2)(a) MCA 1973. The second is that the respondent has behaved in such a way that the petitioner cannot be reasonably be expected to live with the respondent: see s1(2)(b) MCA 1973. The third is that the respondent has deserted the petitioner for a continuous period of at least two years immediately preceding the presentation of the divorce petition (see s1(2)(c) MCA 1973). The other two facts are not fault based. One is that the parties have lived apart for a continuous period of at least two years immediately preceding the presentation of the petition and the respondent consents to the decree being granted: see s1(2)(d) MCA 1973. The second is that the parties have lived apart for a continuous period of at least five years immediately preceding the presentation of the petition: see s1(2)(e) MCA 1973. There is protection for respondent spouses who would suffer grave financial or other hardship – they can defend divorces based on five years living apart on the basis of such hardship: see s5 MCA 1973. These is a limited form of protection to safeguard other respondent spouses in divorces relying on s1(2)(d) and (e): see s10 MCA 1973. Petitions are barred within the first year of marriage: see s3 MCA 1973.

When the existing law was first proposed it was thought that the non-fault-based facts would be relied upon in the majority of cases. In fact the fault-based facts of adultery and behaviour are the most commonly used in divorce petitions. For example, the fact of adultery is used by female petitioners in 22 per cent of cases and by male petitioners in 37 per cent of cases. The fact of behaviour was used by female petitioners in 53 per cent of cases. The reason for the use of the fault-based facts appears to be that this is the quickest way to obtain a divorce in many cases. As a result it was argued that petitioners were encouraged to make allegations (sometimes exaggerated) against their spouses in order to obtain a speedy divorce. This can lead to spouses taking up opposing situations from the beginning of the divorce process.

In May 1988 the Law Commission published a discussion paper *Facing the Future* dealing with the possible reform of divorce law. In 1990 it published its report *The Ground for Divorce* which argued that the objectives of the law should be to support marriages which could be saved and to dissolve as painlessly as possible those marriages which could not be saved. These aims were the same as the previous report which led to the 1969 reforms. It also argued that divorce law should encourage parties to resolve issues relating to the children, the home and finance as amicably as possible having regard to their responsibilities to their children and to each other. In particular the law should aim to reduce the harm suffered by children at the time of divorce and afterwards, and to encourage the continued sharing of parental responsibilities towards the children. The existing law was criticised as being confusing, misleading, discriminating and unjust. The use of the fault-based facts were said to encourage unnecessary hostility and bitterness. It argued that the law did little to save marriage, little to help the children and did not help the parties to consider the future in a calm and reasonable manner. The Commission argued that while irretrievable breakdown should remain the sole ground for divorce it should be proved by a single fact, namely the expiry of a minimum period of one year for the consideration of the practical consequences of the divorce and for reflection upon the possibility of reconciliation. In practice this period would commence by either or both parties making a formal statement that the marriage had broken down and lodging that statement with the court. The court would then supply both parties with an information pack explaining the objectives of the ensuing one year period, the court's powers and about opportunities for reconciliation, counselling, mediation and conciliation. Within that year the court could make orders regarding the children, finance and property. Contested matters could be referred to conciliation before being determined by the court. After 11 months of the one-year period had elapsed either party could apply for a divorce order (or a separation order as judicial separation would be termed) and after one month had elapsed from the making of that application a divorce (or separation) order could be issued. These suggestions for reform came against a background of public concern about divorce and the number of divorcing couples. Great Britain has the highest divorce rate in Europe.

The Lord Chancellor published a Green Paper in December 1993 called *Facing the Future: Mediation and the Ground for Divorce* which followed the recommendations of the Law Commission. He proposed a no-fault divorce after only one year of separation and focusing on mediation rather than the courts. Following consultation, a White Paper was published in 1995 detailing the decisions taken on divorce reform – it largely reflected the views of the Law Commission and the Green Paper. The single ground for divorce would be irretrievable breakdown which would be demonstrated by the passing of a one-year period for reflection and consideration and for the parties to settle the arrangements for the children and financial provision. There would be a compulsory attendance at an information-giving session for the petitioner with the respondent encouraged to attend. At this session couples would be informed of the legal consequences of divorce and of options such as counselling and mediation. Local mediation services would be state funded. While supporting the objectives proposed by the Law Commission, the government was also concerned to minimise the cost to the taxpayer and to the parties of the existing divorce process. The government therefore proposed that legal aid would be limited in the new divorce process so that parties keep control of their own affairs preferably through mediation rather than through lawyers. These provisions were then introduced to the 1995/96 Parliament through the Family Law Bill. They attracted considerable controversy and the passage through Parliament has led to a number of amendments and concessions being made.

The difficulty in the reforms and for those who criticise them is that amendments to the law of divorce do not necessarily maintain the sanctity of marriage. If spouses wish to separate they are likely to go ahead regardless of the law or the ease or difficulty with which they can obtain a divorce. The volume of divorce appears to be largely a product of wider historical and social forces rather than changes in the law. For example, there was a significant increase in marriage breakdowns as a result of the enforced separations and upheavals of the Second World War. This increase has continued ever since. The attitude to divorce has changed considerably and religious attitudes have become far less rigid. There is an argument that reforms to divorce law follow social trends rather than shape them. Even with the extensive use of the existing fault-based facts, most divorces are undefended and amount to divorce by consent. One Member of Parliament put it this way: 'I am nervous about whether we in the House can pick up where 2,000 years of Judeao-Christian traditions appear to have failed to singly and, by the stroke of a legislative pen, safeguard marriage for the foreseeable future. That is wishful thinking.'

In conclusion, the proposals in the Family Law Bill are designed to meet the principal criticisms of the existing law. They are designed to eliminate the unjust and arbitrary use of the fault facts which can engender bitterness. They seek to eliminate fault altogether, and to concentrate on the consequences of divorce and to encourage spouses to prepare for them. They are laudable in these aims. It is unfortunate that some seek to criticise the Bill as not maintaining the sanctity of marriage when its aims and objectives are principally to make the end of marriage less painful. A fault-based divorce law is unlikely to change people's behaviour and lead to fewer marriages ending in divorce. As has already been said, this is likely to be 'wishful thinking'.

5   Rights and Obligations during Marriage

5.1   Introduction

5.2   Key points

5.3   Analysis of questions

5.4   Questions

5.1 Introduction

This chapter looks at the right to maintenance during marriage as part of the mutual rights and obligations of marriage. It must be emphasised that the chapter is *not* concerned with powers to award maintenance as part of divorce proceedings (which is dealt with in chapter 6).

5.2 Key points

a) *Application for maintenance under s27 MCA 1973*

A spouse can apply for maintenance to the High Court or county court under s27(1) MCA 1973 under one or both of the following grounds:

i)   that the respondent has failed to provide reasonable maintenance for the applicant; or

ii) that the respondent has failed to provide or make a proper contribution towards reasonable maintenance for any child of the family.

If one of the grounds is satisfied then the court can make lump sum orders or maintenance orders. The court has regard to the considerations in s25 MCA 1973.

The court is unlikely to have jurisdiction to make child maintenance orders since this is dealt with by child support.

b) *Application for maintenance under DPMCA 1978*

A spouse can apply for maintenance to the magistrates' court under the Domestic Proceedings and Magistrates' Courts Act 1978. Application may be made for an order under s2 DPMCA 1978 if one or more of the following grounds under s1 DMPCA 1978 is satisfied:

i)   the respondent has failed to provide reasonable maintenance for the applicant; or

ii) that the respondent has failed to provide or make a proper contribution towards reasonable maintenance for any child of the family;

iii) the respondent has behaved in such a way that the applicant cannot reasonably be expected to live with the respondent;

iv) the respondent has deserted the applicant.

There is no need to show any *wilful* failure to maintain. The ground of behaviour is dealt with in the same way as the divorce fact under s1(2)(b) MCA 1973 (see *Bergin v Bergin* [1983] 1 WLR 279).

If one or more of the grounds is satisfied then under s2 DMPCA 1978 the magistrates' court can make:

i)   a maintenance order for the applicant;

ii) a maintenance order for a child of the family;

iii) a lump sum for the applicant (subject to a maximum of £1,000);

iv) a lump sum for a child of the family (subject to the same maximum).

In deciding whether to make any order and, if so, in what manner, the court must take into account particular considerations (see s3 DPMCA 1978). These considerations are virtually the same as those in s25(1) and (2) MCA 1973). The clean break provisions do not apply. The authorities on s25 MCA 1973 apply to s3 DPMCA 1978 (see *Macey v Macey* (1982) 3 FLR 7 and *Vasey v Vasey* [1985] FLR 589). The one-third principle may apply but this may be inappropriate for low income families (see *Cann v Cann* [1977] 3 All ER 957).

The court also has power to make consent orders for maintenance which have been agreed between the parties. There is no need for the applicant to prove any grounds. The court will make the agreed order where there is nothing to suggest that so to do would be contrary to the interests of justice and the court is satisfied that proper provision is being made for any child. There is no upper limit on lump sum provisions so long as the other party agrees (see s6 DPMCA 1978).

The magistrates' court is unlikely to have the jurisdiction to make child maintenance orders whether under s2 or s6 DPMCA 1978 since this is largely dealt with by the Child Support Agency.

Applications to the magistrates' court have the advantage of being cheaper and speedier than applications to the county court. Where an applicant is legally aided he/she may be obliged to apply to the magistrates' court to reduce costs.

c) *Reforms under Family Law Act 1996*

The Law Commission in its report *The Ground for Divorce* (1990 (Law Com No 192) recommended the abolition of the grounds of behaviour and desertion in s1 DPMCA 1978 in order to avoid bitterness and conflict which could hinder prospects of saving the marriage. These recommendations have been included in the Family Law Act 1996. The grounds for making a maintenance order under s2 DPMCA 1978 are amended to delete the grounds of behaviour and desertion (see s18(1) FLA 1996 deleting s1(c) and (d) DPMCA 1978). This part of the Family Law Act 1996 is not yet in force.

d) *Child support under the Child Support Act 1991*

A parent with children can apply to the Child Support Agency for a child support assessment against the absent parent. Indeed, in most cases the courts have no jurisdiction to deal with child maintenance (though they retain the right to make capital and/or property orders under the MCA 1973, the DPMCA 1978 or the Children Act 1989). The courts retain the power to make child maintenance orders where:

i)   the child is not the natural child of the absent parent (eg a step-child who has been treated as a child of the family);

ii) in the case of a wealthy absent parent where the amount of child maintenance he/she could pay is in excess of the maximum amount of child support which could be assessed;

iii) the child is over 19 (or is between 16 and 19 and not in education);

iv) where one of the child's parents is not habitually resident in the UK;

v) where the child maintenance is intended solely for educational purposes;

vi) where the child is disabled and the child maintenance is to meet expenses attributable to the child's disability.

Child support is calculated according to a fixed formula which can be summarised as follows:

i) calculating the maintenance requirement (based on income support allowances for the child and parent);

ii) calculating the assessable income of both parents (ie net income less 'exempt income' which is made up of fixed outgoings);

iii) calculating the deduction rate;

iv) comparing the deduction rate with the absent parent's protected income.

The student should be aware of the controversy surrounding child support and the various proposals for reform. This is mentioned in a little more detail in chapter 6.

5.3 Analysis of questions

It is most unlikely that an examination question will be set dealing only with rights and obligatons during marriage. However, parts of examination questions ask the student to give advice to a wife whose husband has left her without any means of financial support. The question may combine with rights of occupation which is dealt with in chapter 11.

5.4 Questions

QUESTION ONE

Arthur and Betty married in 1978 and have two children. Early in 1982 Arthur developed a mental illness, as a result of which he erroneously believed that his wife was having an affair with their bank manager. After many heated arguments, which caused distress to the children as well as to Betty, Betty announced that she was leaving home, taking the children with her, and that she was not going to return. Arthur replied that he was glad she was leaving, as he had never wanted to live with an adulteress, but that he was sorry to see the children go and that he would pay Betty £40 a week for their upkeep. Betty left home a few days later and went to stay with her mother.

Arthur was admitted to a mental hospital a few months later but continued to pay Betty £40 a week out of capital he possessed. Betty visited him occasionally both out of a genuine concern for his health and because she was anxious that he should keep up the payments.

In April 1987 Arthur met Celia, a new nurse at the mental hospital, whom he wishes to marry. Betty does not want a divorce because she thinks Arthur will stop paying her the money if he marries Celia.

Assuming that Arthur does not obtain a divorce, how, if at all, can Betty ensure that Arthur makes financial provision for herself and the children?

Adapted from University of London LLB Examination
(for External Students) Family Law June 1987 Q2

General Comment

Financial provision during marriage is regularly examined; in its original form this question also dealt with whether Arthur could divorce Betty – see chapter 3: *Divorce* for this. In answering the question candidates must remember to discuss, in relation to the magistrates' court proceedings, orders under s7 as well as s2 DPMCA 1978. Advice must also be given on an application by Betty to the Child Support Agency for child support for the two children.

Skeleton Solution

• Discuss the two major jurisdictions available to a spouse to obtain financial relief during a marriage, namely s27 MCA 1973 and s1 DPMCA 1978.

• Explain the grounds to be relied upon, and the orders available under s27 MCA 1973 and ss2 and 7 DPMCA 1978 and the factors to be considered by the court applying the guidelines in s25 MCA 1973 and s3 DPMCA 1978.

• Explain how to make an application for child support and how this is likely to be assessed.

Suggested Solution

On the assumption that Arthur does not obtain a divorce at this time there are two procedures available to Betty to ensure that he makes financial provision for herself.

Betty could apply to the High Court or county court under s27 MCA 1973 for financial provision for herself on the ground that Arthur has failed to provide reasonable maintenance for herself and/or the children, and even though Arthur has been paying maintenance regularly, the sum of £40 for the family's support may not be deemed reasonable. However this will depend on Betty's resources as well as Arthur's and it may be that the provision he has been making is reasonable in all the circumstances.

Alternatively she could apply to the magistrates' court for an order under s2 Domestic Proceedings and Magistrates' Courts Act 1978 (hereinafter DPMCA 1978) on one of the grounds set out in s1, namely that Arthur has failed to provide reasonable maintenance for Betty and/or the children (which ground is similar to that set out in s27 MCA 1973 and therefore the reservations mentioned above must be applied to it); or on the ground of Arthur's unreasonable behaviour (which has the same meaning as under s1(2)(b) MCA 1973); or on the ground that Arthur has deserted her (and desertion in the magistrates' court has the same meaning as under s1(2)(c) MCA 1973 although there is no minimum period of desertion so long as it is continuing at the date of the hearing, and will include constructive desertion).

Betty could rely on Arthur's behaviour, ie his false accusations of adultery, which gave rise to arguments between the parties, and even though such behaviour is attributable to his mental illness the court will take it into account having made allowances for the illness and the performance of marital obligations: *Katz* v *Katz* (1972). Alternatively she could rely on s7 DPMCA 1978 which provides that where the spouses have been separated for a continuous period exceeding three months, neither party being in desertion (which may be the case here particularly in view of Arthur's mental illness which may have prevented him from forming the intention to desert), and one spouse has been making periodical payments for the benefit of the other party and for a child of the family, that other party may apply to the magistrates for an order, specifying in the application the aggregate amount received during the three months preceding the application. On hearing such an application the court may order the respondent to make such periodical payments to the applicant, but the amount ordered must not exceed the aggregate amount stated in the application. However, if as a result of this limitation the magistrates feel that reasonable maintenance cannot be awarded, they may refuse to make an order on this ground and treat the application as one for financial provision under s1 and make a suitable order under s2.

So Betty has a choice of applications before her. If the maintenance paid by Arthur is not reasonable she can rely on s27 MCA 1973 or s1(a) DPMCA 1978. Alternatively, she could rely on s1(b) DPMCA 1978, namely on Arthur's behaviour. If she is satisfied with the maintenance paid by Arthur voluntarily, then a s7 DPMCA 1978 application would seem appropriate.

The orders that can be made under s27 MCA 1973 and s2 DPMCA 1978 are similar and include a periodical payments order in favour of the applicant, but which in the county court can be secured although this cannot be done in the magistrates' court. Further, in both jurisdictions the court may make a lump sum order. However, whereas in the county court there is no limit on the amount of the lump sum, in the magistrates' court it is subject to a limit of £1,000, although on application for variation further lump sum awards can be made. It is unlikely that Betty will require a lump sum in excess of £1,000 in any event. It should be noted that under s7 DPMCA 1978 the magistrates have no power to make lump sum provision so if Betty requires a lump sum, say to pay off existing debts, then a s7 application would be inappropriate.

Under s27 MCA 1973 the court will take into account all the circumstances of the case first consideration being given to the welfare of any minor child of the family, including the matters set out in s25(2) MCA 1973 as substituted by s3 Matrimonial and Family Proceedings Act 1984 (hereinafter MFPA 1984), insofar as they apply to an application which does not affect the status of the marriage. Similarly in the magistrates' court, s3 DPMCA 1978 as substituted by s9 MFPA 1984 which sets out the guidelines to be considered when deciding what if any order to make, follows the provisions of s25 MCA. Therefore in this case the relevant factors will include the income, earning capacity, including any increase in that capacity which the court considers it reasonable to expect a party to take steps to acquire, property and other financial resources of the parties (as well as the income and resources of the children, if any); the financial needs, obligations and responsibilities of the parties (and the children) both immediately and in the foreseeable future; the standard of living enjoyed by the family before the breakdown; the age of the parties and the duration of the marriage; the contribution made by each party to the marriage, including a contribution made by looking after the home; any mental or physical defect of the parties (here Arthur's mental illness must be considered particularly as it may affect his earning capacity and general resources); and the conduct of the parties if the court considers that it would be inequitable to disregard it. Conduct is unlikely to be deemed relevant here as although Arthur seems solely to blame for the breakdown of the marriage there is no evidence to show that it would affect the financial claims. In *Robinson* v *Robinson* (1983) the conduct of a wife reduced her periodical payments award but conduct such as Arthur's is unlikely to increase Betty's award.

Finally the court will consider in respect of the children, the manner in which they were being, or were expected to be trained or educated.

No clear information as to the parties' financial status has been given in this question save that Arthur has been paying maintenance out of capital since he was admitted to hospital. If Betty is working, or can be expected to work at this time (and this will depend largely on the age of their children), then any financial provision for herself will be relatively small and may be of a temporary nature to allow her to adjust to a new job and independence. If she already has a job and sufficient income to provide for her own needs then Arthur will not be ordered to make any periodical payments in her favour. In view of his illness it is difficult to say whether he will be able to work and if not, and he has to pay maintenance out of his capital then this may mean that his capacity to pay maintenance is more restricted. However, more information as to his general resources would be required before full advice on this point can be given. Further it is unclear whether Betty will require lump sum provision and if she does, her needs must be balanced against Arthur's ability to pay.

If Betty obtains orders in either the county court or the magistrates' court under the MCA 1973 or the DPMCA 1978, they can be enforced through the court process if Arthur should default in the payment of the same.

Should Betty wish to pursue financial support for the two children she would have to apply to the Child Support Agency for child support. The courts are unlikely to have any jurisdiction to make maintenance orders for them (see s8 Child Support Act 1991). The courts could make lump sum or property adjustment orders but not maintenance. If Betty did apply for child support she should be advised that the CSA calculate the amount due according to a fixed formula. One of the elements of the formula is Arthur's income. If he has no or a limited income of his own then either a nil or a limited child support assessment will be made. No assessment can be made from any capital or property Arthur has: see *J* v *C (child: financial provision)* (1999). Further advice is difficult in the absence of more information on Arthur's finances.

QUESTION TWO

'The Child Support Act 1991 has largely failed because of the absence of any discretion in the new child maintenance system. When fully implemented, the addition of "departures" from the formula will make the system workable.'

Discuss.

University of London LLB Examination
(for External Students) Family Law June 1996 Q2

General Comment

The Child Support Agency and the formula for calculating child support have been highly controversial since they started to operate. As a result child support has been the subject of a discussion question over the past few years. This has required an outline of how the child support system is meant to operate, together with an analysis of its weaknesses and shortcomings. It also involves a discussion of why it was introduced in the first place and whether it has met the promises made when it first came into force. There has been a steady stream of amendments to the Child Support Act 1991 and its accompanying regulations. One of the most recent has been the introduction of a limited right of appeal (called 'departures') which allow some discretion in an otherwise rigid system. Whether the addition of 'departures' from the formula will make the system workable remains to be seen, but the student is required to set out the arguments for and against.

Skeleton Solution

- Why the Child Support Act 1991 replaced the court-based system for child maintenance with the child support formula.
- The components of the child support formula.
- The difficulties created by the formula-based system.
- The recent reforms to improve the child support formula, including the addition of 'departures'.
- Whether the reforms will make the system workable.

Suggested Solution

The Child Support Act 1991 (hereinafter referred to as the CSA 1991) came into force in April 1993. It has caused considerable controversy ever since. As a result of this controversy the Act has been amended on a number of occasions. In particular, the Child Support Act 1995 has made important reforms to the original formula laid out in the CSA 1991.

From April 1993 the jurisdiction of courts to make maintenance for 'qualifying children' came to an end. The definition of 'qualifying children' includes virtually all children who were the subject of court child maintenance orders so courts largely ceased to make such orders and the Child Support Agency assumed responsibility for most child support. As a result the discretion- based court system with a hearing which both parents were able to attend was replaced by a non-discretionary formula calculated by a government agency behind closed doors. The parents' role is confined to supplying information about their financial circumstances to the Child Support Agency which is then fed into the formula and an assessment of child support is automatically produced.

The government introduced the child support system because it considered that court-based maintenance was not working. It argued that because the calculation of levels of child maintenance was a matter of discretion (with broad guidelines given as to the matters to be considered) there was no consistency between courts in the levels of maintenance fixed. It also argued that the levels of maintenance were too low and did not reflect the true costs of bringing up a child. It further pointed out that few child maintenance orders were actually paid regularly. Most were said to be in arrears and enforcement was perceived to be patchy and ineffective. The government was of the view that this was not fair to separated or divorced parents bringing up children. It also meant that the state was paying large amounts of income support and family credit to families where one parent had left and was either paying too little or no maintenance towards the costs of bringing up the children. As a result it decided to abandon the court-based system and replace it with one operated by a government agency. In order to avoid inconsistency and to increase the levels of financial payments for children it introduced a fixed formula to be used to calculate child support. This formula involves a number of stages and these need to be outlined to show the difficulties caused by this approach.

The first stage is to calculate the maintenance requirement which is the starting point for child support. This is the income support allowance for each qualifying child, plus the income support allowance for the caring parent (ie the rate for a claimant over 25 – though this reduces as the child gets older), plus the income support family premium, plus the income support lone parent premium (where the parent caring for the children – called the 'caring parent' – has no partner) but less the child benefit received. This stage continues to cause controversy because it includes an element for the caring parent, unlike the court-based system.

This can cause a perceived unfairness where separating parents have negotiated a clean break order in terms of property and capital, whereby the parent who has left (called the 'absent parent') has surrendered his/her interest in property or capital in return for reduced or no maintenance payments for the former spouse (the parent with care). This difficulty was highlighted in the case of *Crozier* v *Crozier* (1994) where an absent parent attempted to recover his interest in the former matrimonial home because of this element in the child support assessment made against him. He failed to persuade the court to change its original order.

This stage also caused controversy because it produced much higher amounts of child support than the old child maintenance system. The following stages of calculating child support are meant to ensure that the final amount of child support to be paid could be afforded by the absent parent, but the level of protest from absent parents indicated that this was often hotly disputed. The next stage in the calculation of child support is to work out the 'assessable incomes' of the parent with care and the absent parent. This is done by calculating the net income of each parent and deducting from that what is called 'exempt income'. 'Exempt income' is the income support allowance for a claimant over 25, plus housing costs up to a certain amount, plus other allowances if a parent is a lone parent or is disabled and/or has dependent children. This part of the of the calculation has perhaps caused the greatest controversy since it makes little or no allowance for many kinds of expenditure. Payments for debts taken on when the parents were together and in the absent parent's name are not considered. Travelling costs for work or the costs of travelling to see children for contact visits were not considered. The full costs of an absent parent's second family were not allowed. This latter point represented a radical departure from the court-based system. The courts took the view that an absent parent was allowed to start life afresh and allowed him or her to treat the reasonable costs of maintaining a second family as priority items of his or her expenditure. The first family would be maintained out of any balance (if any) even if this left the first family dependent on state benefit because the absent parent could not reasonably maintain two families: see *Barnes* v *Barnes* (1972) and *Delaney* v *Delaney* (1990). The child support formula makes a full allowance for the financial support of the first family with only a limited allowance for the costs of keeping the second family – a complete reversal of the court approach.

The next stage of the child support formula is the deduction rate. This involves sharing the assessable income of the absent parent equally between the children and the absent parent until the maintenance requirement is met. If the parent with care has an assessable income he or she will also contribute towards the maintenance requirement. If the absent parent is particularly well off and his or her income allows more than the maintenance requirement to be paid there are provisions to allow for an extra amount of child support to be paid (called the 'additional element'). The deduction rate for the absent parent is then compared with his or her 'protected income' which is designed to provide a safety net whereby his or income is not reduced to poverty levels by the amount of child support to be paid. 'Protected income' is the income support allowance for a single claimant over 25 (or the allowance for a couple if he or she has a partner), plus other allowances, plus £30 a week, plus council tax payments, plus 15 per cent of any spare income after the allowances have been taken off. This part of the formula was also subject to considerable criticism since many absent parents argued that they were left with insufficient to live on.

The above general outline of the formula for calculating child support gives an indication of how complicated the formula actually is. The formula is meant to be rigid in order to produce consistency. However, it is also designed to take into account the different situations families find themselves in after separation. As a result further complications are introduced. This has led to the Child Support Agency being accused of incompetency in that it takes too long to collect the required information to make the necessary calculations, and then takes too long to do the calculations. It is also accused of getting many of the calculations wrong because of the complexity of the formula. As a result the CSA has been criticised not only by the absent parents (who complain that they are required to pay too much) but also by parents with care (who face delays and mistakes in the calculation of child support). As a result of the perceived injustices of the system there has been a concerted campaign by a number of absent parents to avoid having to pay child support. In other cases the CSA has failed to trace or enforce payments against absent parents who prefer to avoid payment. This has led to critics saying that the child support system has failed to provide the advantages over the court-based system which the government promised.

The criticisms of absent parents have been supplemented by criticisms from some parents with care. While some parents with care have benefited from the child support system by receiving much greater financial support, others have either not benefited in any way or have been left worse off. Those on benefits have accused the government of using child support to reduce expenditure on those benefits by transferring the burden of child support onto the absent parent. In some cases families became worse off because of the inefficiencies of the Child Support Agency. There is an element of compulsion on a parent with care on benefit to co-operate with a child support assessment. If he or she does not co-operate he or she runs the risk of having his or her benefit reduced by 20 per cent for the first six months and by 10 per cent for the following year. It is possible for such a parent to persuade the Child Support Agency that to provide information would lead to undue distress or harm (eg violence from the absent parent). However, this element of compulsion illustrates that the government is seeking to reduce its expenditure on benefits through the child support system. The government has tried to improve the service provided to parents with care (eg by allowing lone parents on income support to keep an extra amount of child support before losing their benefit and by trying to improve the service provided by the CSA).

The government appears to have accepted many of the criticisms from absent parents and has significantly amended the formula in the years following 1993. For example, it has amended the calculation of exempt income whereby an absent parent should not pay any more than 30 per cent of his or her income in child support. It has raised the fixed figure of £30 a week to £40 a week. From April 1995 the CSA will take into account property or capital transfers of at least £5,000 made before 5 April 1993 by the absent parent. An allowance for this is included in exempt income. This is to allow for absent parents who have previously agreed to a clean break settlement in divorce proceedings to get some recognition of this (and so attempting to overcome the problem identified in *Crozier* v *Crozier*). Another amendment has been to allow 100 per cent of pension contributions to be included in the exempt income rather than the previous figure of 50 per cent. An extra allowance will be made for parents who have high travelling costs to their work. Full housing costs will be allowed for absent parents who have new partners and step-children. The maximum additional element a parent can be asked to pay has been halved. These changes have been introduced largely through the Child Support Act 1995 (and accompanying regulations).

Even with these amendments the government has accepted that the formula may still produce serious injustice in some cases. As a result it has now created an appeal system which introduces some discretion. These appeals are called 'departures' and the idea is to provide a final 'safety net' for any problems caused by the rigid application of the child support formula:

see ss28A–28H CSA 1991, as added by the Child Support Act 1995. The first appeal is to the CSA and is called an 'application for a departure direction'. The application can be made subject to a condition that the absent parent pays a fixed amount of child support regularly. There is a further appeal to an independent child support appeal tribunal. The right of appeal is limited. In particular the CSA has to have regard to the general principle that parents should be responsible for maintaining their children whenever they can afford to do so and that they are liable to pay for each child equally. The CSA has to have regard to various factors (in Schedule 4 CSA 1991) and must consider whether it would be just and equitable to allow the appeal having regard to the financial circumstances of both parents and the welfare of the child. The appeal will not necessarily be available in all cases where an absent parent considers a serious injustice has been caused by the child support formula.

Whether the addition of 'departures' from the formula will make the child support system workable remains to be seen. The problems of applying a rigid formula have been manifold and has led to a steady stream of amendments to meet those problems. The system remains largely based on the formula so many problems may still remain even with the safety net of 'departures'. The system has had its successes. It has collected increasing amounts of child support and reduced government expenditure on benefits, as well as increasing the income of parents with care. However, its deep unpopularity and perceived inefficiency and unfairness may still mean that the system would not survive a change of government following a general election.

6 The Financial Consequences of Divorce

6.1 Introduction

6.2 Key points

6.3 Recent cases and statutes

6.4 Analysis of questions

6.5 Questions

6.1 Introduction

This is an important topic both in practice and as far as the examination is concerned. Invariably at least one question on ancillary relief is included in the examination paper each year.

The courts powers are contained in ss23, 24 and 24A of the Matrimonial Causes Act (MCA) 1973 and allow the court to make wide-ranging orders for periodical payments, lump sums, settlement and sale of property and division of the proceeds to either spouse and/or the children. Sections 25 and 25A give guidelines to the court on how to exercise those powers. The student must demonstrate a clear knowledge and understanding of those powers and guidelines, together with the important case law in this area.

It must be remembered that maintenance orders for children are now almost solely dealt with by way of child support through the Child Support Agency (see the Child Support Act 1991). A sound knowledge of when the rules on child support apply and a general awareness of how child support is calculated is also essential for the student.

6.2 Key points

a) *The wide powers under ss23, 24 and 24A MCA 1973*

A question about ancillary relief should start with an outline of the wide powers of the court under s23 (power to make periodical payments), s24 (power to settle property on one or both spouses) and s24A (power to order the sale of property and divide the proceeds of sale). Where children are involved it should be made clear where the court's jurisdiction to make maintenance order ends and is replaced by the Child Support Agency's power to order child support.

b) *The s25 guidelines*

If there are children involved their welfare is the first consideration (s25(1)). This does not mean that their welfare is paramount and overrides other considerations but it will be of the first importance (see *Suter v Suter and Jones* [1987] 2 All ER 336).

The court will consider all the circumstances but must have regard to particular matters.

First, the income, earning capacity, property and other financial resources which each of the parties has or is likely to have in the foreseeable future, including in the case of earning capacity any increase in that capacity which it would in the opinion of the court be reasonable to expect a party to the marriage to take steps to acquire (see s25(2)(a)). This will largely be a factual matter based on the information given in the question, though the student will often be expected to highlight any earning capacity and comment on it (eg whether a non-working wife with the care of children has any earning capacity). The student may also be required to consider any interest by way of damages or under a will or by way of third parties (eg wealthy members of a spouse's family). Students will need to know such cases as *Michael* v *Michael* [1986] 2 FLR 389 (interests under a will), *Wagstaff* v *Wagstaff* [1992] 1 WLR 320 and *Thomas* v *Thomas* [1995] 2 FLR 668 (assets of third party).

Second, the financial needs, obligations and responsibilities which each of the parties to a marriage has or is likely to have in the foreseeable future have to be considered (s25(2)(b)). The costs and responsibilities of bringing up any children for the parent with whom they live or are to live must be emphasised. This may be particularly important in terms of any property orders since the need for any children to be properly housed will be of the first importance. This may favour an outright transfer to the parent with the children or a *Mesher* order (though the dangers of *Mesher* orders need to be known). The costs of any second family must also be considered (applying *Delaney* v *Delaney* [1990] 2 FLR 457).

Third, the student should mention the standard of living enjoyed by the parties before the breakdown of the marriage (see s25(2)(c) MCA 1973). The point which needs to be made in most cases is that there is likely to be a reduction in that standard as a a result of the breakdown of the marriage, but that the court will seek to spread such a reduction fairly between the parties. Where the spouses are wealthy the court will seek to maintain both parties to the standard they are accustomed to. Mention should also be made of the age of the parties and the duration of the marriage (see s25(2)(d) MCA 1973). The age of the parties may be more relevant when it comes to the clean break provisions and in assessing the earning capacity of either party. Where there has been a long marriage both parties are likely to be given credit for that, whereas a short marriage is likely to lead to a clean break and limited financial provision. The student will be expected to be aware that cohabitation before marriage is not normally considered to be relevant (see *H* v *H* (1981) 2 FLR 392, but contrast *Day* v *Day* [1988] 1 FLR 278). Questions do not normally disclose any physical or mental disability of either party so this consideration rarely needs mention (see s25(2)(e) MCA 1973).

An important consideration is the contribution made by each of the parties to the welfare of the family, including any contribution made by looking after the home or caring for the family (see s25(2)(f) MCA 1973). Where a question includes a non-earning wife who has looked after the children this will be an important foundation of her claim for financial provision (see *Wachtel* v *Wachtel* [1973] 2 WLR 366). Any contributions to establishing a successful business will also be considered under this heading (see *Gojkovic* v *Gojkovic* [1991] 3 WLR 621). Any lack of contribution would be a minus factor.

The student should be aware of the place of conduct in assessing financial provision. Financial provision is more of a mathematical exercise than a moral one (see *Duxbury* v *Duxbury* [1987] 1 FLR 7). The court will only consider conduct if it is such that it would be inequitable to ignore it (see s25(2)(g) MCA 1973). The student will need to be aware of the kinds of conduct which the court has taken into account (eg financial misconduct as *Day* v *Day* (above))

The importance of the loss of any pension rights is currently much in vogue. The student should be aware of ss25B–25D MCA 1973 (as introduced by the Pensions Act 1995). The student does not need to have a detailed knowledge of these provisions. Suffice he/she must stress that the court will consider the pension provision of the parties and may make a pension 'ear marking' order, namely provision for one spouse from the pension of the other, but only when that pension provision comes into effect (ie on retirement or death). At present there is no power to make a pension 'splitting' order, ie an order providing for immediate provision for one spouse from the pension provision for the other spouse.

The student must then move on to deal with the clean break provisions. He/she must state that in deciding what orders to make the court has a duty to consider making orders whereby the obligations of one party towards the other will be terminated as soon after the grant of the decree as the court considers just and reasonable (see s25A(1) MCA 1973). If the court decides to make a maintenance order for a spouse it must consider whether it would be appropriate to limit the term of the maintenance for such period as to enable that spouse to adjust without undue hardship to the end of his/her financial dependence on the other party (see s25A(2) MCA 1973). The student should stress that the court does not have a duty to impose a clean break but must consider it (see *Barrett* v *Barrett* [1988] 2 FLR 516). In advising on the effect of these provisions the age of the spouses and their work experience and/or earning capacity will be important. If there are children this will not rule out a clean break but will make it less appropriate. Where one spouse is older, and has no or limited work experience, the courts have shown considerable reluctance to impose a clean break (see *M* v *M* [1987] 2 FLR 1). The clean break provisions are relevant to property orders since they favour an outright transfer or, where this would not be fair to one party, a *Martin* style order (see *Clutton* v *Clutton* [1991] 1 All ER 340). Where one of the parties is wealthy the possibility of a lump sum calculated by the *Duxbury* calculation may be relevant. However, it should be emphasised that such a calculation is only a tool to assist the court and should not supplant s25 considerations.

The relevance and application of the one-third guideline may be relevant (see *Wachtel* v *Wachtel* (above). The student will need to know how it operates and when it is unlikely to be applied (eg in low or high income cases).

The Legal Aid Board charge may be an additional complication in the question. Where one party is legally aided the student must be able to describe the effects of the Legal Aid Board charge and how to avoid it or minimise its consequences. This will include advice to either party to minimise his/her costs and not to contest trivial issues or to unnecessarily raise matters (eg conduct) which may increase costs. It will also include advice on limiting lump sums of £2,500 and making use of the exemption on maintenance orders. It will also include advice on postponing any charge on the home or proceeds of sale used to house the spouse/children.

The relevance of state benefits may also be an important feature. This both includes the fact that the maintenance of the children will be invariably outside the court's jurisdiction and will be a matter for the Child Support Agency by way of child support. An important exception is where there are step-children which can be made the subject of court maintenance orders. Where there are only limited financial resources the fact that the courts will accept one spouse having to rely on state benefit rather than making financial provision orders which will financially cripple the other spouse needs to be highlighted (see *Delaney* v *Delaney* [1990] 2 FLR 457).

c) *Child Support Act 1991*

Although the Child Support Act (CSA) 1991 has been mentioned already a fuller outline of how child support is provided since some questions deal exclusively with this area. As from 5 April 1993 courts lost the jurisdiction to make maintenance orders for children (see s8(3) CSA 1991) with the following exceptions:

i)   Only natural or adopted children are included in child support so courts can make maintenance orders for step-children who are 'children of the family'.

ii) Lump sum and property orders for children may still be made by the courts.

iii) In the case of wealthy parents the courts may still make child maintenance orders which exceed the maximum levels of child support.

iv) Where the child is over 19 (or is between 16 and 19 and not in education) the court can make a child maintenance order.

v)   Where one parent is not habitually resident in the United Kingdom the court can make a child maintenance order.

vi) Where the child maintenance order is intended solely for education purposes (eg school fees) a child maintenance order may be made for such purposes.

vii) Where the child is disabled and the child maintenance is to meet expenses attributable to the child's disability again a child maintenance order can be made for such purposes.

A parent with children who is in receipt of benefit is obliged to supply details of the absent parent to the Child Support Agency (CSA) should the CSA wish to make a child support assessment against the absent parent. The parent with children (called the parent with care) may be penalised if he/she does not supply this information unless he/she can show that he/she or the children would suffer undue harm or distress. The penalty is a 20 per cent reduction in the parent with care's benefit for the first six months and a 10 per cent reduction for the following year.

Child support is calculated using the following stages:

i)   calculating the maintenance requirement (which is the income support allowance for each qualifying child plus the income support allowance for the caring parent plus the income support family premium plus the income support lone parent premium if the parent with care is single less the child benefit for each child – the income support allowance for the caring parent reduces as the youngest child gets older);

ii) calculating the assessable incomes of the parent with care and the absent parent (which is net income less exempt income – 'exempt' income is the income support allowance for a single parent plus reasonable housing costs plus other allowances plus certain travel to work costs – allowance is given for property or capital transfers of at least £5,000 made by the absent parent before 5 April 1993);

iii) calculating the deduction rate (which is 50 per cent of the combined assessable incomes of both parents – there is provision for 'top up' payments if the deduction rate is more than the maintenance requirement);

iv) comparing the deduction rate with the absent parent's protected income (protected income is the income support allowance for an adult/couple plus reasonable housing costs plus other allowances plus £30 a week plus council tax plus 15 per cent of any

63

spare income – any deduction of child support must not bring the absent parent's income below his/her protected income).

Where an absent parent has contact with his/her children for 104 nights a year there are provisions to reduce the amount of child support.

A particular source of grievance for absent parents is the consequence of child support for existing court orders, particularly clean break orders imposed by the court on the basis that the absent parent did not have any ongoing financial commitment to the former spouse and/or children. As outlined above child support includes an element for the parent with care – a kind of indirect spouse maintenance. It was confirmed in *Crozier* v *Crozier* [1994] 2 WLR 444 that a child support assessment was not a reason to set aside a clean break consent order made in full and final settlement of a spouse's claim for herself and the children. The consequences of *Crozier* have been recognised in that allowance is now given for clean break property or capital settlements of a value of £5,000 or more. The courts will take into account child support in fixing its orders for financial provision. See *Mawson* v *Mawson* [1994] 2 FLR 985 where a spouse's financial provision was varied to take into account the child support position.

The Child Support Act 1991 has proved very controversial. Its provisions have attracted much criticism as being unfair, rigid and bureaucratic. The CSA has a considerable backlog of work. As a result it has abandoned plans to take over existing court maintenance orders where the spouse in receipt of the maintenance is not in receipt of benefit.

The Child Support Act 1995 has introduced, inter alia, provision to allow for a limited right of appeal against child support assessment. The appeals are called 'departure directions' and allow a limited discretion to deal with cases where unfairness may have been caused as a result of the child support assessment

6.3 Recent cases and statutes

Conran v *Conran* [1997] 2 FLR 615 (on a wife's 'outstanding' contribution to the husband's business and welfare of the family giving her a large award)

C v *C (financial relief: short marriage)* [1997] 2 FLR 26 (showing caution in applying a clean break even after a short marriage)

G v *G (periodical payments: jurisdiction to vary)* [1997] 1 FLR 368 and *Flavell* v *Flavell* [1997] 1 FLR 353 (advising caution in relation to term maintenance orders as part of a clean break)

Section 31(7A)–(7F) MCA 1973 (as inserted by the Family Law Act 1996 on 1 November 1998) giving courts the power to make property adjustment and lump sum orders when dealing with a variation application

6.4 Analysis of questions

There will always be at least one question on this area in every examination. The question is usually a problem-solving question (as opposed to an essay question) since the examiner is looking for a practical understanding of how the principles are applied to particular circumstances. The question is normally solely concerned with ss23–25A MCA 1973, but additional matters (eg the Legal Aid Board charge) may also be included. It is also possible for the question to include advice on the grounds for nullity or divorce.

6.5 Questions

QUESTION ONE

Judith and Michael married in 1984 and have twin girls who were born in 1986. The couple have lived separately since 1988. Judith, who works as a dentist, remains in the jointly owned matrimonial home with the girls and Michael rents a small flat. In December 1990, Michael, who is a teacher, began cohabiting with Stella who owns a large house and is extremely wealthy. He now wishes to divorce Judith and she has indicated that she will consent to the divorce.

Advise Michael, who wishes to know the likely financial orders which the divorce court may make.

University of London LLB Examination
(for External Students) Family Law June 1991 Q5

General Comment

This is a straightforward question on financial provision and property adjustment on divorce. The only difficulty with it lies in the fact that candidates are given no detailed information as to the value of the property or the value of the parties' interests in that property, so the advice given on the property adjustment aspect of the question is necessarily rather general.

Skeleton Solution

• Outline orders available under s23, 24 and 24A MCA 1973.
• Discuss in some detail the relevant factors in s25(2) referring first to the welfare condition in s25(1) MCA 1973.
• Discuss s25(2)(a), (b), (c), (d), (f), (g) and discount (h).
• Discuss the clean break principle in s25A MCA1973.
• Discuss child support for the children, discount such an order for a spouse. Discuss property adjustment orders – consider the options. Discuss in detail an outright transfer and *Mesher* order.

Suggested Solution

The court has power to make various orders for financial provision for a party to the marriage and/or any children of the family pursuant to divorce proceedings under s23 Matrimonial Causes Act 1973 (hereinafter MCA 1973), namely periodical payments and lump sum payments for a spouse. Further, under s24 MCA 1973 the court may make a property adjustment order, that is, it can, inter alia, order one party to transfer to the other party such property, or an interest in such property, as may be specified by the court, or to order the settlement of such property for the benefit of the other party and/or the children. It can also order the sale of property under s24A MCA 1973. Maintenance of the children is now dealt with separately by the Child Support Agency which operates independently to the courts.

When deciding what, if any, orders to make the court will consider the matters set out in s25 MCA 1973 as substituted by s3 Matrimonial and Family Proceedings Act 1984. The court is under a duty to have regard to all the circumstances of the case and must give first consideration to the welfare of any minor children of the family (s25(1) MCA 1973). This means that the twins' welfare will be a first consideration for the court although it will not be paramount (*Suter v Suter & Jones* (1987)).

In addition the court will have regard to the matters set out in s25(2) MCA 1973 in respect of a spouse's claim.

Under s25(2)(a) MCA 1973 the court will consider the income, earning capacity, property and other financial resources which each of the parties has or is likely to have in the foreseeable future, including any increase in earning capacity which it is reasonable to expect a party to take steps to acquire. In this case we are given no details of the spouses' incomes but it is clear that both parties have secure jobs which will earn them reasonable incomes. It is likely that Judith earns more than Michael, particularly if she is working full time. Michael is now cohabiting with Stella who is wealthy. The court has no power to make an order which would in effect provide for the children out of Stella's resources (*Macey* v *Macey* (1982)). However, the court may consider Stella's resources to the extent that they will release more of Michael's own income to discharge his obligations towards his family (*Slater* v *Slater* (1982), *Suter* v *Suter & Jones*).

The resources of the parties must be balanced against their financial needs and obligations both now and in the foreseeable future (s25(2)(b) MCA 1973). These needs include the everyday living expenses of the family such as food, clothing and accommodation costs. The children live with Judith and therefore their needs will be greater than those of Michael, who has only his own needs to cater for, particularly in relation to accommodation. The children's welfare requires that they be provided with adequate accommodation so far as practicable (*Harman* v *Glencross* (1986)). At the moment Judith and the children live in the former matrimonial home and, in the absence of evidence to the contrary, it is likely to be adequate accommodation and not excessive to their needs.

The standard of living enjoyed by the family before the breakdown of the marriage will be considered under s25(2)(c) MCA 1973, not so as to place the parties in the position they would have been in had the marriage not broken down, for this is seen as an impossible task, rather, to distribute any drop in living standards as evenly as possible so far as this is reasonable and fair. In this case Judith and Michael earn reasonable salaries so it is unlikely that there has been any appreciable drop in living standards since they separated in 1988. This factor in s25(2)(c) is likely to be considered more relevant in relation to the accommodation requirements, particularly of the children. The court will wish to ensure that they are provided with accommodation of the same standard as that enjoyed during the marriage, so far as this is practicable. Clearly this would be practicable and reasonable in this case.

The age of the parties is relevant when assessing the future earning capacities of the parties and their ability to be financially independent of one another. The duration of the marriage is relevant under s25(2)(d) also, and linked to this will be the consideration of the contribution made by each party to the marriage, including any future contribution likely to be made to the welfare of the family (s25(2)(f); *Wachtel* v *Wachtel* (1973)). It is probable that both Judith and Michael have made equal contributions during the marriage which effectively lasted four years. Judith will continue to make a contribution in the future in that she will be responsible for the care of their children.

Conduct, if it is considered inequitable to disregard it, will be taken into account under s25(2)(g) MCA 1973. Generally the court is unwilling to investigate the cause of the breakdown of the marriage particularly, as in a case such as this, where it is likely that both parties are responsible for the breakdown. We are given no reason why Judith and Michael separated in 1988. If, as seems likely, it occurred because of mutual incompatibility then the conduct issue is irrelevant in this case and will not affect the outcome of their financial proceedings.

Finally, it is unlikely that the court will have to consider losses of benefits under s25(2)(h) MCA 1973 in view of the parties' ages and financial independence.

The court is now also under a duty to consider the clean break provisions contained in s25A MCA 1973, that is to decide whether it is appropriate to terminate all further financial obligations of each party towards the other pursuant to orders made under ss23 and 24 MCA 1973, or in the case of a periodical payments order in favour of an applicant, to limit the period for which such payments are made. It is clear from caselaw (see *Suter* v *Suter & Jones*) that even if orders are made in favour of children, it is not inconsistent to impose a clean break as between the spouses themselves.

It is submitted that a periodical payments order in Judith's favour is inappropriate because she is financially independent and will continue to be so. Therefore a clean break under s25A MCA as between Judith and Michael is appropriate. There is no suggestion either that Michael should receive financial assistance from Judith even if she is earning more than him unless their earnings were very disparate.

With regard to the matrimonial home, it is jointly owned but we are given no information as to its value or any equity value therein. It is likely, unless it is excessive to the needs of Judith and the children, that the court will be minded to retain it to provide suitable accommodation for the children. Generally if it was of great value and provided accommodation in excess of the family's needs then it could be sold immediately and the proceeds divided between Judith and Michael, enabling them to obtain alternative, more appropriate accommodation for themselves. In such a case it would be likely that Judith would be granted a greater share than half in respect of the proceeds to reflect the fact that she would be seeking new accommodation for herself and the children.

It is more likely that the house provides no more than adequately for the family's accommodation needs. It may also be the case that the equity in the property would not be sufficient to enable Judith to easily acquire alternative accommodation with her share of the proceeds, even if that share was enlarged. Other options therefore should be considered. The court could order that Michael transfer his interest in the property outright to Judith so that the home becomes hers absolutely. This has the advantage of providing certainty as to the future in that the children have secure accommodation while they need it, and Judith's future accommodation requirements are adequately provided for as well. Michael is now living with Stella and certainly, if the relationship is a stable one, the court could take the view that he does not require his share of the equity in the house to secure alternative accommodation for himself. It is, however, difficult to be certain as to the relevance of such an order as we have no idea of the value of any interest we would be transferring to Judith if such an order was made. If the equity in the property was large and the value of the shares was great it may do an injustice to Michael to transfer his entire share to Judith.

A more appropriate option may be to retain the property in joint names and to suspend sale of it until the children reach school leaving age, that is for twelve or thirteen years. Thereafter the property could be sold and the proceeds divided between Judith and Michael in the shares deemed appropriate by the court at this time. If necessary the court could give Judith a greater share in those proceeds to reflect the fact of her continued contribution to the welfare of the children in her looking after them and also the fact that she will be using her share to finance the purchase of alternative accommodation (*Mesher* v *Mesher* (1980)). As Judith has a good income it is unlikely that she would suffer such hardship at the time when the house was sold as was envisaged in cases such as *Carson* v *Carson* (1983). However, the *Mesher* order does create a possible problem in that if Judith wished to move before the end of the period for which the sale is postponed, she would not be entitled to use Michael's share of the proceeds when purchasing alternative accommodation for herself and the children (*Thompson* v *Thompson* (1985)).

Another, perhaps more appropriate option, may be to transfer the house to Judith outright but to give to Michael a charge over the property in respect of his share in the proceeds of sale (see *Knibb* v *Knibb* (1987)). The charge could provide that the statutory power of sale would arise in certain circumstances such as Judith's remarriage or cohabitation with another man for a specified period, or when she voluntarily left the house.

As an alternative to that order the house could be transferred to Judith outright and she would make an immediate payment to Michael effectively in settlement of his interest. Such an order may be appropriate if Judith could raise the sums necessary to buy Michael out. In such circumstances it is unlikely that she would have to pay him the equivalent of a half share as the court may be minded to increase her share to take into account her continued contribution to the family in the case of the children, the needs of heself and the children for suitable accommodation and the fact that Michael is receiving his share immediately.

QUESTION TWO

In 1990, Deborah, who was then 30, married Edward, a successful barrister, who was then 50 years old. Deborah, whose first husband, Frederick, an accountant, had died in a car accident in 1988, originally trained as an actress, but has not been employed outside the home since the birth of her twins in 1987.

After her marriage to Edward, Deborah and the twins moved into Edward's Chelsea home, which he had inherited from his mother and is valued at £500,000. As his current income is approximately £70,000 per annum she and the twins enjoyed a comfortable lifestyle. Indeed, Edward employed a full time nanny so Deborah was able to secure a small part in a film.

In 1992 Deborah discovered that Edward was incapable of being faithful and she has filed a petition for divorce.

Advise Deborah of the likely financial provision, if any, she can obtain for herself and the twins.

University of London LLB Examination
(for External Students) Family Law June 1993 Q3

General Comment

This question deals with one of the few areas of child maintenance where courts continue to exercise jurisdiction, the maintenance of step-children or 'children of the family'. The term 'child of the family' needs to be explained as well as the considerations in ss25 and 25A of the Matrimonial Causes Act 1973 which a court will take into account in deciding whether to exercise its wide powers of financial provision in ss23, 24 and 24A of the 1973 Act. The likelihood of a clean break order for Deborah and the particular considerations in s25(3) as far as the twins are concerned need discussion in advising on what kind of orders could be made against Edward. The fact that the children are stepchildren means that the Child Support Act 1991 does not apply so the court can order child maintenance.

Skeleton Solution

- The jurisdiction of the court to deal with financial provision for step-children in light of the Child Support Act 1991.
- Definition of 'child of the family' and whether the twins are children of Edward and Deborah's family.
- The considerations in ss25 and 25A MCA 1973.
- The likely order for Deborah in light of the clean break provisions.
- Section 25(3) MCA 1973 and the likely orders for the twins.

Suggested Solution

Advice is requested concerning the likely financial provision, if any, Deborah can obtain from Edward for herself and the twins. Since Deborah has filed for divorce she can seek orders for financial provision under ss23, 24 and 24A of the Matrimonial Causes Act (MCA) 1973. These sections give the court wide powers to make financial provision on divorce including orders transferring, settling or selling property, lump sum orders and maintenance orders.

Two matters need to be considered as far as financial provision for the twins is concerned. Firstly courts have largely lost the jurisdiction to make maintenance orders for children since the Child Support Act 1991 came into force on 5 April 1993 and a government agency (the Child Support Agency) took over the assessment and collection of financial support for children. Deborah can be advised that the Child Support Act 1991 only applies to the natural or adopted children of the absent parent (see s8 Child Support Act 1991). Since the twins are the step-children of Edward the court would retain the jurisdiction to make financial provision for them. Secondly the court could only order Edward to make financial provision for the twins if they were each a 'child of the family' ie they had been treated by both parties as children of the family (see s52 MCA 1973). The test is an objective test which looks at how Edward treated the twins. In this case it appears that Edward did treat the twins as children of his family by having them live with him and Deborah, employing a nanny to look after them and giving them a comfortable lifestyle over the two years of the marriage.

In deciding whether and, if so, how to exercise its wide powers to order financial provision, the court will have particular regard to certain considerations. The court will give first consideration to the welfare of the twins (se s25(1) MCA 1973). This does not mean that their welfare will outweigh all other considerations but will be of first importance in deciding what financial provision is just (see *Suter* v *Suter and Jones* (1987)). The need for the twins to be properly housed and maintained will be of first importance. The court will have regard to the income, property and other financial resources of Edward and of Deborah. It will take Edward's relative wealth and his inheritance into account. The court will consider both his and Deborah's earning capacity both now and in the foreseeable future including any increase in that capacity which it would be reasonable, in the court's opinion, for a party to take steps to acquire (see 25(2)(a) MCA 1973). The twins are now six years old and presumably attending primary school. Deborah has trained as an actress and has recently started to make use of her earning capacity in this respect. She should be prepared to make the most of her earning capacity in these circumstances.

The court will consider the financial needs, obligations and responsibilities of both Edward and Deborah as they are now and will be in the foreseeable future (see s25(2)(b) MCA 1973). Deborah's obligations will include the need to house the children and provide for them. Such needs will be particularly important since the welfare of the children is the first consideration. The court will consider the standard of living enjoyed by each party before the breakdown of the marriage (see s25(2)(c) MCA 1973). The court will have regard to the comfortable lifestyle Deborah and the children had while living with Edward for the two years of the marriage and may make orders reflecting that lifestyle (see *Foley* v *Foley* (1981)). The court will have regard to the age of the parties and the duration of the marriage (see s25(2)(d) MCA 1973). Deborah is of an age where she could reasonably be expected to have an earning capacity and enough time to establish some independence, though her obligations to her children limit her in this respect. The marriage was relatively short. This may persuade the court to limit Edward's duty to provide financially for Deborah though his duty towards the twins is likely to be more long term. The court will have regard to the contributions made by both Edward and Deborah to the welfare of the family, including looking after the home and caring for the children (see s25(2)(f) MCA 1973). Credit will be given to Deborah's contribution in looking after the twins though her contribution may not be counted as great as a full time mother given that a nanny was employed to look after the children. Edward will also be given credit for providing the family with a comfortable lifestyle and providing the nanny. If Edward neglected his responsibilities to Deborah and the twins this could be considered as a lack of contribution (see *West* v *West* (1977)) but there is no specific information on this point. Deborah should be advised that the court will only consider the conduct of the parties if it is such that, in the opinion of the court, it would be inequitable to disregard it (see s25(2)(g) MCA 1973). The court is unlikely to have regard to Edward's conduct since the ordering of financial provision is usually a mathematical exercise rather than a moral one (see *Duxbury* v *Duxbury* (1987)). A court would not be likely to increase any order for financial provision in order to punish Edward for his infidelities. If Deborah attempted to use the court in this way it would probably lengthen the proceedings with no likelihood of gain to her. Conduct has been considered relevant in some instances but these have been exceptional (eg where a spouse has unilaterally and unreasonably abandoned the other spouse who has been blameless – see *Cuzner* v *Underdown* (1974) and *Robinson* v *Robinson* (1983)). The court will also consider the value of any benefit Deborah would lose as a result of the divorce (eg a pension right) (see s25(2)(h) MCA 1973) but there is no information on this point.

Deborah should be advised that in considering financial provision for her the court will consider whether it would be appropriate to exercise its powers so that the financial obligations of each party towards the other will be terminated as soon after the divorce as the court thinks just and reasonable (see s25A(1) MCA 1973). If the court decides to make a maintenance order for her it must consider whether it is appropriate to require the payments under such an order to be made for only such term as would be sufficient to enable her to adjust without undue hardship to the termination of her financial dependence on Edward (see s25A(2) MCA 1973). The court will consider Deborah's age, her present work and how secure it is and her future job security in light of her need to care for the twins. If the court concludes that Deborah has little job security particularly in light of her responsibilities to the twins it may consider that a clean break is not appropriate (see *Day* v *Day* (1988)). If the court considers that she has job security even with her responsibilities for the children and the uncertain nature of the acting profession it may make no maintenance order for her or limit the period of any maintenance order it makes.

In considering financial provision for the children the court will take into account their financial needs and the way they are being educated, including what plans Deborah and Edward had for their education (see s25(3)(a) to (d) MCA 1973). Since the twins are not Edward's natural children the court will consider the extent to which he assumed responsibility for their maintenance over the two years of the marriage and on what basis (see s25(4) MCA 1973). He appears to have assumed full responsibility for them and is likely to be obliged to provide for them financially (see *Day* v *Day*).

In all the circumstances the court is likely to order that Edward make some financial provision for Deborah. The marriage was short, Deborah is relatively young and in work, albeit not very secure work. She enjoyed a comfortable lifestyle with Edward. The court is likely to make a clean break order by obliging Edward to pay a lump sum for her and/or provide her with a property for her and the twins to live in. The court may also make a limited period maintenance order. Such orders would provide her and the children with secure accommodation and Deborah with sufficient to enable her to adjust to the end of the marriage and maintain something of the lifestyle she has become used to. Edward appears to have the financial resources to comply with such orders. The court is unlikely to oblige Edward to maintain Deborah until her death or remarriage given the shortness of the marriage and the clean break provisions. Edward is likely to be obliged to maintain the twins until they finish full time education. Providing for their accommodation and enabling them to have a reasonable lifestyle will be the court's first consideration. The court may also take into account the twins' need to be looked after while Deborah is at work (though they will now be attending school). This could increase any maintenance order made for the children.

QUESTION THREE

Imogen and John married in 1973. They had one child, Kate, who is now 19 and studying at a drama college in London. John, who is a dentist, established a successful practice in the matrimonial home. His elderly parents, who are very wealthy, regularly supplemented his comfortable income with significant cash sums. Imogen had trained as a teacher, but she chose not to work outside the home after her marriage, preferring to act as a homemaker and mother and occasionally assisting John in his practice.

The family enjoyed a comfortable lifestyle. The matrimonial home, which John inherited from his grandmother, was refurbished more than once, the couple acquired a holiday home in Scotland and took yearly holidays abroad. To provide for their future, John invested in a valuable private pension scheme and collected twentieth-century paintings.

In 1992, John began a public affair with Laura, one of Kate's schoolfriends. Imogen was hurt and humiliated, but encouraged a reconciliation. However, the affair continued and Imogen divorced him in March 1994. Imogen and Kate now seek your advice with regard to the financial provision that they can expect from John.

Advise Imogen and Kate

University of London LLB Examination
(for External Students) Family Law June 1994 Q4

General Comment

The question deals with the likely orders for financial relief for a wife and 'adult child' as a result of a recent divorce. It requires discussion of the wide powers of the court under ss23, 24 and 24A and the considerations in ss25 and 25A of the Matrimonial Causes Act 1973. From Imogen's point of view particular attention needs to be given to the credit she will receive for the length of the marriage, her contribution to the household and bringing up the family, the standard of living enjoyed during the marriage and possible loss of pension rights. John's behaviour may also be relevant. The significance of his wealthy family needs to be discussed. This is also relevant as far as Kate is concerned, as are her plans to attend drama college. Given her age the court is able to make orders for her despite the Child Support Act 1991.

Skeleton Solution

- Wide powers to order financial provision under ss23, 24 and 24A of the Matrimonial Causes Act 1973.
- General considerations under ss25 and 25A MCA 1973.
- Considerations for Imogen:
  - John's financial resources including his wealthy family;
  - Imogen's financial resources and earning capacity;
  - the standard of living enjoyed by Imogen and John during the marriage;
  - the age of the parties and duration of the marriage;
  - Imogen's contribution to the family and household;
  - John's conduct;
  - Imogen's loss of pension rights;
  - whether the clean break provisions are likely to be applied.

- Considerations for Kate:
  - Child Support Act 1991 does not apply;
  - her financial needs and the way she expects to continue her education;
  - John's financial resources;
  - the duration of any maintenance order.

Suggested Solution

Imogen and Kate should be advised that the court has wide-ranging powers to make maintenance, lump sum and property orders (including transferring the ownership or ordering the sale of the matrimonial home and/or holiday home) (see ss23, 24 and 24A of the Matrimonial Causes Act (MCA) 1973). In deciding whether to exercise its wide powers and, if so, in what manner, the court will have regard to all the circumstances and make such orders as it considers just and reasonable. It is bound to have regard to particular matters which will affect the likely financial provision for Imogen and Kate.

In Imogen's case the court will have regard to the income, earning capacity, property and other financial resources she and John each have and are likely to have in the foreseeable future (see s25(2)(a) MCA 1973). In the case of earning capacity the court will have regard to any increase in that capacity which it would be reasonable to expect either party to take steps to acquire. The court will consider John's successful dental practice. It will consider the financial assistance given to him by his wealthy parents. This may include his inheritance prospects but only if this is a reasonable possibility in the foreseeable future. This will depend on the age and health of his parents. If such prospects are too vague and remote the court will not consider them (see *Michael* v *Michael* (1986)). The court will take into account the matrimonial home and holiday home and John's collection of twentieth-century paintings. Imogen and Kate should be advised that the court will not be bound by strict rules of who owns what. It may distribute the property or order its sale as it sees fit. From Imogen's point of view the court will note that she has not worked full time for many years. She may have a earning capacity either as a teacher (though the world of teaching has undergone many changes in recent years) or by virtue of her experience in helping in John's practice. If she is able to make use of these skills to acquire an income the court will expect her to do all that is reasonable to take steps to acquire that income.

The court will then look at the financial needs, obligations and responsibilities which each have now and will have in the foreseeable future (see s25(2)(b) MCA 1973). This will include the need for either party to find alternative accommodation if the other party remains in the former matrimonial home. Since John's business is established there it is likely that the court will allow him to remain there so that he can carry on with his successful business. However, the court will require him to make provision whereby Imogen is rehoused in as equivalent style of housing as is reasonable. Expenses could also include any expenses either parent will have in supporting or accommodating Kate while she is at college or when she returns home to visit either parent. It could also include John's obligations towards Laura if he intends to marry or support her. The standard of living enjoyed by the family before the breakdown of the marriage will also be considered (see s25(2)(c) MCA 1973). In this case the parties enjoyed a comfortable standard of living. Now that the marriage has broken down it may not be possible to maintain this standard. However, the court will seek to ensure that any decline in that standard of living is equally shared so that, for example, John is not left with a far better standard of living than Imogen.

The court will consider the age of Imogen and John and the duration of the marriage (see s25(2)(d) MCA 1973). Both parties will be given credit for the length of the marriage. Imogen's age may be particularly relevant in terms of her earning capacity since the older she is the more difficult it may be for her to find full time employment. The court will consider any physical or mental disability of either party (see s25(2)(e) MCA 1973) and the contributions made by John and Imogen to the welfare of the family, including Imogen's contribution in looking after the home and caring for Kate as she grew up (see s25(2)(f) MCA 1973). Imogen is likely to be given considerable credit for her contribution for more than twenty years in acting as homemaker, bringing up Kate and occasionally assisting John in his practice and thereby foregoing her own chance of establishing employment as a teacher. The court will only consider the conduct of the parties if it would, in the court's opinion, be inequitable to disregard it (see s25(2)(g) MCA 1973). Normally the court considers that determining financial provision is largely a mathematical exercise rather than a moral one. It normally would wish to avoid any kind of post mortem into the breakdown of the marriage. However, in this case conduct may be in issue if it appears that John has behaved particularly badly in abandoning a 'blameless spouse', in making his affair with Laura so public and in rejecting a reasonable offer of reconciliation (see *Robinson* v *Robinson* (1983)). If the court is of this view then John may be required to make greater provision for Imogen. The court will also consider any loss of pension rights which may result from the divorce (see s25B MCA 1973). This may be particularly important for Imogen since she may have very poor pension provision. If the marriage had continued she would have been covered by John's pension cover either as his spouse or as his widow. The court may seek to compensate her for the loss of her pension rights or make a pension ear-marking order under s25B MCA 1973.

In relation to deciding what provision to make for Imogen the court is under a duty to consider whether it would be appropriate to exercise its powers so that the financial obligations between

John and Imogen will be terminated as soon after the grant of the decree as the court considers just and reasonable (see s25A(1) MCA 1973). If the court decides that John should pay maintenance to Imogen the court must consider whether it would be appropriate to require those payments to be made only for such term as would in the court's opinion be sufficient to enable Imogen to adjust without undue hardship to the termination of her financial dependence on John (see s25A(2) MCA 1973). Imogen may find it difficult to attain financial independence given her age and lack of work experience. Unless a generous capital and property settlement is made in her favour the court may feel unable to impose a clean financial break between the parties. The courts have shown considerable reluctance to impose such a clean break where a late middle-aged wife is left in a situation of financial weakness and uncertainty (see for example *M* v *M* (1987)).

Financial provision for children of separated parents is mostly dealt with by the Child Support Agency (see s8 Child Support Act (CSA) 1991). However, Kate is of such an age that the divorce court would be able to deal with the question of financial provision for her (see s55 CSA 1991). Normally the court only orders financial provision in relation to children aged under 18 years, but it can make provision for children above this age who are receiving training or education (see s29(3) MCA 1973). Since Kate is going to drama school the court can consider her case. It will consider her financial needs, her income, financial resources and earning capacity (eg whether she can work during holiday periods) and the manner in which she is being, and in which John and Imogen expected her to be, educated or trained. The court will also consider the matters already discussed in relations to s25(2)(a), (b), (c) and (e) MCA 1973). Given that Kate also enjoyed a comfortable lifestyle while her parents were together, and that her parents may well have supported her wish to study at drama school, it is likely that John will be ordered to make financial provision for her while she is studying full time at the drama school.

In conclusion, given all the considerations outlined above and the court's duty to achieve a fair result having regard to all the circumstances, it is likely that John will remain in the former matrimonial home where his business has been established. The court is likely to order him to make generous financial provision for Imogen so that she can be rehoused and is able to continue to live as close as possible to the lifestyle she has become accustomed to. The provision will need to reflect Imogen's possible weak financial position having regard to her sacrifices and contribution to the welfare of the family. This may involve John in having to sell his paintings and the holiday home or transfer them to Imogen in order to increase the provision for her. That provision may also be increased having regard to John's conduct in breaking up the marriage. A clean-break settlement seems unlikely unless John can provide a sufficiently large capital settlement to give Imogen long-term financial security. Kate is also likely to receive financial provision to allow her to continue her education and the lifestyle she has enjoyed while her parents were together.

QUESTION FOUR

Discuss the applications for financial relief of the following petitioners:

a) Fiona, now 40, who married Gerard in 1975. Although a qualified accountant, Fiona did not work outside the home during the marriage, but devoted herself to the care of the household and the upbringing of Harry and Imogen, the children of Gerard's dead sister and brother-in-law, who are now aged 12 and 11 respectively. During the marriage, Gerard, a merchant banker, earning over £100,000 per annum, accumulated a number of properties, including the large home that the family have lived in since 1980 which is now valued at £1,000,000. He also established a valuable private pension scheme. Gerard is now living with Jane, his former secretary who is 22, in a new flat he has acquired, while Fiona, who still has care of the children, is currently living in the former matrimonial home.

b) Kelvin, an unemployed actor, now 35, who married Lia, a barrister, now 43, in 1985. The couple have no children and Kelvin, who developed an ulcer in 1990, largely as a result of alcohol abuse which is still continuing, will be unable to work for some time. Lia earns £80,000 per annum and her assets include the former matrimonial home, which Kelvin continues to occupy, valued at £120,000 and the small flat she lives in, worth £70,000, acquired since the breakdown of the marriage.

University of London LLB Examination
(for External Students) Family Law June 1995 Q3

General Comment

The two parts of the question deal with ancillary relief after the breakdown of the marriage (and presumably as a result of divorce proceedings, though the question does not make this clear). Part (a) asks the student to evaluate the claim of a wife of some 20 years who has no work experience and who made a significant contribution to the welfare of the family. Her contribution includes caring for children who are 'children of the family'. She is likely to have a strong claim against her wealthy spouse. Her lack of pension provision and his valuable pension scheme merit special consideration. Part (b) reverses the situation in that the husband has no income and it is the wife who is in the stronger financial position. The conduct of the husband is a particular factor in these circumstances.

Skeleton Solution

a) • Wide range of powers under ss23, 24 and 24A MCA 1973 to make financial provision for Fiona.
  • Welfare of children of family is first consideration (s25(1) MCA 1973) – definition of 'child of the family' and whether Harry and Imogen are children of the family.
  • Section 25(2) MCA 1973 considerations, particularly in terms of respective incomes and outgoings, Fiona's contribution to the welfare of the family and the respective pension provisions of the parties.
  • Clean-break provisions under s25A MCA 1973 and whether they might apply in Fiona's case.

b) • Wide range of powers under ss23, 24 and 24A MCA 1973 to make financial provision for Kelvin.
  • Section 25(2) MCA 1973 considerations, particularly the respective income and outgoings of the parties, Kelvin's earning capacity and whether his conduct might be relevant.

Suggested Solution

The question does not make it clear what kind of petitions have been lodged by Fiona or Kelvin. It is assumed that they have petitioned for divorce though since the provisions for financial relief also apply to petitions for nullity or judicial separation the advice given could apply to these applications as well.

a) Fiona should be advised that the court has wide powers to make financial provision for her. It can order Gerard to pay maintenance and/or a lump sum payment to her and make orders either settling property on her or transferring it to her or ordering its sale and the division of the proceeds (see ss23, 24 and 24A of the Matrimonial Causes Act 1973 – hereinafter called MCA 1973). In deciding what provision, if any, it should order it will do what it considers just and reasonable taking into account particular factors.

First, the court must give first consideration to the welfare of any children of the family under the age of 18 (see s25(1) MCA 1973). This does not mean that the welfare of such a child overrides all other considerations but it will be of first importance (see *Suter* v *Suter and Jones* (1987)). Harry and Imogen are not the natural children of Fiona and Gerard. They will nevertheless be children of the family if they have been treated by both parties as children of Fiona and Gerard's family (see s52(1) MCA 1973). The court will look at the situation objectively and ask whether both Fiona and Gerard have treated and looked after Harry and Imogen as they would have their own children (see *W* v *W* (1972)). Assuming that the children have been treated as children of the family the court will give first consideration to their need to be housed, maintained and looked after. Since Fiona is living with them and they remain in the former matrimonial home the court will give first consideration to making orders which preserve this situation.

Second, the court will look at the income, earning capacity, property and other financial resources which each of the parties to the marriage has or is likely to have in the foreseeable future. In the case of earning capacity the court will expect either party to take reasonable steps to increase that capacity (see s25(2)(a) MCA 1973). Fiona has no income of her own. She appears to have a very limited earning capacity since she has not worked outside during the 20 years of marriage. Though she is a qualified accountant it is likely that her skills will be significantly out of date so that she is unlikely to find well-paid accountancy work. Having said that, she should make all efforts to find employment now that the children are in full-time education. By contrast, Gerard is well paid and has various properties, including his own independent accommodation.

The court will then look at the financial needs, obligations and responsibilities the parties have now and in the foreseeable future (see s25(2)(b) MCA 1973). This will include Fiona's and the children's need to be housed and to have sufficient income to live on. It may include Gerard's obligations towards Jane if he intends to marry her or have a long-term relationship with her. In relation to the children, Gerard is likely to be required by the court to make financial provision for them, taking into account the fact that he has accepted responsibility for them (together with Fiona) over what may be a considerable period of time (see s25(3) and (4) MCA 1973). He is likely therefore to bear the financial burden of their maintenance. Fiona should be advised that the Child Support Agency cannot be involved since Harry and Imogen are not his natural children. The court will look at the standard of living enjoyed by the parties before the breakdown of the marriage (see s25(2)(c) MCA 1973). Fiona is likely to have enjoyed a high standard of living as the wife of a wealthy merchant banker and the court will seek to avoid any unnecessary drop in her standard of living. The court will look at the age of Fiona and Gerard and the duration of the marriage (see s25(2)(d) MCA 1973). Fiona's age may count against her obtaining suitably paid employment. Gerard's age is not given. Both parties will be given credit for the 20 years of marriage. No physical or mental disabilities are disclosed for the court to consider (see s25(2)(e) MCA 1973). The court will give credit to Fiona for her contribution over the 20 years of marriage in looking after the home and in looking after Harry and

Imogen (see s25(2)(f) MCA 1973). Gerard will similarly be given credit for his contribution to the welfare of the family. The court will not take the conduct of either Fiona or Gerard into account unless any conduct was such as it would be inequitable to disregard it (see s25(2)(g) MCA 1973). Financial provision is treated by the courts more as a mathematical exercise than a moral one and the court is likely to want to avoid any post mortem into why the marriage broke down. It may be possible that Gerard's conduct might be relevant if the court took the view that he abandoned a blameless wife, but this is not likely unless he behaved in a particularly reprehensible manner (see *Robinson* v *Robinson* (1983)).

In the case of a divorce or nullity, the court will have regard to any pension rights Fiona may lose as a result of the end of the marriage (see s25B MCA 1973). Fiona may well lose generous pension rights under Gerard's valuable pension scheme, and the court will seek to compensate her for that, particularly in view of the fact that she is unlikely to be able to provide sufficient pension cover for herself.

The court has to consider whether to exercise its powers in such a way that the financial obligations of each party towards the other terminate as soon after the decree as the court considers just and reasonable (see s25A(1) MCA 1973). In the case of any maintenance order Gerard might have to pay for Fiona, the court will consider whether it should limit the term of the order to such term as would enable Fiona to adjust to the termination of her financial dependence on Gerard without undue hardship (see s25A(2) MCA 1973). The courts have shown themselves to be cautious in imposing a clean break after a long marriage and where a spouse has limited earning capacity (see *Morris* v *Morris* (1985) and *M* v *M* (1987)).

While insufficient information is given to be more precise about what will happen to Fiona's application for financial relief, it appears that unless Gerard can provide a sufficiently large lump-sum payment which would generate sufficient income to meet Fiona's reasonable living expenses (called a *Duxbury* calculation), in addition to providing for the children he is likely to be required to pay maintenance to her. It is possible that the court will make an order that the former matrimonial home be held on trust for Fiona and the children to stay there until the children have finished their education when the house can be sold and the proceeds divided so that Fiona can find suitable accommodation (see *Mesher* v *Mesher* (1980)). An outright transfer of the home to her is unlikely, given its value. Alternatively, Gerard may be required to provide Fiona with a sufficient lump sum to allow her to rehouse herself and the children. Since the children may have lived in the same home for most of their lives this may persuade the court that they should continue to live in it for as long as they need to.

b) The same statutory provisions apply in Kelvin's case and so there is no need to repeat them. There are no children so s25(1) MCA 1973 will not apply in this context. The court will look at Kelvin's lack of income but also at his earning capacity. The condition of his ulcer suggests that he will be unable to work for some time. By contrast, Lia is a well-paid barrister. Their respective financial needs, obligations and responsibilities will be considered, as will the ages of the parties and the duration of the marriage. Credit will be given to both parties for the ten years of marriage. Lia may receive greater credit for her contribution to the welfare of the family unit since she has borne the brunt of financially maintaining Kelvin. Kelvin's physical disability will be considered. If Kelvin's disability has been largely self inflicted this may count as behaviour which it would be inequitable to disregard (see s25(2)(g) MCA 1973). In a case with similar circumstances the husband's poor financial state was considered to be largely self inflicted, in contrast to the wife's efforts to improve herself. Having said that, financial provision was still made whereby he could accommodate himself (see *K* v *K* (1990)). The clean-break provisions will also be relevant. In one case a husband had so reduced the quality of his life because of his drinking the court concluded that there would be no point in ordering the wife to pay maintenance since it would add nothing to his quality of life (see *Seaton* v *Seaton* (1986)). Kelvin's case does not seem to be in this somewhat extreme category. Following the decision in *K* v *K* the court may consider ordering the sale of the former matrimonial home and providing Kelvin with sufficient proceeds of sale to rehouse himself. This could be combined with a maintenance order whereby Lia provides financial support for Kelvin, if the court considers this just and reasonable, or a maintenance order for a limited period during which Kelvin would be expected to adjust to the end of any financial dependence on her (whereupon Kelvin would have to find work or rely on state benefits).

QUESTION FIVE

Rebecca and Andrew, now aged 37 and 48 respectively, married in 1982. The matrimonial home was inherited by Andrew from his grandparents and is now worth £500,000. At the time of the marriage it was Andrew's wish that Rebecca act as a housewife and look after any children they might have and support him in his career as owner of a large newspaper chain. Rebecca, who had had a short career as a nanny prior to her marriage, was happy to agree to this plan. Rebecca was an excellent homemaker during the marriage and by virtue of her skills as a hostess, she proved to be an enormous asset to Andrew in expanding his business. Unfortunately, Rebecca and Andrew were unable to have children of their own, but in 1990 took over the care of Sabrina, Andrew's niece, who is now aged eight, whose parents, charity workers, had been killed in a car accident.

In 1992, Rebecca discovered that Andrew was having an affair with Lucy. Believing that this was a result of a short-term crisis, Rebecca was at first understanding and sought to retain the marriage. However, Andrew continued the affair and began to take Lucy, rather than Rebecca, to social functions and began to refer to her to his business associates as 'my true partner'. In early 1996, Rebecca divorced Andrew on the basis of his adultery.

Rebecca now wishes to be advised as to the likely financial provision she can expect for herself and Sabrina. As well as owning the matrimonial home, Andrew owns a country house outside Oxford, worth £200,000. The newspaper chain, which is partly owned by his sister, is worth £12 million and he draws a personal salary of £150,000 per annum. He has also invested in a number of private pension plans so that his future will be secure. Sabrina, whose parents left no assets, attends a private day school and is a promising pianist.

Advise Rebecca.

University of London LLB Examination
(for External Students) Family Law June 1996 Q4

General Comment

This is a standard question on ancillary relief after divorce. It involves a wealthy husband and a wife with no apparent means but who has made a substantial contribution to the family and helped her husband in his business. It also involves a 'child of the family' who is not the natural child of the parties. These points need to be brought out in the outline of the considerations under the Matrimonial Causes Act 1973 which the court will have regard to.

Skeleton Solution

- Wide powers of the court under the MCA 1973 to make orders for financial consideration.
- Discretion to make orders as is just and reasonable but subject to certain considerations.
- Welfare of child of family is first consideration (s25(1) MCA 1973) – definition of child of family and considerations which apply (ss23 and 52 MCA 1973).
- Considerations under s25(2) MCA 1973:
  - income, property and earning capacity;
  - outgoings;
  - standard of living before marriage ended;
  - age of parties and duration of marriage;
  - contribution to welfare of family by looking after the home and child and contribution towards business;
  - relevance of conduct;
  - need to consider pension position.
- Clean break provisions under s25A MCA 1973 – the *Duxbury* calculation as a basis for a clean break.
- Conclusion:
  - provision of accommodation for wife and child;
  - provision for child (especially education);
  - clean break lump sum for wife.

Suggested Solution

Rebecca asks for advice on the likely financial provision she can expect for herself and for Sabrina following her divorce from Andrew. Rebecca should first be advised that the courts have wide powers to make orders for maintenance payments, lump sum orders and for the sale or settlement of property owned by either her or Andrew: see ss23, 24 and 24A Matrimonial Causes Act 1973 – hereinafter referred to as MCA 1973. The court has a wide discretion to make such orders as it considers just and reasonable but must take into account particular considerations: see ss25 and 25A MCA 1973. Rebecca can be advised that these particular considerations will have considerable influence on the likely financial provision for herself and Sabrina.

The court will give first consideration to the welfare of Sabrina as a child of Rebecca's and Andrew's family: see s25(1) MCA 1973. This does not mean that her welfare will determine what orders are made but the need for her to be maintained and to be properly housed and educated will be of the first importance: see *Suter* v *Suter and Jones* (1987). It is noted that Sabrina is not the natural child of Andrew and Rebecca. However, if she has been treated by both as a child of their family she will be a 'child of the family': see s52(1) MCA 1973. Since Sabrina appears to have been so treated from 1992 until the parties separated the court is likely to conclude that she is a child of the family. In deciding on financial provision for her, the court will take into account her financial needs and any income, earning capacity, property and other financial resources she has. It will consider the manner in which she is being educated or trained, as well as the manner in which Andrew and Rebecca expected her to be educated or trained: see s23(3) MCA 1973. This is likely to include Andrew continuing to pay for her private day school and for any piano tuition if this is what he and Rebecca provided and planned for. The court will also have regard to the extent to which he assumed responsibility for Sabrina knowing she was not his child and the liability of any other person to support her: see s23(4) MCA 1973. Andrew and Rebecca appear to have accepted sole and full responsibility for her since she is an orphan and has no assets of her own.

The court will then go on to consider the income, earning capacity, property and other financial resources which each of Rebecca and Andrew has now or is likely to have in the foreseeable future, including any increase in earning capacity which it would be reasonable to expect either party to take steps to acquire: see s25(2)(a) MCA 1973. Rebecca appears to have no income or assets of her own. She may have a limited earning capacity but appears to have been away from the world of work since her marriage in 1982. She is unlikely to have either the qualifications or work experience to have any realistic ability to get a well-paid job. Sabrina is also still quite young and at a day school, which may further limit Rebecca's employment options. However, if she has any earning capacity she will be expected to take steps to realise it. Andrew has considerable assets. He has an income of £150,000, owns the matrimonial home worth £500,000 and a country house worth £200,000. He has interests in a business worth £12 million. It is noted that this is part-owned by his sister. The court will take a realistic approach to the wealth to which he has access via the business and also to the assets he could have access to should the court make an order he could not meet from his immediate liquid assets: see *Thomas* v *Thomas* (1995). He also appears to have private pension plans to secure his retirement. The court will then look at the financial needs, obligations and responsibilities which each of the parties has or is likely to have in the foreseeable future: see s25(2)(b) MCA 1973. Since Rebecca appears to be continuing to care for Sabrina, this financial obligation and responsibility will be of first importance in the court's mind. Rebecca needs to be housed appropriately and to receive an appropriate income to live on. If Andrew wishes to remarry he can argue that he will have the obligation and responsibility for maintaining Lucy. The court will also have regard to the standard of living enjoyed by the family before the breakdown of the marriage: see s25(2)(c) MCA 1973. It is assumed that Rebecca and Andrew had a rich lifestyle in keeping with Andrew's income and status. The court will seek to ensure that Rebecca is either able to maintain an equivalent lifestyle or that any drop in lifestyle is shared equitably between the parties. However, in light of Andrew's apparent wealth Rebecca should be advised that there is a possibility that the court will only make provision which maintains her to the lifestyle to which she is accustomed as opposed to any higher provision: see *Thyssen-Bornemisza* v *Thyssen-Bornemisza (No 2)* (1985). English courts tend to order what they consider to be reasonable financial provision to meet reasonable needs rather than make higher orders in order to give a former spouse a larger share of the other spouse's wealth. The court will have regard to the age of the parties and the duration of the marriage: see s25(2)(d) MCA 1973. Rebecca is still relatively young but has a limited earning capacity. Andrew is at an age when he is likely to carry on working for another ten years or so but where retirement may be an option. Both parties will be given credit for a marriage which has lasted 14 years, particularly Rebecca who has made considerable efforts to keep the marriage going.

The court will look at the contributions which each of the parties has made or is likely to make in the foreseeable future to the welfare of the family. This will include any contribution by looking after the home or caring for the family: see s25(2)(f) MCA 1973. Rebecca can be advised that this consideration is likely to be a significant factor since she gave up work to act as a housewife and to support up Andrew in his career. The court will note that she was described as an 'excellent homemaker' during the marriage and her skills as a hostess were an 'enormous asset' to Andrew in expanding his business. She will also receive credit for taking over the care of Sabrina who was no relation to her. She is also likely to receive credit for her understanding after discovering Andrew's adultery in 1982 and trying to keep the marriage going. Her future contribution in caring for Sabrina will also be noted by the court. Rebecca can be advised that these factors are likely to increase any award for financial provision: see *Wachtel* v *Wachtel* (1973) and *Vicary* v *Vicary* (1992). Rebecca can be advised that the court is unlikely to consider the conduct of the parties unless that conduct is such that it would in the opinion of the court be inequitable to disregard it: see s25(2)(g) MCA 1973. The courts tend to treat financial provision as more of an arithmetical exercise than a moral one: see *Wachtel* v *Wachtel* and *Duxbury* v *Duxbury* (1987). The court may take Rebecca's positive conduct into account in that she appears to have made considerable efforts to keep the marriage going and to help Andrew and to care for Sabrina. It may possibly consider Andrew's conduct if it considers that he abandoned a blameless spouse for no good reason: see *Robinson* v *Robinson* (1983), but more recent authorities suggest a greater reluctance to take conduct into account.

The court will also consider the value of any benefit which each party will lose as a result of the divorce: see s25(2)(h) MCA 1973. Rebecca may lose any rights to any pension cover which may be included in Andrew's private pension plans. She can be advised that the loss of pension rights is a matter of considerable debate at the present time. The court is likely to be concerned that Rebecca has some kind of provision for the future given her lack of any kind of cover in her own right. This concern may be emphasised by amendments to the Matrimonial Causes Act 1973 introduced by the Pensions Act 1995 (which added ss25B–25D to the MCA 1973). These changes do not affect Rebecca's case since they were not in force at the time of her divorce petition, but the spirit of them may still influence the court. The new provisions place a duty on the court to consider the pension provision of the parties and give new powers to make orders so that when Andrew's pensions come into effect provision can be made for Rebecca. In her case, though these new provisions do not apply, the court can compensate her with a lump sum payment. It may also be possible to vary Andrew's pensions plans if they fall within the definition of a post-nuptial settlement in order to provide for Rebecca: see *Brooks* v *Brooks* (1995) and s24(1)(c) MCA 1973.

The court will also consider whether it would appropriate to make orders whereby the financial obligations of Andrew to Rebecca will terminate as soon after the divorce decree as the court considers just and reasonable: see s25A(1) MCA 1973. If the court makes a maintenance order in her favour the court must consider whether it would be appropriate to limit the term of the order to such a term as would enable Rebecca to adjust without undue hardship to the termination of her financial dependence on Andrew: see s25A(2) MCA 1973. Rebecca can be advised that the courts have shown some reluctance in imposing a clean break where a former wife is in a financially weak position, particularly where she is of an age where it is difficult to get back into the job market or to find any work with a reasonable income. However, if Andrew is able to provide a lump sum payment which will give her security then a clean break order may well be considered. Given Andrew's apparent wealth this may be a real possibility. Rebecca should be advised that one way of achieving a clean break is via the *Duxbury* calculation (named after the case of *Duxbury* v *Duxbury*). This involves calculating a lump sum which if invested (with assumptions made as to life expectancy, rates of inflation, return on investments, growth on capital and tax rates) would produce enough to meet Rebecca's needs for life. Such a figure can then be used as a guide to produce a settlement which the court considers just and reasonable (eg *Vicary* v *Vicary*).

Rebecca should be advised that the court is likely to provide her with accommodation suitable to her standard of living and suitable for Sabrina. If the former matrimonial home is considered too large and lavish for their needs the court may order that Andrew provide a lump sum to buy a suitable property (even if this means the sale of one of the properties and a division of the proceeds). It is likely to require Andrew to provide for Sabrina's education including her school fees and any expenses for her piano tuition. Normally the court cannot provide for any child maintenance since this is dealt with by the Child Support Agency. However, child support only applies to natural children so the court could make a maintenance order to a child of the family. In addition, the likely financial provision would be well above child support provision. It is also likely to require Andrew to provide a lump sum clean break settlement for Rebecca to give her security and to provide for her retirement. Such provision is likely to be generous given her substantial contribution to the home and to caring for Sabrina and her help in Andrew's business.

7 Domestic Violence

7.1 Introduction

In this chapter we look at the way the law attempts to deal with the social problem of domestic violence. The emphasis here is on violence by a husband or male partner towards his wife or female partner (though violence by the wife or female partner towards the husband or male partner does occur). Child abuse is dealt with in chapter 10. It is possible that a question combines violence towards both wife/partner and her children but the answer normally only requires a discussion of the remedies under the Family Law Act 1996 rather than local authority child protection procedures. The student has to demonstrate a knowledge of Part IV of the Family Law Act 1996 which has codified the law on matrimonial home rights, occupation orders and non-molestation orders.

7.2 Key points – Family Law Act 1996

Occupation and non-molestation orders

a) *To which court should application be made?*

Application can be made to the High Court, county court or magistrates' court (see s57 FLA 1996). There is provision allowing magistrates' courts to transfer more difficult cases to the county court. Magistrates' courts will not be allowed to deal with any application involving disputes concerning a party's entitlement to occupy a property by virtue of a beneficial interest estate or interest or contract unless it is unnecessary to determine the question in order to deal with the application or make the order (see s59(1) FLA 1996). This is because magistrates' courts do not have the expertise to deal with such applications. The magistrates can decline to deal with applications which may be more conveniently dealt with in another court (eg a county court) (see s59(2) FLA 1996).

b) *Definition of terms*

'Cohabitants' are a man and woman who, although not married to each other, are living together as husband and wife (see s62(1)(a) FLA 1996). 'Former cohabitants' is to be read accordingly but does not include cohabitants who have subsequently married each other (see s62(1)(b) FLA 1996).

'Relevant child' means any child who is living with or might reasonably be expected to live with either party to the proceedings and any child in relation to whom an order under the Children Act (CA) 1989 or Adoption Act (AA) 1976 is in question in relation to the proceedings and any other child whose interests the court considers relevant (see s62(2) FLA 1996). A 'child' means a person under the age of 18 years (see s63(1) FLA 1996).

The phrase 'significant harm' carries a similar meaning as in the CA 1989 (see s63(1) and (3) FLA 1996).

A person is 'associated' with another person if –

i)   they are or have been married to each other;

ii) they are cohabitants or former cohabitants;

iii) they live or have lived in the same household otherwise than merely by reason of one of them being the other's employee, tenant, lodger or boarder;

iv) they are relatives;

v)   they are engaged (whether or not that engagement has been terminated);

vi) they are parents of a child or have parental responsibility for the child (or are a natural parent of a child and the adoptive parents or a child who has been or is in the process of being adopted);

vii) they are parties to the same family proceedings (other than proceedings under Part IV FLA 1996).

See s62(3), (4) and (5) FLA 1996.

'Relative' is defined by reference to a list (which includes fathers, mothers, stepparents, siblings, stepsiblings, grandparents and grandchildren including by virtue of that person's spouse or former spouse or cohabiting partner, brothers, sisters, uncles, aunts, nephews and nieces) (see s63(1) FLA 1996).

c) *Application for occupation orders*

There are five kinds of application for occupation orders:

i)   application by a person with occupation rights or with matrimonial home rights against an 'associated' person (pursuant to s33 FLA 1996);

ii) application by a former spouse with no existing right to occupy against the other former spouse who has a right to occupy (pursuant to s35 FLA 1996);

iii) application by a cohabitants/former cohabitants with no right to occupy against a cohabitant/former cohabitant with a right to occupy (pursuant to s36 FLA 1996);

iv) application by a spouse with no right to occupy against a spouse who also has no right to occupy (pursuant to s37 FLA 1996); and

v)   application by a cohabitant/former cohabitant with no right to occupy against the cohabitant/former cohabitant who also has no right to occupy (pursuant to s38 FLA 1996).

It may be important to make the right kind of application since different provisions apply depending on the kind of application to be made. Applicants may have to clarify their rights of occupation in order to determine which kind of application should be made. However, if an applicant makes an application under one section but the court considers it should have been made under another section then the court can make the order under the correct section (see s39(3) FLA 1996).

d) *Application for an occupation order by a person with occupation rights or with matrimonial home rights (the s33 occupation order)*

   i) Who may apply for a s33 occupation order?

If a person is entitled to occupy a dwelling-house by virtue of a beneficial estate or interest or contract or by virtue of any enactment giving him/her the right to remain in occupation or has matrimonial home rights in relation to a dwelling-house (eg under s30(2) FLA 1996) and the dwelling-house is, or at any time has been, or is intended to be, the home of the person entitled and of another person with whom he/she is associated, then the person entitled may apply for an occupation order against that other person ('the respondent') (see s33(1) FLA 1996).

For these purposes if an agreement to marry is terminated no application can be made under s33 FLA 1996 by reference to that agreement after the end of three years beginning with the date on which it is terminated (see s33(2) FLA 1996).

   ii) What is a s33 occupation order?

A s33 occupation order is an order which:

- enforces the applicant's entitlement to remain in occupation as against the respondent; or
- requires the respondent to permit the applicant to enter and remain in the dwelling-house or part of the dwelling-house; or
- regulates the occupation of the dwelling-house by either or both parties; or
- prohibits, suspends or restricts the exercise by the respondent of his/her rights to occupy the dwelling-house by virtue of his/her beneficial estate or interest or contract or enactment giving him/her the right to remain in occupation; or
- if the respondent has matrimonial rights in relation to the dwelling-house and the applicant is the other spouse, restricts or terminates those rights; or
- requires the respondent to leave the dwelling-house or part of the dwelling-house; or
- excludes the respondent from a defined area in which the dwelling-house is situated.

See s33(3) FLA 1996.

A s33 occupation order may also declare that the applicant is entitled to occupy a dwelling-house or has matrimonial home rights (see s33(4) FLA 1996). If the applicant has matrimonial home rights and the respondent is the other spouse an occupation order made during the marriage may provide that those rights are not brought to an end by the death of the other spouse or the termination (otherwise than by death) of the marriage (see s33(5) FLA 1996). The court may exercise such powers in any case where it considers that in all the circumstances it is just and reasonable to do so (see s33(8) FLA 1996). Otherwise a s33 occupation order ceases to have effect on the death of either party and may not be made after the death of either party (see s33(9) FLA 1996). A s33 occupation order may be made for a specified period or until the occurrence of a specified event or until further order (see s33(10) FLA 1996).

  iii) What the court must consider before making a s33 occupation order

Under s33(6) FLA 1996 the court must have regard to all the circumstances including:

- the housing needs and housing resources of each of the parties and of any relevant child; and
- the financial resources of each of the parties; and
- the likely effect of any order, or of any decision by the court not to exercise its powers, on the health, safety or well-being of the parties and of any relevant child; and
- the conduct of the parties in relation to each other and otherwise.

The court must balance the risk of significant harm – if it appears to the court that the applicant or any relevant child is likely to suffer significant harm attributable to conduct of the respondent if an occupation order is not made the court shall make the occupation order unless it appears to the court that: (a) the respondent or any relevant child is likely to suffer significant harm if the order is made; and (b) the harm likely to be suffered by the respondent or child in that event is as great as, or greater than, the harm attributable to the conduct of the respondent which is likely to be suffered by the applicant or child if the order is not made (see s33(7) FLA 1996).

In *Chalmers* v *John* [1999] Fam Law 26 it was confirmed that s33(7) did not come into play where only minor acts of violence were involved. An occupation order was a draconian order which was not suited to the facts of that case. A non-molestation order was the more appropriate remedy.

e) *Application by former spouse with no existing right to occupy (a s35 occupation order)*

i) What is a s35 occupation order?

If one former spouse is entitled to occupy a dwelling-house by virtue of a beneficial estate or interest or contract or has a right of occupation by virtue of any enactment, and the other former spouse is not so entitled, and the dwellling-house was at any time their matrimonial home or was at any time intended by them to be their matrimonial home, then the former spouse not so entitled may apply to the court for an occupation order against the other former spouse (see s35(1) and (2) FLA 1996).

For these purposes a former spouse who has an equitable interest in the dwelling-house or in the proceeds of sale, but who has no legal interest, is treated as not being entitled to occupy the dwelling-house (see s35(11) FLA 1996).

ii) Meaning of a s35 occupation order

For these purposes a s35 occupation order must include the following provisions:

- where the applicant is in occupation –
  - an order giving the applicant the right not to be evicted or excluded from the dwelling-house or any part of it by the respondent for the period specified in the order; and
  - prohibiting the respondent from evicting or excluding the applicant during that period.
- where the applicant is not in occupation –
  - an order giving the applicant the right to enter into and occupy the dwelling-house for such period specified in the order; and

– requiring the respondent to permit the exercise of that right (see s34(4) FLA 1996).

A s35 order may also:

- regulate the occupation of the dwelling-house by either or both of the parties;
- prohibit, suspend or restrict the exercise by the respondent of his/her right to occupy the dwelling-house;
- require the respondent to leave the dwelling-house or part of the dwelling-house; or
- exclude the respondent from a defined area in which the dwelling-house is situated (see s35(5) FLA 1996).

iii) What the court must consider

In deciding whether to make an occupation order under s35(3) or (4) and, if so, in what manner, the court shall have regard to all the circumstances.

In particular the court must consider the same matters as for a s33 occupation order.

In addition the court must consider:

- the length of time that elapsed since the parties ceased to live together;
- the length of time that has elapsed since the marriage was dissolved or annulled; and
- the existence of any pending proceedings between the parties –
  - for an order under s23A or 24 MCA 1973;
  - for an order under para 1(2)(d) or (e) Sched 1 of the CA 1989; or
  - relating to the legal or beneficial ownership of the dwelling-house.

In deciding whether to add a s35(5) provision (eg an order excluding the respondent) and, if so, in what manner, the court shall have regard to all the circumstances including the matters mentioned in s35(6)(a)–(e) FLA 1996.

The balance of harm test (which applies to s33 occupation orders) also applies. If the balance of harm is in favour of the applicant or relevant child a s35(5) provision must be added.

An order may not be made under s35 after the death of either of the former spouses and ceases to have effect on the death of either of them (s35(9) FLA 1996). An order under s35 must be limited so as to have effect for a specified period not exceeding six months. It may be extended on one or more occasions for a further specified period not exceeding six months (s35(10) FLA 1996).

So long as a s35 order remains in force s30(3)–(6) apply in relation to the applicant as if he/she were the spouse entitled to occupy the dwelling-house by virtue of s30, and as if the respondent were the other spouse (s35(11) FLA 1996).

f) *Where the applicant is an unmarried cohabitant or former cohabitant with no existing right to occupy (a s36 occupation order)*

i)   What is a s36 occupation order ?

Where one cohabitant or former cohabitant is entitled to occupy a dwelling-house by virtue of a beneficial estate or interest or contract or by virtue of any enactment giving him/her the right to remain in occupation, and the other cohabitant or former cohabitant is not so entitled, and that dwelling-house is the home in which they live together as husband and wife or a home in which they at any time so lived together or intended so to live together, then the cohabitant or former cohabitant not so entitled may apply for an occupation order against the other cohabitant or former cohabitant ('the respondent') (s36(1), (2) FLA 1996).

ii) Meaning of a s36 occupation order

If the applicant is in occupation a s36 order must contain provision (see s36(3) FLA 1996):

- giving the applicant the right not to be evicted or excluded from the dwelling-house or any part of it by the respondent for the period specified in the order; and
- prohibiting the respondent from evicting or excluding the applicant during that period.

If the applicant is not in occupation a s36 order must contain provision (see s36(4) FLA 1996):

- giving the applicant the right to enter into and occupy the dwelling-house for the period specified in the order; and
- requiring the respondent to permit the exercise of that right.

A s36 order may also (see s36(5) FLA 1996):

- regulate the occupation of the dwelling-house by either or both of the parties;
- prohibit, suspend or restrict the exercise by the respondent of his/her right to occupy the dwelling-house;
- require the respondent to leave the dwelling-house or part of the dwelling-house; or
- exclude the respondent from a defined area in which the dwelling-house is included.

For these purposes a person who has an equitable interest in the dwelling-house or in the proceeds of sale, but has no legal interest, is to be treated as not being entitled to occupy the dwelling-house (see s36(11) FLA 1996).

iii) What the court must consider

In deciding whether to make a s36(3) or (4) order and, if so, in what manner, s36(6) provides that the court shall have regard to all the circumstances including the same matters as for a s33 occupation order. In addition, the court must consider:

- the nature of the parties' relationship;
- the length of time during which they lived together as husband and wife;
- whether there are or have been any children who are children of both parties or for whom both parties have or have had parental responsibility;
- the length of time that has elapsed since the parties ceased to live together; and
- the existence of any pending proceedings between the parties –
  - for an order under para 1(2)(d) or (e) Sch 1 CA 1989; or
  - relating to the legal or beneficial ownership of the dwelling-house.

In deciding whether to exercise its powers to include any s36(5) provision (eg an order excluding the respondent) and, if so, in what manner, the court must have regard to all the circumstances including the matters mentioned in s36(6)(a)–(d) (see s36(7)(a) FLA 1996).

The balance of harm test applies *but* if the balance is in favour of the applicant or relevant child there is *no* obligation to include a s36(5) provision – only a discretion.

In considering the nature of the parties' relationship the court must have regard to the fact that they have not given each other the commitment involved in marriage (see s41 FLA 1996).

iv) Duration of the order

A s36 order must be limited so as to have effect for a specified period not exceeding 6 months, but may be extended on one occasion for a further specified period not exceeding six months (see s36(10) FLA 1996). A s36 order may not be made after the death of either of the parties and ceases to have effect on the death of either of them (see s36(9) FLA 1996).

So long as the order remains in force s30(3)–(6) apply in relation to the applicant as if he/she were a spouse entitled to occupy the dwelling-house by virtue of s30 and as if the respondent were the other spouse (see s36(13) FLA 1996).

g) *Where neither spouse entitled to occupy (a s37 occupation order)*

i) What is a s37 occupation order?

Where a spouse or former spouse and the other spouse or former spouse occupy a dwelling-house which is or was the matrimonial home but neither of them is entitled to remain in occupation, then either may apply to the court for an occupation order (see s37(1) and (2) FLA 1996).

ii) Meaning of a s37 occupation order

A s37 occupation order means an order (see s37(3) FLA 1996):

• requiring the respondent to permit the applicant to enter and remain in the dwelling-house or part of the dwelling-house;
• regulating the occupation of the dwelling-house by either or both of the spouses;
• requiring the respondent to leave the dwelling-house or part of it; or
• excluding the respondent from a defined area in which the dwelling-house is included.

iii) What the court must consider

In deciding whether to exercise its powers and, if so, in what manner, the court shall have regard to all the circumstances including the same matters as for a s33 occupation order.

The balance of harm test applies as for a s33 occupation order.

iv) Period of the order

A s37(3) order must be limited to have effect for a specified period not exceeding six months but may be extended on one or more occasions for a further specified period not exceeding six months (see s37(5) FLA 1996).

v) Effect of the order

The order will only operate between the parties and will not, for example, affect a third person who is entitled to occupy the property.

h) *Where neither cohabitant nor former cohabitant is entitled to occupy (a s38 occupation order)*

i) Who may apply for a s38 occupation order?

If one cohabitant or former cohabitant and the other cohabitant or former cohabitant occupy a dwelling-house which is the home in which they live or lived together as husband and wife but neither of them is entitled to remain in occupation then either of them may apply to the court for an order against the other (see s38(1) and (2) FLA 1996).

ii) Meaning of a s38 occupation order

A s38 occupation order means an order (see s38(3) FLA 1996):

• requiring the respondent to permit the applicant to enter and remain in the dwelling-house or part of the dwelling-house;

• regulate the occupation of the dwelling-house by either or both of the parties;

• requiring the respondent to leave the dwelling-house or part of the dwelling-house; or

• excluding the respondent from a defined area in which the dwelling-house is included.

iii) What the court must consider

In deciding whether to exercise its powers to make a s38(3) order and, if so, in what manner the court must have regard to all the circumstances including the same matters as for a s33 occupation order.

The balance of harm test also applies *but* if the balance is in favour of the applicant or relevant child there is *no* obligation to include a s38(3) provision.

iv) Period of a s38(3) order

A s38(3) order shall be limited so as to have effect for a specified period not exceeding six months but may be extended on one occasion for a further specified period not exceeding six months (see s38(6) FLA 1996).

i) *General provisions concerning occupation orders*

An occupation order under ss33, 35, 36, 37 or 38 may be made in other family proceedings or without any other family proceedings being instituted (see s39(2) FLA 1996). If an application is made for an occupation order under one of those sections and the court considers that it has no power to make the order under the section concerned, but that it has power to make an order under one of the other sections, the court may make an order under that other section (see s39(3) FLA 1996).

The fact that a person has applied for an occupation order, or that an occupation has been made, does not affect the right of any person to claim a legal or equitable interest in any property in any subsequent proceedings (see s39(4) FLA 1996).

Under s40(1) FLA 1996 the court may on, or at any time after, making an occupation order under ss33, 35 or 36 provide for the payment of rent and mortgage and for the repair of the property. It can also make orders about furniture or other contents of the dwelling-house.

j) *Non-molestation orders*

   i) Meaning of non-molestation order

A non-molestation order means an order prohibiting the respondent from molesting another person who is associated with the respondent and/or prohibiting the respondent from molesting a relevant child (see s42(1) FLA 1996). The order may refer to molestation in general or to particular acts of molestation or both (see s42(6) FLA 1996).

   ii) Who can apply for a non-molestation order?

Application can be made by a person who is associated with another person. The definition of a person 'associated' with another person has already been given.

   iii) When can a non-molestation order be made?

The court may make a non-molestation order if an application for a non-molestation order has been made (whether or not in other family proceedings) by a person associated with the respondent or on the court's own motion if it is hearing family proceedings to which the respondent is a party and the court considers such an order should be made for the benefit of any other party to the proceedings or any relevant child (even though no such application has been made) (see s42(2) FLA 1996).

Where an agreement to marry is terminated no application can be made for a non-molestation order by reference to that agreement after the end of the period of three years beginning with the date on which it is terminated (see s42(4) FLA 1996).

   iv) What the court must consider

In deciding whether to make a non-molestation order and, if so, in what manner the court must have regard to all the circumstances, including the need to secure the health, safety and well-being of the applicant (or, where the court is making the order of its own motion, the person for whose benefit the order would be made) and of any relevant child (see s42(5) FLA 1996).

In *C v C (application for non-molestation order)* [1998] 2 WLR 599 it was held that molestation meant some deliberate conduct which was aimed at a high degree of harassment of the other party so as to justify the intervention of the court. It did not include enforcing an invasion of privacy per se. In that case newspaper articles which spoke about the applicant in unflattering terms did not amount to molestation.

   v) How long can a non-molestation order last?

A non-molestation order may be made for a specified period or until further order (see s42(7) FLA 1996). However, if the order is made in other family proceedings it ceases to have effect if those proceedings are withdrawn or dismissed (see s42(8) FLA 1996).

k) *Ex parte orders*

An occupation or non-molestation order can be made ex parte where the court considers that it is just and convenient to do so (see s45(1) FLA 1996).

Under s45(3) FLA 1996 the court must have regard to all the circumstances including:

i) any risk of significant harm to the applicant or a relevant child attributable to conduct of the respondent if the order is not made immediately;

ii) whether it is likely that the applicant will be deterred or prevented from pursuing the application if an order is not made immediately; and

iii) whether there is reason to believe that the respondent is aware of the proceedings but is deliberately evading service and the applicant or a relevant child will be seriously prejudiced by the delay involved in effecting service (or substituted service) of the proceedings.

If the court makes an ex parte order it must give the respondent an opportunity to make representations relating to the order as soon as just and convenient at a full hearing (ie a hearing notice of which has been given to all the parties) (see s45(3) FLA 1996). The length of an order made at a full hearing is treated as starting from the date of the ex parte order, and any extension may be made as if the ex parte order and the order made at the full hearing are one order (see s45(4) FLA 1996).

l) *Undertakings*

Instead of making an occupation or non-molestation order the court may accept an undertaking from any party to the proceedings. Such an undertaking is enforceable as a court order (see s46(1) and (4) FLA 1996). A power of arrest cannot be attached to an undertaking and an undertaking cannot be accepted where a power of arrest would be attached to an order (see s46(2) and (3) FLA 1996).

m) *Attaching a power of arrest*

If a court makes an occupation order or non-molestation order and it appears to the court that the respondent has used or threatened violence against the applicant or relevant child, it *must* attach a power of arrest to the order unless satisfied that in all the circumstances of the case the applicant or child will be adequately protected without such a power of arrest (see s46(2) FLA 1996).

A power of arrest cannot be attached to an ex parte order unless it appears to the court that the respondent has used or threatened violence against the applicant or a relevant child and that there is a risk of significant harm to the applicant or child attributable to the conduct of the respondent if the power of arrest is not attached immediately (see s46(3) FLA 1996). If the court does attach a power of arrest to an ex parte order it may provide that the power of arrest is to have effect for a shorter period than the occupation or non-molestation order (see s46(4) FLA 1996). Any such period may be extended by the court on one or more occasions on an application to vary or discharge the occupation or non-molestation order (see s46(5) FLA 1996).

Where a power of arrest is attached a constable may arrest without warrant a person whom he has reasonable cause for suspecting to be in breach of the occupation or non-molestation order (see s46(6) FLA 1996). The person must be produced before a court within 24 hours of his/her arrest (excluding Christmas Day, Good Friday or any Sunday) where he/she may be dealt with or remanded to appear before a later court (see s46(7) FLA 1996). The power to remand includes a remand for medical examination and report (whether on bail or in custody) (see s48 FLA 1996).

Where no power of arrest is attached to an order the applicant may apply to the court for the issue or a warrant for the respondent's arrest if the applicant considers that the respondent has failed to comply with the order. The application must be substantiated on oath and the court must be satisfied that there are reasonable grounds for believing that the respondent has failed to comply with the order (see s46(8) and (9) FLA 1996).

n) *Enforcement of an occupation or non-molestation order*

The High Court, county court and (to a lesser extent) the magistrates' court have power to commit a respondent to prison for disobeying an occupation or non-molestation order. This committal power may be suspended for such period or on such terms and conditions as the court may specify.

7.3 Recent cases

C v *C (application for non-molestation order)* [1998] 2 WLR 599

Chalmers v *John* [1999] Fam Law 26

7.4 Analysis of questions

Usually this area is examined by way of a problem question; it is not unusual for it to be combined with another aspect of family law eg nullity or divorce. Essay questions are sometimes set – they tend to require the candidate to critically assess the existing law and comment on its adequacy or otherwise in dealing with domestic violence.

7.5 Questions

QUESTION ONE

Robert and Nellie married in 1987. They have one child and Nellie is expecting another in September 1992. The matrimonial home, Rose Cottage, was purchased by Robert out of money he inherited from his grandparents and registered in his own name. Since the birth of their first child, Nellie has acted as a housewife and Robert has paid her a weekly allowance to run the household and purchase clothes for herself and the children. Nellie, who is good with money, saved some of this allowance, using it to buy shares and art deco china.

In 1992 Robert developed a mental illness, as a result of which he enjoys frightening Nellie and their child, sometimes by brandishing imitation weapons. Nellie has become extremely tense as a result of this behaviour.

In March this year Robert and Nellie had a violent quarrel in the course of which Robert threatened to throw her and the child out. The following day Nellie left Rose Cottage to stay with her brother Joseph and his wife. In April Robert met Joseph in the local post office and threatened to kill him if he did not return Nellie and the child to the home.

Advise Nellie who wishes to return, safely, to Rose Cottage and would like, further, to dispose of the shares and china.

University of London LLB Examination
(for External Students) Family Law June 1992 Q6

General Comment

This question concerns occupation of the matrimonial home and the ways in which a party to the marriage may be excluded from the home. It also deals with ownership of marital property.

Skeleton Solution

a) • Consider matrimonial home rights under s30 Family Law Act 1996.

   • Consider application for s33 occupation order:

      – apply s33(6) factors;

      – apply s33(7) balance of harm test.

   • Consider application for non-molestation order under s42 FLA 1996.

b) Regarding the shares and the china:

   • consider common law position;

   • s1 Married Women's Property Act 1964.

Suggested Solution

a) *'Rose Cottage'*

   Nellie wishes to return to the matrimonial home, 'Rose Cottage'. Initially one must consider whether she has a right of occupation by virtue of ownership. Here the property was purchased by Robert out of his own money and registered in his sole name. Therefore Nellie does not have a right of occupation by virtue of ownership.

   Next one must consider s30 Family Law Act 1996. This creates a statutory right of occupation in the matrimonial home for the non-owning spouse. Nellie falls within this section as Robert alone has the legal title. She can come under s30 even though she is not in occupation at the moment.

   The right of occupation constitutes:

   i) the right of a spouse in occupation not to be evicted or excluded from the home or any part thereof without the leave of the court; and

   ii) the right of a spouse not in occupation to enter and occupy the home with the leave of the court.

   In order to enforce her right of occupation Nellie should seek an occupation order under s33 FLA 1996 to enforce her entitlement to occupy Rose Cottage and to require Robert to leave. In deciding whether to make such an order the court would have regard to all the circumstances including particular matters (see s33(6) FLA 1996). The court would consider the housing needs and housing resources of each of the parties and the child and the financial resources of the parties. Nellie has no job and no income of her own. She has to provide for the child plus the baby about to be born. She and the children will have greater housing needs than Robert and less resources (though it is not clear whether he is still working). The availability of council housing is likely to be relevant (see *Thurley v Smith* (1985)). The court will also consider the likely effect of an order on Robert's health, safety and well-being and the likely effect of a refusal to make an order on the health, safety and well-being of Nellie and the child. The court will also consider the conduct of Robert and Nellie in relation to each other and otherwise. The court will look at how reasonable Nellie's refusal to live with Robert is. Robert's behaviour has caused problems for Nellie and even though his behaviour is involuntary to the extent that it derives from his illness, it will be taken into account in strengthening Nellie's case (see *Wootton* v *Wootton* (1984)). His behaviour appears extreme, particularly taking into account the brandishing of imitation weapons. The behaviour has clearly made Nellie extremely tense. His threats to her (even though she is pregnant) and their child is aggravated by his threat of violence to kill Joseph. If it appears to the court that Nellie and the child are likely to suffer significant harm attributable to Robert's conduct if an order excluding him is not made, the court must make the order unless it appears to the court that Robert is likely to suffer significant harm if the order is made and that harm is greater than the harm Nellie and the child are likely to suffer if the order is not made (see s33(7) FLA 1996). The effect of Robert's behaviour is likely to be accepted as significant harm. The balance of harm test in s33(7) is likely to go in Nellie's favour whereby the court will be obliged to make the occupation order she seeks. Even if the balance of harm is equal (taking into the account the consequences of excluding a mentally ill man from his home) then the occupation order would still have to be made.

In addition, Nellie should apply for a non-molestation order under s42 FLA 1996. The court will have regard to all the circumstances including the need to safeguard the health, safety and well-being of Nellie and the child (see s42(5)). In these circumstances a non-molestation order is likely to be made prohibiting Robert from threatening or using violence against Nellie and her child. Since there has been a threat of violence by Robert against Nellie it must attach a power of arrest to the occupation and non-molestation order unless satisfied that in all the circumstances she and the child will be adequately protected without such a power of arrest (see s47(1) FLA 1996). The court is unlikely to be so satisfied so a power of arrest is likely to be attached. This will allow Nellie to enforce the order by calling the police if Robert were to breach the occupation or non-molestation order so that he could be immediately arrested and brought before the court for contempt.

Nellie should be advised that she will have to consider a long term solution to her difficulties. Any occupation and non-molestation order is likely to be treated as a remedy only for the short term (since they are likely to be subject to a time limit). In the long term she may have to contemplate divorce proceedings and apply for a property transfer order whereby the former matrimonial home is transferred into her name.

b)   *The shares and the china*

Nellie saved some of the allowance paid to her by Robert to buy the shares and the china.

At common law if a husband provided an allowance out of his income to his wife to pay housekeeping expenses, any sums not spent for that purpose prima facie remained his and he would be entitled to any property purchased with such savings: *Blackwell* v *Blackwell* (1943).

This principle was altered by s1 Married Women's Property Act 1964 which provides that:

'Where any question arises as to the right of a husband or wife to money derived from any allowance made by the husband for the expenses of the matrimonial home or for similar purposes, or any property acquired out of such money the money or property shall, in the absence of any agreement between them to the contrary, be treated as belonging to the husband and wife in equal shares.'

Here the shares and the art deco china are bought with money from the housekeeping allowance therefore prima facie Robert and Nellie will have equal shares in them.

Robert and Nellie may be able to reach an agreement as to the ownership of the shares and china but if they cannot, an application may be made to the High Court or county court (probably county court here) under s17 Married Women's Property Act 1882. The court has the power to resolve disputes between the spouses as to their property, and the court may order a sale of the property in which case Robert and Nellie would each get a half share in the proceeds.

QUESTION TWO

Sarah and Timothy became lovers in 1989. In 1990, they began cohabiting in a house which they had purchased in their joint names. Although their relationship was turbulent and they had many arguments, it was rarely violent. In January 1994, Sarah became pregnant and since that time the relationship between the couple has deteriorated. Their arguments became even more frequent and Timothy slapped Sarah across the face more than once.

In late April 1994, Sarah, concerned at the effect the situation was having on the unborn child, decided to move out of the house she was sharing with Timothy and into a one-bedroomed flat occupied by her friend Ursula. Timothy blamed Ursula for Sarah's decision and began a campaign of harassment against Ursula, following her constantly and phoning her at all hours. Sarah now wishes to move back into her home. However, she is not prepared to do so while Timothy is living there.

Advise Sarah and Ursula.

University of London LLB Examination
(for External Students) Family Law June 1994 Q7

General Comment

The problems of violence within an unmarried relationship and which then involve a third party are covered in this question. The situation requires discussion of s33 Family Law Act 1996 as an immediate remedy together with an application for a property transfer under s15 and Schedule 1 Children Act 1989 as a longer term solution. In addition, non-molestation orders under s42 Family Law Act 1996 need to be discussed.

Skeleton Solution

• Application under s33 Family Law Act 1996 for an occupation order excluding Timothy from the family home – consideration of:
  – housing needs and resources;
  – financial resources;
  – health, safety and well-being of the parties;
  – balance of harm test.

• Application for a non-molestation order under s42 FLA 1996.

• Application for a property transfer order under s15 and Schedule 1 Children Act 1989.

• Protection of third party from harassment – Protection from Harassment Act 1997.

Suggested Solution

In view of the violence used by Timothy against Sarah she may apply to either the magistrates' court or the county court under s33 Family Law Act 1996 for an occupation order excluding him from the jointly owned matrimonial home. Such an order would enforce her entitlement to occupy the home and require Timothy to leave. She could apply under s33 since, as a joint owner, she is entitled to apply and Timothy is an 'associated person' against whom application may be made. In deciding whether to make an order the court will have regard to all the circumstances, including particular matters (see s33(6) FLA 1996). The court would consider the housing needs and housing resources of each of the parties and their financial resources. It is not clear whether Sarah has a job but in light of her pregnancy she is assumed to have no income or a limited one. She will have to provide for the new baby. She is therefore likely to have greater housing needs than Timothy and less resources (though it is not clear whether he is working). The availability of council housing is likely to be relevant (see *Thurley* v *Smith* (1985)). The court will also consider the likely effect of an order on Timothy's health, safety and well-being if an occupation order is made and the likely effect of a refusal to make an order on Sarah's health, safety and well-being. The court will also consider the conduct of Timothy and Sarah in relation to each other and otherwise. The court will look at how reasonable Sarah's refusal to live with Timothy is. His behaviour appears serious particularly taking into account Sarah's pregnancy. The court may find that Sarah is justified in refusing to live in the same house as Timothy in light of his physical violence. However, the court has to make a judgement about the violence. If it finds the violence to be trivial it may consider that it does not justify the draconian step of ordering Timothy to leave his home (see *Chalmers* v *John* (1999)). If it appears to the court that Sarah is likely to suffer significant harm attributable to Timothy's conduct if an order excluding him is not made, the court must make the order unless it appears to the court that Timothy is likely to suffer significant harm if the order is made and that harm is greater than the harm Sarah is likely to suffer if the order is not made (see s33(7) FLA 1996). This will depend on whether Timothy's violence and other behaviour is sufficiently serious for the court to make a finding of significant harm. If the violence is serious the balance of harm test in s33(7) is likely to go in Sarah's favour whereby the court will be obliged to make the occupation order she seeks. Even if the balance of harm is equal (taking into account the consequences of excluding a man from his home) then the occupation order would still have to be made. Timothy's harassment of Ursula does put his violence towards Sarah in a worse light.

In addition, Sarah should apply for a non-molestation order under s42 FLA 1996. The court will have regard to all the circumstances, including the need to safeguard the health, safety and well-being of Sarah (see s42(5)). In these circumstances a non-molestation order is likely to be made prohibiting Timothy from threatening or using violence against Sarah. In addition, because Timothy has used physical violence towards her, the court would be obliged to attach a power of arrest to an occupation or non-molestation order made unless it was satisfied that in all the circumstances Sarah will be adequately protected without such a power of arrest (see s47 FLA 1996). It is unlikely that the court would be so satisfied (given Timothy's harassment of Ursula), so a power of arrest is likely to be attached. This will enable Sarah to contact the police immediately should Timothy breach an occupation or non-molestation order whereby he would be arrested and brought before the court for contempt.

It is possible to deal with the occupation and non-molestation orders by way of Timothy giving undertakings which would avoid the need for a contested court hearing (see s46 FLA

1996). However Sarah may not find this acceptable since a power of arrest cannot be attached to an undertaking.

Sarah should be aware that any occupation or non-molestation order is likely to be made for a specified period as a short term remedy. She will have to consider a long term solution to her difficulties. Once her child is born she should apply under s15 and Schedule 1 Children Act 1989 to the county court for a transfer of property order to her for the benefit of the child (see para 1(2)(e) Schedule 1 CA 1989). In considering whether to grant such an application the welfare of the child would not be paramount. The court would have regard to all the circumstances and in particular the income, earning capacity and property of both parties as balanced against their financial outgoings and responsibilities. This will include the financial needs of the child.

In relation to Ursula, she should be advised that the police should be informed of the campaign of harassment. They can prosecute Timothy under s2 Protection from Harassment Act (PHA) 1997, whereby he can be fined or imprisoned for the offence of harassment. The court would have to be satisfied that he had harassed Ursula on at least two separate occasions (in order to be satisfied that he had pursued a course of conduct which amounted to harassment and which he knew or ought to have known amounted to harassment). In addition to any fine or imprisonment, the court can make a restraining order whereby Timothy could not further harass Ursula. Breach of the restraining order would be a separate criminal offence (see s5 PHA 1997). There was a civil remedy to an invasion of the right to privacy but doubt has been cast on whether such a remedy exists (see *Hunter* v *Canary Wharf Ltd* (1997)). As a result of this doubt Ursula is advised that she should seek the remedy available under criminal law.

QUESTION THREE

Advise the parties in the following cases:

a) Annabel and Brian, who have been married for 25 years, have two children, Clara 21, a law student, who shares a house with a group of friends, and Deborah, 14, who lives in the matrimonial home and attends a school nearby. Since January 1993, Brian, who is jealous and suspicious, has had frequent arguments with Annabel. Although the arguments have never been violent, they have grown in intensity and frequency and frighten Deborah, whose school work has suffered. In May 1995, Annabel left the matrimonial home with Deborah and they are both now sleeping on the floor of Clara's bedroom.

b) Edwina and Frederick, who have two children aged 4 and 5, divorced in 1992, but continued to occupy the large jointly-owned matrimonial home. Edwina met George in December 1994 and they are planning to marry. Edwina wants to remain in her present home with the children and George, but she wants Frederick to leave. Frederick, who is shocked that Edwina is remarrying, refuses to leave what he describes as 'his home'.

c) Helen and Ian, who had lived together since 1990, separated in November 1994 after Ian attacked Helen with a belt. Although Helen no longer wished to have any contact with him, Ian considered that it was still possible to resume their relationship. He sends flowers to Helen each week, telephones her daily and often follows her. Helen is afraid of Ian and her health has begun to suffer.

University of London LLB Examination
(for External Students) Family Law June 1995 Q8

General Comment

The first two parts of this question require discussion of the rights of occupation of first, a married couple, and second, a divorced couple. The third part requires knowledge of how an unmarried woman can be protected from molestation. The student needs to demonstrate a knowledge of the Family Law Act 1996 and the remedies it provides in these situations. The Family Law Act 1996 has codified the law in relation to the occupation of the family home. The question tests the student's knowledge in applying that code and the different considerations and remedies it applies.

Skeleton Solution

a) • Right of occupation of married spouse under s30 Family Law Act 1996.

   • Application for an occupation order under s33 FLA 1996:
     – s33(6) considerations;
     – s33(7) balance of harm test.

b) Rights of occupation of divorced couple – application for an occupation order under s33 FLA 1996 on basis of joint ownership with same considerations and balance of harm test.

c) Application for a non-molestation order under s42 FLA 1996.

Suggested Solution

a) Since Annabel and Brian are married one must consider s30 Family Law Act 1996. This creates a statutory right of occupation in the matrimonial home for a spouse, including a right of occupation for a non-owning spouse. If, for example, Annabel has no legal rights of ownership she is given the following rights:

   i) the right of a spouse in occupation not to be evicted or excluded from the home or any part thereof without the leave of the court; and

   ii) the right of a spouse not in occupation to enter and occupy the home with the leave of the court.

   Either she or Brian can enforce their rights of occupation by seeking an occupation order under s33 FLA 1996 to enforce the entitlement to occupy the home and to require the other to leave. In deciding whether to make such an order the court would have regard to all the circumstances including particular matters (see s33(6) FLA 1996). The court would consider the housing needs and housing resources of each of the parties and youngest child, and the financial resources of the parties. If Annabel has no job and no income of her own and has to provide for Deborah, she and Deborah will have greater housing needs than Brian and less resources (though it is not clear whether he has an income). The availability of council housing is likely to be relevant (see *Thurley* v *Smith* (1985)). The court will also consider the likely effect of an order on Brian's health, safety and well-being if he is ordered to leave the home and the likely effect of a refusal to make an order on the health, safety and well-being of Annabel and Deborah. The court will also consider the conduct of Brian and Annabel in relation to each other and otherwise. The court will look at how reasonable Annabel's refusal to live with Brian is. The court will have to make a judgement on his behaviour and the effect it has had on both Annabel and Deborah. It is assumed that his behaviour has been serious because it has frightened his daughter and obliged both mother and daughter to move to unsatisfactory accommodation. If it appears to the court that Annabel and Deborah are likely to suffer significant harm attributable to Brian's conduct if an order excluding him is not made, the court must make the order unless it appears to the court that Brian is likely to suffer significant harm if the order is made and that harm is greater than the harm Annabel and Deborah are likely to suffer if the order is not made (see s33(7) FLA 1996). If the balance of harm test in s33(7) is either equal or in Annabel and Deborah's favour, the court will be obliged to make the occupation order she seeks. It is noted that the arguments are frequent and intense rather than violent. They have frightened Deborah and affected her schoolwork. The fact that she and her mother are living in unsatisfactory living conditions is also likely to harm her. As a result it is likely that the court will consider that Brian's behaviour has caused Deborah significant harm and that the balance of harm test will cause an occupation order to be made.

b) The advice follows that for Annabel and Brian. Though the parties are no longer married they jointly own the matrimonial home. As a result either may apply for an occupation order under s33 FLA 1996. The considerations outlined above equally apply. However, the balance of harm test would not lead to an obvious result since there is no information to suggest that Edwina or the children are suffering from significant harm as a result of any behaviour attributable to Frederick. Indeed, if they have suffered no significant harm then the balance of harm test would not apply (see *Chalmers* v *John* (1999)). The courts will treat the making of an occupation order as a draconian step so it is unlikely to make an occupation order unless Frederick's conduct is sufficiently serious and the consequences for Edwina and the children similarly serious. The most appropriate solution remains that of seeking property orders under ss24 and 24A MCA 1973 if the claims for ancillary relief have not yet been resolved.

c) Helen would be able to apply for a non-molestation order against Ian (see s42 FLA 1996). Ian is an 'associated person' (namely a former cohabitant – s62 FLA 1996) against whom Helen can bring proceedings. The court would have regard to all the circumstances, including the need to secure the health, safety and well-being of Helen. If a non-molestation order is made the court would be obliged to attach a power of arrest to it given the attack with the belt, unless it considered Helen would be adequately protected without such a power of arrest (see s47 FLA 1996). The attack with the belt was some time ago and this may persuade the court that attaching the power of arrest is not needed. However, if Ian's behaviour is so persistent and unreasonable so as to make Helen's health suffer it is likely that the power would be attached. This would enable Helen to enforce any breach of the court order by contacting the police who would arrest Ian and bring him before the court for contempt.

8 Parental Disputes Concerning Children

8.1 Introduction

8.2 Key points

8.3 Recent cases

8.4 Analysis of questions

8.5 Questions

8.1 Introduction

Disputes between parents concerning their children are resolved through orders available under the Children Act (CA) 1989. The student needs to know the range of orders available under the CA 1989 and the principles to be applied by a court in determining whether to make an order.

8.2 Key points

Parental responsibility

a) *What is parental responsibility?*

'All the rights, duties powers, responsibilities and authority which by law a parent of a child has in relation to the child and his property' (s3(1) CA 1989).

Parental wishes give way to the exercise of choice by the child according to that child's age, maturity and understanding. See *Hewer v Bryant* [1970] 1 QB 357, quoted with approval in *Gillick v West Norfolk and Wisbech Area Health Authority* [1985] 3 All ER 402 – 'parental rights to control a child do not exist for the benefit of the parent. They exist for the benefit of the child and they are justified only insofar as they enable the parent to perform his duties towards the child ...' per Lord Fraser of Tullybelton in *Gillick*.

b) *Incidents of parental responsibility*

   i) Determining the child's surname

   Where both parents have parental responsibility both must agree to a change in the child's surname or obtain a court order in the event of a dispute (see *Practice Direction (child: change of surname)* [1995] 1 WLR 365 and *Re PC (change of surname)* [1997] 2 FLR 730. Similarly, where a residence order is in force no one can change the child's surname without the written consent of each person with parental responsibility or the leave of the court (see s13(1) CA 1989). Where the parents are unmarried and only the mother has parental responsibility the mother can unilaterally change the child's surname but the father can seek to prevent this by a prohibited steps or specific issues order (see *Dearson v Wearmouth* [1997] 2 FLR 629.

   In deciding whether to allow a change of surname the child's welfare is paramount. Courts treat a change of surname as a serious matter, particularly in relation to the link it may provide with the father. The welfare checklist applies (see *Re C (a minor) (change of surname)* [1998] 2 FLR 656.

ii) Leaving the jurisdiction

Where a residence order is in force no one can remove the child from the jurisdiction without the written consent of every person who has parental responsibility or with the leave of the court (see s13(1) CA 1989). This does not prevent the child from being removed for a period of up to one month (eg for a foreign holiday).

The Court of Appeal laid down the general approach in *Re H (application to remove from jurisdiction)* [1998] 1 FLR 848 which followed the decision in *Poel* v *Poel* [1970] 1 WLR 1469. The first question is whether the proposed move is a reasonable one from the point of view of the adults involved? Had it been properly thought out and planned? If the answer was 'yes' then leave should only be refused if it is clearly shown beyond any doubt that the interests of the child and the residential parent were incompatible. The court would not interfere with the reasonable decision of the residential parent. Otherwise the bitterness or disappointment of the applicant may harm the child.

iii) Education of the child

Parents have a duty to ensure that their children aged between five and 16 receive a full time education (see s36 Education Act 1944). Failure to do so amounts to an offence.

iv) Consent to marriage

The consent of the parents with parental responsibility is required to the marriage of child between the age of 16 and 18 (see s3 Marriage Act 1949). The child can apply to a court for consent which replaces parental consent. If no consent has been given the marriage will not be void in any event.

v) Medical treatment

A child over the age of 16 may validly consent to medical treatment (see s8(3) Family Law Reform Act 1969). Under that age the parent may give consent on the child's behalf or the child may give consent him/herself provided the child is of sufficient maturity and understanding to make an informed decision (see *Gillick* v *West Norfolk and Wisbech Area Health Authority* (above) – this gives rise to the phrase '*Gillick* competent' child).

The court retains the power to override the wishes of a child where a particular child lacks sufficient maturity and understanding to make an informed decision about his/her medical treatment, ie is not *Gillick* competent (see *Re R (a minor)(wardship: medical treatment)* [1991] 4 All ER 177).

The court retains the power to override the wishes of the child's parents where the court considers that the parents' decision is not in the child's best interests. See *Re E (a minor) (wardship: medical treatment)* [1993] 1 FLR 179 where a court overruled the wishes of 15-year-old boy and his parents in authorising a blood transfusion which was required to save his life.

c) *Who has parental responsibility?*

Where a child's parents are married to each other at the time of birth they each have parental responsibility (s2(1) CA 1989).

Where a child's parents are not married to each other at the time of birth the mother has sole parental responsibility for the child (s2(2)(a) CA 1989).

The unmarried father can only acquire parental responsibility through:

i) a parental responsibility agreement signed by him and the mother and witnessed (eg by a magistrate) (see s2(2)(b) and s4(1)(b) CA 1989 and Parental Responsibility Agreement Regulations 1991); or

ii) an order from the court giving him parental responsibility (see s2(2)(b) and s4(1)(a) CA 1989).

A court in deciding whether to make a parental responsibility order must consider:

i) the degree of commitment shown by the father towards his child;

ii) the degree of attachment between the father and his child; and

iii) whether or not he is motivated by a concern for the welfare of the child in asking the court to make a parental responsibility application.

See *Re C (minors)* [1992] 2 All ER 86 and *Re G (a minor)(parental responsibility order)* [1994] 1 FLR 504.

If an unmarried father is able to satisfy these three criteria then he is entitled to a parental responsibility order unless there are clear reasons not to do so. The fact that he has no contact with the child, or that the mother will not allow him to be involved in decisions affecting the child, are not reasons for not making the order. The order confers a status on the father which may be important in the future (see *Re P (a minor) (parental responsibility order)* [1994] 1 FLR 578 and *Re S (parental responsibility)* [1995] 2 FLR 648). A parental responsibility order does not entitle the father to interfere with the day-to-day management of the child's life but he should be involved in important decisions (see *Re P*).

A person in whose favour a residence order is made shall acquire parental responsibility for the child (see s12(2) CA 1989).

A person with parental responsibility does not lose it because some one else acquires parental responsibility (eg a local authority acquiring parental responsibility when a care order is made), but shares it with that other person (though subject to not being able to act in a way incompatible with any court order) (see s2(6) and (8) CA 1989).

A person without parental responsibility may do what is reasonable in all the circumstances to safeguard or promote the child's welfare (see s3(5) CA 1989).

Determining disputes concerning a child

a) *Section 8 orders*

There are four main types of order available to a court when deciding on a dispute between parents (or other persons) concerning a child (see s8 CA 1989):

i) The residence order (determining with whom a child should reside).

ii) The contact order (requiring the person with whom a child lives, or is to live, to allow the child to visit or stay with the person named in the order or for that person and the child to otherwise have contact with each other).

iii) The prohibited steps order (whereby a specified act of a kind which could be taken by a parent in meeting his/her parental responsibility for a child shall not be taken by any person without the consent of the court).

iv) The specific issues order (determining a specific question which has arisen or may arise in connection with any aspect of a parental responsibility for a child).

The court can make a shared residence order whereby the child lives with one parent for part of the time and with the other parent for the rest of the time. The court will be reluctant to make such an order if it leave the child in a state of limbo without a stable base. It will make the order if it confirms arrangements which clearly benefit the child and confirm the equality of the parents (see *Re H (a minor)(shared residence)* [1994] 1 FLR 717 and *A v A (minors) (shared residence order)* [1994] 1 FLR 669).

In deciding whether to make any of the above orders that court must take into account particular considerations:

i) The welfare of the child is paramount

In determining any question concerning the upbringing of a child, the child's welfare shall be the paramount consideration (see s1(1) CA 1989). This means that the child's welfare determines the course to be followed (see *J v C* [1969] 2 WLR 540).

ii) Delay is assumed to be harmful to the child's welfare

The court must assume that any delay in making its decision is likely to harm the child's welfare (see s1(2) CA 1989). To this end the court will make directions as to the conduct of the case in order to avoid delay.

iii) The no order principle

The court cannot make any order unless it is satisfied that making the order is better than making no order at all, ie the order will positively benefit the child (see s1(5) CA 1989).

iv) The welfare checklist

If the making of a s8 order is opposed the court must consider a number of particular factors – these are known as the welfare checklist (see s1(3) and (4) CA 1989):

- The ascertainable wishes and feelings of the child considered the light of his/her age and understanding (s1(3)(a)).
- The child's physical, emotional and educational needs (s1(3)(b)).
- The likely effect on the child on any change in his/her circumstances (s1(3)(c)).
- The child's age, sex, background and other relevant characteristics (s1(3)(d)).
- Any harm the child has suffered or is at risk of suffering (s1(3)(e)).
- How capable each of his parents and any other relevant person is of meeting the child's needs (s1(3)(f)).
- The court's full range of powers (s1(3)(g)).

Case law can assist in applying the checklist:

- The views of children aged nine years or more tend to be regarded as important – the older the more important (see *M v M (a minor: custody appeal)* [1987] 1 WLR 404).

- There is no longer any presumption that mothers should look after young children – each parent must be carefully assessed (see *Re S (a minor)(custody)* [1991] 2 FLR 388 and *Re A (a minor)(custody)* [1991] 2 FLR 394).

- There may be advantages in keeping siblings together since they can given themselves emotional support after a family has split up (see *C v C (minors: custody)* [1988] 2 FLR 291).

- The court recognises that stability is important in a child's life – if a child has been in the care of one parent for a long time the court may be slow the change the child's residence given the upset this may cause (see *Stephenson v Stephenson* [1985] FLR 1140).

- The court also recognises the importance of a child being looked after continuously by one adult rather than a child being looked after in a fragmented way by a succession of adults (see *Re K (minors)(children: care and control)* [1977] 2 WLR 3).

- Though the court is not bound by the recommendation in a welfare report it should give reasons if it is departing from that recommendation (see *Stephenson v Stephenson* (above)).

In relation to contact orders the courts assume that the emotional needs of a child are best met by continued contact with both parents (see *Re H (minors)(access)* [1992] 1 FLR 148 and *Re M (contact: welfare test)* [1995] 1 FLR 274). The court is likely to ask whether that fundamental emotional need is outweighed by any harm which may befall the child and taking into account the child's wishes and feelings.

b) *Who can apply for a s8 order?*

Applications can be made in the context of family proceedings or an application. A parent or guardian or person in whose favour a residence order has been made can apply for any s8 order.

A person who is a party to the marriage in respect of a child of the marriage who is a child of the family (ie a step-parent), or a person with whom the child has lived for at least three years, or a person with the consent of those with parental responsibility, can apply for a residence or contact order.

Other persons have to obtain the leave of the court to apply. An example would be grandparents applying for leave to apply for a residence or contact order. In deciding whether to grant leave under s10(9) CA 1989 the court must have particular regard to:

i)   the nature of the proposed application;

ii) the applicant's connection with the child;

iii) any risk there might be of the proposed application disrupting the child's life to such an extent that he/she would be harmed by it; and

iv) where the child is being looked after by a local authority, the authority's plans for the child's future and the wishes and feelings of the child's parents.

The welfare of the child is not paramount in deciding on leave (see *Re A (minors)(residence orders: leave to apply)* [1992] 3 WLR 422). The prospect of success of the intended application is a relevant factor (see *G v Kirklees MBC* [1993] 1 FLR 805).

A child can apply for leave to make an application of a s8 order in his/her own right.

The court must be satisfied that the child has sufficient understanding to make the application. The child's welfare is important but not paramount. The court has to be cautious and balance two considerations. Firstly, a child is an individual with wishes and feelings which should command serious attention. Secondly, a child may be vulnerable and impressionable, may lack maturity and be unable to weigh the long term against the short term. If a child was given party status he/she would be present when parents gave evidence and were cross-examined and may hear things it would be better for the child not to hear. The child could be cross-examined (see *Re C (residence: child's application for leave)* [1995] 1 FLR 927). An application by a child for leave to apply for a s8 order should be transferred to the High Court because of the difficult issues raised (see *Practice Direction* [1993] 1 All ER 820).

Resolving disputes over the paternity of a child

Questions involving disputes over a child can include disputes over the paternity or parentage of a child and the student must demonstrate a knowledge of how such disputes can be resolved.

a) *Presumption of legitimacy*

A child conceived by or born to a mother who is married at the time of the conception or birth is presumed at common law to be the child of the mother and her husband. This presumption applies even if the marriage is dissolved after the child has been conceived but before the child is born.

b) *Rebutting the presumption of legitimacy*

The presumption may be rebutted on a balance of probabilities (see s26 Family Law Reform Act 1969). However, the courts have considered the status of a child to be a grave matter and the standard of proof is more than a narrow balance of probabilities (see *W v K (proof of paternity)* [1988] 1 FLR 86; *Serio v Serio* [1983] 4 FLR 756).

Examples of how to rebut the presumption include:

i) the sterility of the husband (see *W v K* (above)).

ii) the absence of the husband at the time of conception – the court will apply the present-day standards of medical science in deciding the possible dates of conception, taking into account the nature of the pregnancy and when the child was born (see *Preston-Jones v Preston-Jones* [1951] 1 All ER 124).

iii) registration of the name of the father on the birth certificate under the Births and Deaths Registration Act 1953.

iv) blood tests (see below).

c) *Blood tests*

The court may direct that blood tests be carried out to ascertain the paternity of the child (see s20 Family Law Reform Act 1969). In most cases the blood tests will be DNA tests. The courts assume that DNA tests are virtually conclusive so will determine whether or not a particular man is the father of a child.

Blood tests are directed. There is no power to order a person to provide a blood sample. A person (and in the case of a child under 16, the child's parent) has to consent to a blood sample being taken (see s21(1) and (3) Family Law Reform Act 1969). If a person fails to taken any step required of him/her to comply with a blood test direction then the court may draw such inferences from that failure as appear proper in the circumstances (see s23(1) Family Law Reform Act 1969). In the case of DNA tests a failure by a putative father to comply is likely to lead to the inference that he is the father because any man unsure of paternity could put his doubts at rest by submitting to a test (see *Re A (a minor) (paternity: refusal of blood test)* [1994] 2 FLR 463).

A blood test direction can be made even where the mother refused to consent to undergo blood testing of herself and the child. An inference could be drawn from the mother's refusal irrespective of whether the refusal was made before or after a blood test direction had been made. Though the child's welfare is paramount in deciding on such issues as parental responsibility and contact, the child's welfare is not paramount in deciding whether to direct blood tests. However, a court should normally refuse to direct blood tests if satisfied that it would against the child's interests to direct blood tests (following *S* v *McC* [1972] AC 24).

The court should take into account the prospects of success in the proceedings. Any gain to the child from preventing any disturbance to his or her security had to be balanced against the loss to him or her of the certainty of knowing who he or she was. Whether to direct a blood test should not be treated as a disguised application for leave to apply for a s8 order. The paternity issue should not be judged by the criteria set down in s10(9).

While a mother might wish to deny the truth it was the child's welfare which was more important. A child had the right to know the truth unless his or her welfare clearly justified the truth being covered up. A child should grow up knowing that he may have two fathers: one, his psychological father who lived with him and his mother, and the second, his biological father, rather than having a time-bomb ticking away (see *Re H (a minor)(blood tests: parental rights)* [1996] 3 WLR 506; [1996] 4 All ER 28 in which *Re G (a minor)(blood tests)* [1994] 1 FLR 495 was followed and *Re CB (a minor)(blood test)* [1994] 2 FLR 762 disapproved).

For an example of where a husband successfully persuaded a court not to order blood tests see *B* v *B and E* [1969] 3 All ER 1106 where a married couple had a child. Three years after the birth the mother suggested that her husband was not the father and asked for blood tests to determine the child's parentage. It was held to be reasonable for the husband to refuse to submit to the blood tests in these circumstances and rely on the presumption of legitimacy. Where it would be unfair to disturb the presumption that the parents bringing the child up were anything other than the child's parents and disturb the stability of the family unit upon which the child's welfare depended blood tests may not be ordered (see *Re F (a minor)(blood tests: paternity rights)* [1993] 3 All ER 596).

8.3 Recent cases

A v *United Kingdom* [1998] 2 FLR 959

Re C (minors)(change of name) [1998] 1 FLR 549

Re H (a minor)(parental responsibility) [1998] 1 FLR 855

Re H (application to remove from jurisdiction) [1998] 1 FLR 848

Re T (change of surname) [1998] 2 FLR 620

8.4 Analysis of questions

Questions on this area often combine applications for s8 orders with other disputes, eg over parentage or adoption. Questions on s8 orders require an application of the welfare principle, the delay principle, the no order principle and the welfare checklist to the facts.

8.5 Questions

QUESTION ONE

'Current case law reflects judicial realism over the degree to which a child needs to know about his or her genetic origins.'

Discuss.

University of London LLB Examination
(for External Students) Family Law June 1996 Q3

General Comment

The question is aimed at the link between a child and his or her genetic origins. Normally a child remains linked to those origins by being brought up by his or her genetic parents. Problems can arise if parents separate or where children leave or are removed from their natural parents. Disputes which then arise often come before the courts and involve a decision being made which affects that link. The answer involves a discussion of how judges approach such disputes. Case law dealing with applications for contact by absent parents, resolving disputes as to parentage, contact after care proceedings and contact after adoption illustrates the 'judicial realism' in favour of a child needing to know about his or her genetic origins.

Skeleton Solution

- General presumption in favour of maintaining child's links with his or her genetic origins.
- Case law on contact disputes – presumption in favour of contact.
- Case law on disputes on parentage – presumption on learning the truth of a child's parentage.
- Case law on contact between child made the subject of a care order and his or her natural parents (reflecting statutory presumption in favour of contact).
- Adoption – normally the severance between the child and his genetic origins – but now open adoptions and case law.

Suggested Solution

The question asks about the courts' approach to disputes about children whereby the children may lose touch with one or both natural parents, ie with their genetic origins. When families split up a child may lose touch with the parent who leaves (usually the child's father). That parent may then apply for a contact order in order to keep in touch with his son or daughter. The courts' approach is to favour contact on the basis that the child needs to keep in contact with the absent parent because of a perceived fundamental need for a child to know about his or her genetic origins. Equally, when there is a dispute about the parentage of a child the courts tend to favour the use of blood tests to establish the truth of a child's genetic origins. In other areas, such as adoption, the courts have also been more flexible in allowing a child some link with his or her natural parents where this is appropriate. In care proceedings both statute and case law favour some kind of contact between a child made the subject of a care order and his or her natural parents.

The situation in which a child is most likely to lose touch with a natural parent is when his or her parents separate and one parent leaves the family home. The parent with whom the child remains may wish to sever all links with the departing parent which may include preventing any contact between that parent and the child. If the departing parent applies to the court for a contact order pursuant to the Children Act 1989 (hereinafter referred to as the CA 1989) how does current case law approach such an application? Statute provides some guidelines. The welfare of the child is paramount, so outweighs the wishes and feelings of the parents: see s1(1) CA 1989. The court should not make an order unless it is satisfied that such an order will make things better for the child than making no order at all: see s1(5) CA 1989. If the application is opposed, then the court is obliged to consider various matters called 'the welfare checklist': see s1(3) and (4) CA 1989. Provided the court makes its decision within that statutory framework it is given a fairly wide discretion. However, case law clearly indicates that no court should deprive a child of contact with either parent unless it is wholly satisfied that it is in the interests of the child that there should be no contact. This is a conclusion which a court should be extremely slow to arrive at because of the perceived long-term benefits of a child keeping in touch with the absent parent. Save in exceptional cases it is assumed that to deprive a child of such contact is to deprive a child of an important contribution of the child's emotional and material growing up in the long term: see *Re H (minors)(access)* (1992). This approach has also been formulated by reference to the welfare checklist. In *Re M (contact: welfare test)* (1995) the recommended approach was to ask whether the fundamental emotional need of every child to have an enduring relationship with both parents (see s1(3)(b) CA 1989) was outweighed by the harm, in the light of the child's wishes and feelings (see s1(3)(a) CA 1989), the child would be at risk of suffering (see s1(3)(e) CA 1989) if a contact order was made. This illustrates the importance judges show for preserving a child's link with his or her genetic origins, ie his or her absent parent.

In some case there will be a dispute as to who a child's parents really are. For example, the parents of a child may separate. The departing parent applies to the court for an order for contact and the parent with whom the child is living denies that the departing parent is in fact the genetic parent of the child. How do the courts approach the question of establishing the truth of a child's parentage? Case law states that it is usually more important to a child's welfare that the truth of that child's parentage is established: see *S v S; W v Official Solicitor* (1970). A more recent example of this approach can be found in *Re G (a minor) (blood tests)* (1994) where a child was born to married parents shortly before they separated. The paternal grandmother applied for contact with her grandchild. The child's mother then disputed the child's paternity by saying that the child was conceived while she and her husband were separated and that another man was the real father. Both the husband and the paternal grandmother applied for blood tests to ascertain the child's parentage. The mother said that she would refuse to comply with a blood test direction made by the court. The court directed that blood tests be carried out because it was in the general interests of the child for the truth to be ascertained (following *S v S; W v Official Solicitor*). It held that it was not in the child's long term interests for the rights and responsibilities enshrined in the Children Act 1989 to remain unresolved. Such rights and responsibilities could be asserted by the child when older, which could lead to great distress. The adults needed to found their future relationship with the child on facts rather than what they wished the situation to be. The mother's refusal to comply with a blood test direction did not prevent a direction from being made. If she failed to comply with the direction, appropriate inferences could be drawn and a finding of paternity made.

In some cases the court has held that it is in the child's interests that the truth of his or her genetic origins need not be established by blood tests. In *Re F (a minor) (blood tests: paternity rights)* (1993) a child was conceived by a married woman when she was having sexual intercourse with her husband and another man (A). The relationship between the mother and A ended when she discovered she was pregnant. The child was born and brought up by the mother and her husband. A had nothing to do with the child. A then applied for blood tests to determine the child's paternity with a view to applying for parental responsibility and contact. The mother opposed the tests. The court refused to direct tests, holding that although normally the truth of a child's parentage should be ascertained, in this case the chance of A successfully obtaining a parental responsibility order or contact order were remote. It was considered unfair to the child to disturb the presumption that her parents were anything other than her legitimate parents. The court would not disturb the stability of the family unit upon which the child's physical and emotional welfare depended.

More recently the situation was restated in *Re H (a minor) (blood tests: parental rights)* (1996). While the child's welfare was not paramount in deciding whether to direct blood tests, the court had to balance the importance of the child knowing the truth against the risk of the truth damaging the child's security. A child should grow up knowing the truth rather than having a time bomb ticking away whereby his or her psychological father was not the same person as his or her biological father.

When a child's parents have harmed the child and the child has suffered significant harm a care order may be made pursuant to s31 CA 1989. Even though such a care order is likely to mean that the child is accommodated with foster parents or in a children's home, there is a presumption that contact between the child and his or her parents should continue unless it is not reasonably practicable or consistent with the child's welfare: see s34(1) CA 1989. This statutory presumption in favour of keeping the links with the child's genetic origins can only be overturned by a court order refusing or limiting such contact: see s34(4) and (5) CA 1989. The courts' approach is to consider the child's welfare as paramount. If the local authority's plans involve stopping contact between the child and his or her parents, the court will look at those plans with the greatest respect and consideration. However, the court can require the local authority to justify its long term plans to the extent that those plans exclude contact between parent and child. Where appropriate the court will overrule the local authority's plan and make a contact order: see *Re B (minors) (termination of contact: paramount consideration)* (1993) and *Re E (a minor)* (1993).

The one kind of order which normally requires a complete severance between the child and his or her parents is an adoption order which extinguishes the parental responsibility of the genetic parents: see s12(3) Adoption Act 1976. However, the need for a complete break between the child and his or her genetic parents is not an inflexible one. It may be that the adoptive parents agree to such links being maintained and the court may include a condition allowing such a link even though an adoption order has been made: see *Re C (a minor) (adoption: conditions)* (1988). After adoption a parent may not be allowed to seek a contact order. In *Re C (a minor) (adopted child: contact)* (1993) a child's mother applied for leave to apply for a contact order with respect to her child after the child had been adopted. She argued that recent research recognised the importance of the biological family and that adopted children should be able to re-establish contact with their roots. The court refused her application, holding that unless provision were made for contact as a condition when an adoption was made then there should be no re-opening of the issue of contact unless there was a fundamental change in circumstances. Adoption orders were intended to be permanent and final and that remains the position of the current law, notwithstanding any changes in society's understanding of what ought best be done for children. Even this approach appears to be softening. Research now appears to favour 'open adoptions' whereby links are maintained with the child's genetic family. However case law still stresses that this must be with the agreement of the adopters: see *Re T (adoption: contact)* (1995). If adopters do agree to contact but then renege on that agreement then the court may allow a contact application to be made: see *Re T (minors) (adopted children: contact)* (1995) which involved the child's half-sister being given leave to apply for contact with the adopted child.

In conclusion, current case law does reflect the view founded on research that a child needs to know about his or her genetic origins. This is particularly true in the court's approach to the child maintaining links with an absent genetic parent. It is also reflected in links between parents and children taken into care and to a lesser extent between genetic parents and adopted children. Where there is a dispute about a child's genetic origins then the courts favour the truth being discovered rather than being concealed.

QUESTION TWO

John and Norma, who married in 1975, have two children, Sophia, born in 1982 and Ben, born in 1984. John and Norma separated in 1994 and it was agreed that Norma, who is a writer, would look after the children in the former matrimonial home in London from Monday to Thursday and John, a freelance photographer, who lives in Oxford would care for the children for the rest of the week.

This agreement continued until March 1996, when a disagreement arose concerning Sophia's education. John wants her to attend a boarding school close to his home in Oxford, while Norma would like her to attend the local comprehensive that she already attends. Sophia herself, who has a part-time job as a model, told her parents that she would like to leave school and devote herself to modelling. In mid-April, Ben, who enjoys outdoor pursuits, announced that he and a friend had decided to go trekking in the Himalayas during the summer holidays. Norma was horrified and forbade him to go on the trip, but John was undecided. Two weeks ago, Sophia told her mother that she was pregnant and would be leaving school to have the baby. Norma immediately made arrangements for Sophia to have an abortion. Last weekend, John refused to return the children after their weekend visit.

Advise Norma how the questions concerning the children can be resolved. She tells you that John is still adamant about Sophia's schooling and Sophia, supported by John, is still refusing to consider having an abortion. She also tells you that Ben is still planning to go on his trekking trip over the summer and has threatened to leave home and move in with the parents of the friend who aims to accompany him.

Advise Norma.

University of London LLB Examination
(for External Students) Family Law June 1996 Q8

General Comment

The question reveals a range of problems involving residence, the employment of a child, abortion and foreign travel. The legal key to most of these problems lies in the Children Act

1989 and the considerations in making residence, prohibited steps and specific issues orders. This involves an application of the welfare checklist to the problems. One particularly interesting topic for debate is that of shared residence which appears to find greater favour with the courts than in the past. A brief outline of the law relating to the employment of a 14 year old and the legal position of parents with regard to education is also required.

Skeleton Solution

- Making of residence, specific issues and prohibited steps orders under the Children Act 1989.
- The considerations which the court must apply:
  – welfare of each child is paramount;
  – the delay principle;
  – the no order principle;
  – the welfare checklist.
- The legal position on employing a 14 year old and the obligation on parents to secure the education of their child.
- Application of welfare checklist to:
  – question of residence (including approach to shared residence);
  – question of abortion (including possibility of wardship);
  – question of holiday to Himalayas.

Suggested Solution

Norma asks for advice how the questions concerning Sophie and Ben can be resolved. The difficulties include the schooling of Sophie and her wish to go into employment, whether she should have an abortion and Ben's wish to go abroad on his Himalayan trek and the fact that John has refused to return the children after their weekend visit.

Taking the matter of the residence of the children first, Norma can be advised that she can ask the court to make a residence order determining where the children should reside: see s8 Children Act 1989 – hereinafter referred to as the CA 1989. In relation to the disagreement concerning Sophia's education, Norma can apply to the court for a specific issues order (an order giving directions for the purpose of determining the specific question of Sophia's education): see s8 CA 1989. Regarding Ben's trip to the Himalayas, she can apply to the court for a prohibited steps order (an order that no step which could be taken by a parent in meeting his parental responsibility for a child shall be taken by any person without the consent of the court): see s8 CA 1989. The prohibited steps order could seek to prohibit Ben from going to the Himalayas. In relation to Sophia's pregnancy, she can ask the court to make an order resolving the matter of the abortion either through a specific issues order or through wardship in the High Court.

In deciding whether to make such orders, the court must consider the welfare of each child as its paramount consideration: see s1(1) CA 1989. This means that their welfare will determine the decisions to be made and will take priority over such factors as the wishes and feelings of John and Norma: see *J* v *C* (1969). The court will also assume that any delay in determining the questions is likely to be prejudicial to the welfare of each child: see s1(2) CA 1989. Therefore, the court will wish to deal with any applications with the least possible delay. The court will also not make an order unless it is satisfied that the order will improve matters for the child: see s1(5) CA 1989. If it is not so satisfied, then it will not interfere in the children's lives by making the order. Should an application be opposed, the court must consider a list of particular considerations called the 'welfare checklist': see s1(3) and (4) CA 1989. These considerations will be discussed in relation to each of the orders Norma may wish to seek to resolve the questions concerning Sophia and Ben.

Sophia is now aged 14 years. She is still therefore of compulsory school age, and so both John and Norma would be liable to be prosecuted if they did not ensure that she attended school regularly: see s36 Education Act 1944 and s199 Education Act 1993. If Sophia fails to attend school regularly, proceedings could be taken by the local education authority to persuade and encourage her to attend school, or an order could be obtained obliging her to attend. If this fails, she should be warned that the local authority could take proceedings to take her into care if she is suffering significant harm as a result of her failure to attend school: see *Re O (a minor) (care proceedings: education)* (1992). The court will not regard very favourably a parent who is not using his or her best efforts to ensure that Sophia continues to attend school.

In relation to Sophia's part-time work, Norma should be advised that there are restrictions on Sophia doing work which interferes with her school work: see s18 Children and Young Persons Act 1969. These restrictions cover working in the evening after 7pm and not working for more than two hours on any school day, and restrictions on working on Sunday. These restrictions apply until she is over compulsory school age, normally when she is between the ages of 16 and 17: see s35 Education Act 1944. If Sophia is employed in contravention of these restrictions, the employer and any person who has caused the illegal working by any act or default is liable to be prosecuted and fined: see s21 Children and Young Persons Act 1933. Thus, if either John or Norma were to encourage Sophia to work in contravention of those restrictions they could be prosecuted. This should resolve the issue of Sophia wanting to leave school and devote herself to modelling once it is pointed out to her that no law-abiding employer can employ her and that she is obliged to remain at school or risk her parents being prosecuted and the local authority taking proceedings to secure her attendance.

The above considerations should ensure that Sophia does attend school and that any work she does both complies with the law and does not affect her schooling. The remaining dispute is where she should be educated – at the boarding school close to John's home or the local comprehensive that she already attends. This dispute is likely to be decided in tandem with the dispute as to with whom the children should reside, so advice will now be given on how the court is likely to approach those two questions. In considering the 'welfare checklist', the court will have regard to the wishes and feelings of each child, having regard to his or her age and understanding: see s1(3)(a) CA 1989. Sophia is aged 14 years so her wishes and feelings may carry weight with the court. This will depend on her maturity. The court may take the view that her views about modelling work and about schooling do not show a great level of maturity or understanding about what is really in her interests. Her wishes and feelings may be put into that context. Ben is 12 years old. Again, depending on his maturity, his wishes and feeling are likely to carry weight with the court. Again the court may doubt his maturity given his wish to go the Himalayas which the court may conclude does not show a great understanding of what is in his interests. It is unlikely to pay much regard to his wish to leave home and move in with his friends' parents because he does not agree with his mother about the Himalayan trip. This again shows immaturity and impulsiveness on his part. The court will also consider each child's physical, educational and emotional needs as well as his or her age, sex, background and other relevant characteristics: see s1(3)(b) and (d) CA 1989. Sophie's pregnancy is likely to be considered here. The court will also consider the likely effect on each child of any change in his or her circumstances: see s1(3)(c) CA 1989. The children have been used to a shared residence arrangement over the last two years. Any change in their residence may upset their schooling and mean less involvement with one of their parents. If the court is satisfied that this arrangement is in the children's best interests it will require reasons to be given as to why it should be changed. It is likely to assume that there should be stability and security in the children's lives and any change to their arrangements may harm them. The court will also consider any harm each child is suffering or is likely to suffer: see s1(3)(e) CA 1989. Sophia's wish to stop her schooling is likely to be regarded as harmful. The effect of the pregnancy and having a baby at such a young age may also be considered to be harmful in terms of Sophia's schooling and emotional and physical development. The court will also consider how capable each parent is of meeting each child's needs: see s1(3)(f) CA 1989. It may not be impressed with John if it is of the view that he has acted unilaterally and with insufficient reason in failing to return the children. It may also not be impressed with his equivocal attitude to Ben's proposed Himalayan trip if it considers such a trip inappropriate for a 12-year-old boy. It may ask about the circumstances in which Sophia came to be pregnant in case this reflects on the capabilities of either parent. The court will also consider its full range of powers: see s1(3)(g) CA 1989.

The court will consider the arrangement reached between John and Norma to share the residence of the children. In the past the courts have frowned on such arrangements, since the view was taken that children needed one stable home and that having two homes was unsettling and confusing. Norma can be advised that the courts appear to be more prepared to accept shared residence arrangements where the children clearly benefit from it and where it confirms the equal status of each parent in the children's lives: see *A v A (minors) (shared residence order)* (1994) and *Re H (a minor) (shared residence)* (1994).

If the court decides to confirm the existing residence arrangements, it is likely to favour Sophia continuing to go to the school she already attends. At her age a change of school may be disruptive, particularly if she is following particular studies leading to exams. As a result John would have to persuade the court that a change to a boarding school (which would also mean a change in lifestyle) is in Sophia's best interests. If Ben goes to the same school there may also be an argument that he and his sister should be kept together and treated equally. A boarding school may mean that Sophia and Ben are separated. The courts tend to favour keeping siblings together, particularly where they are close in age.

In relation to Ben's trip to the Himalayas, as if the court makes a residence order (including a shared residence order) then Ben would not be allowed to leave the United Kingdom without the written consent of both John and Norma or the leave of the court: see s13 CA 1989. If there is a shared residence order this provision would not prevent John removing Ben from the United Kingdom for a period of less than one month: see s13(2) CA 1989. If the intended trip is for more than one month then Norma can prevent it by not providing consent. John would have to apply to the court for leave to allow Ben to go. If the trip is for less than one month then Norma could apply for a prohibited steps order to prevent Ben from going on the trip to the Himalayas. The court would apply the welfare checklist. It would consider Ben's age and the hazards of such a trip. If it took the view that the trip was not in his interests it would make an order prohibiting him from going. The order could apply to his friend's parents if it was thought they might still try to take Ben on the holiday.

With regard to Sophia's abortion, Norma can be advised that Sophia is of an age where the court will give weight to her wishes and feelings. The court is likely to start by asking whether Sophia has sufficient understanding and intelligence to make an informed decision about her pregnancy. If she has sufficient understanding and intelligence it is likely to approach its decision by favouring her wishes. Having said that, Sophia does not have the absolute right to refuse an abortion so her veto is not binding on the court: see *Re W (a minor) (medical treatment)* (1992) and *Re E (a minor) (wardship: medical treatment)* (1993). The court will treat her welfare as the paramount consideration and ask itself whether allowing the pregnancy to continue is in her best interests. If is not, then it can order a termination: see *Re P (a minor)* (1986). Since such a decision is likely to be difficult and complex, it is likely to be dealt with by the High Court, either through a specific issues order or via wardship whereby Sophia is made a ward of court. These days provisions can be made for teenage mothers to continue schooling, so the court may be of the view that the pregnancy and subsequent baby may not be as detrimental to her welfare in terms of her schooling as Norma thinks.

In conclusion, Norma can apply to the court for orders dealing with the residence, schooling and Himalayan holiday disputes. The law on the employment of children should deal with the difficulties caused by Sophia's wish to work rather than go to school. The matter of the abortion can be dealt with by court order or through wardship.

QUESTION THREE

Camilla and David, who married in 1978, have two children, Edwina and Fred, aged 14 and 10 respectively. David, a television journalist, has played little part in the care of the children, while Camilla, a barrister, chose to take leave from her career until the children were both of school age. Since Camilla's return to work in 1989, she and David employed a nanny, Gemma, to help look after the children.

In January 1994, Edwina, who had been suffering from depression for some months, was diagnosed as suffering from anorexia nervosa and began treatment with a specialist in eating disorders, Dr Hart. Initially, Edwina's condition improved, but then it deteriorated. Dr Hart discovered that Edwina was refusing to follow her treatment, and, afraid that Edwina might ultimately suffer permanent damage, proposed that she be admitted to a hospital unit dedicated to such cases. Both Edwina and her mother opposed Dr Hart's suggestion, but David was prepared to give his consent. Edwina's condition has now deteriorated further and Dr Hart seeks your advice as to the steps she can take to have Edwina admitted to the unit. David, convinced that Edwina's condition is related to her relationship with Camilla, has decided that both Edwina and Fred would be better off at a strict boarding school. Camilla, who is ideologically opposed to boarding schools, seeks your advice as to how she can prevent David sending the children away.

Advise Dr Hart and Camilla.

University of London LLB Examination
(for External Students) Family Law June 1994 Q3

General Comment

This question deals with firstly the medical treatment of a 14–year-old child. The issue of the child's wishes and feelings, in particular her refusal to co-operate with treatment, needs to be addressed, as does the place of parental consent in the situation where one parent disagrees with the other. The second part of the question deals with a parental dispute over schooling. This can be resolved through an application for a specific issues order or prohibited steps order under the Children Act 1989 and the considerations the court would apply need to be outlined.

Skeleton Solution

- The medical treatment of a teenage child – whether the child is '*Gillick*' competent and the importance of her wishes and feelings – the decision in *Re W* (1992).
- Parental consent to medical treatment where one parent disagrees with the other – one parent can act without the other (s2(7) of the Children Act 1989).
- Application for a specific issues or prohibited steps order under s8 Children Act 1989 – the consideration that the welfare of the children is paramount (s1(1)), that delay is assumed to be harmful (s1(2)), the welfare checklist (s1(3),(4)) and the no order principle (s1(5) Children Act 1989).

Suggested Solution

The first and most urgent issue to be resolved is the medical treatment of Edwina. Her condition has deteriorated and Dr Hart wishes to admit her to a specialist unit. Both Edwina and her mother oppose this move for reasons which are not disclosed. Her father is willing to agree. Both Dr Hart and Edwina's mother, Camilla, need to be advised of the legal position.

Does Edwina's refusal prevent Dr Hart from moving her to the specialist hospital unit? The significance of her refusal depends on her age, maturity and understanding. She may be able to act independently of her parents in certain circumstances if she has sufficient understanding and intelligence to know what is involved in the decision she wishes to make (see *Gillick v West Norfolk and Wisbech Area Health Authority* (1985)). If Edwina is immature and has no real understanding of her medical position her refusal to give consent would not carry weight and would not prevent Dr Hart from treating her. If her condition is such that she is sometimes rational (and has *Gillick* capacity) and sometimes not then, because her understanding is not on a lasting basis, her refusal again will not carry weight (see *Re R (a minor) (wardship: medical treatment)* (1991)). If she is mature, intelligent and has full understanding (ie is *Gillick* competent) then her refusal may carry weight and Dr Hart would have to take them into account. Her situation has parallels with the case of *Re W (a minor) (medical treatment)* (1992) where a 16-year-old girl, in the care of the local authority and suffering from anorexia nervosa, refused to be moved to a specialist hospital which doctors recommended for treatment. The local authority, as her 'parents', wished to move her there despite the fact that she would not consent. Edwina's case is different to *Re W* in that Edwina is only 14. *Re W* involved discussion of s8 of the Family Law Reform Act 1969 which provides that a child over 16 may effectively consent to medical treatment. This does not apply in Edwina's case. However *Re W* does establish some important principles which are relevant to Edwina's case. A court can override the wishes of a child in the child's best interests, even where a child had sufficient understanding and intelligence to make an informed decision about refusing medical treatment, where such refusal could lead to death or serious injury. A court would approach its decision by strongly favouring the child's wishes but the child had no absolute right to refuse medical treatment. A similar approach was followed in the case of a 15-year-old boy who refused to have blood transfusions in *Re E (a minor) (wardship: medical treatment)* (1993). His parents also refused to consent to such treatment. The court dispensed with the consent of the boy and of the parents because his welfare was paramount and if he was not given the treatment he would die. Dr Hart and Camilla should consider Edwina's wishes and feelings in this context. The more life threatening her condition the more likely a court is to override her refusal even if it is an informed refusal. If Edwina is *Gillick* competent Dr Hart may be advised to safeguard his position by asking the court to confirm that he may continue with her treatment.

Does Camilla's refusal prevent Edwina's treatment? Similar principles will apply. As in *Re E*, if a child's medical condition is life-threatening the court is likely to override a refusal whether from the child or her parents or both. In Edwina's case her father, David, is willing to give consent. Since he is married to Camilla he shares parental responsibility (which includes the responsibility for consenting to medical treatment) for Edwina with Camilla (see s2(1) of the Children Act (CA) 1989). Even though parental responsibility is shared he may act alone and without Camilla in meeting that responsibility (see s2(7) CA 1989). This means that his consent could be sufficient to allow Dr Hart to transfer Edwina to the specialist unit even though Camilla does not consent. In addition, if Dr Hart has the actual care of Edwina, he may also do what is reasonable in all the circumstances for the purpose of safeguarding or promoting Edwina's welfare (see s3(5) CA 1989). The reasonableness of Dr Hart acting against Camilla's wishes will again depend on how life-threatening Edwina's condition is. Should Camilla wish to prevent the medical treatment Dr Hart proposes she could apply to the court for an order prohibiting the treatment under the terms of a prohibited steps order (see s8 CA 1989). In deciding whether to make such an order the welfare of Edwina would be paramount and would override the wishes of either Camilla or David (see s1(1) CA 1989). The court would consider Edwina's wishes and feelings (considered in the light of her age and understanding) and any harm she was at risk of suffering, as well as the capabilities of Camilla and David as parents and Edwina's medical needs (see s1(3),(4) CA 1989). As has already been discussed the more life-threatening Edwina's condition the less likely that Camilla could prevent Dr Hart from treating her.

Why is Camilla refusing to give her consent? If her refusal is based on unsound grounds then her capability as a parent would be brought into question and her views would carry little weight with the court.

The second issue relates to the schooling of Edwina and Fred. Camilla and David have clearly conflicting views. Each shares parental responsibility with the other so neither view can override the other. In order to resolve this dispute Camilla or David may apply to the court for a specific issues order settling this dispute, or Camilla can apply for a prohibited steps order preventing David from changing the children's schooling (see s8 CA 1989). In deciding what order to make the court would be bound by particular considerations. Firstly, the welfare of each child is paramount (see s1(1) Children Act 1989). Their welfare overrides the views of the parents. Camilla's ideological opposition to boarding schools would not prevent the court from ordering this form of education if this was in the children's best interests. Secondly, the court would assume that any delay in settling this dispute would be likely to be harmful to the children (see s1(2) CA 1989). This means that the court would seek to make a decision as soon as was possible. Thirdly, the court would be bound to take account of particular matters (see s1(3),(4) CA 1989). It would have regard to the wishes and feelings of Edwina and Fred in the light of their ages and understanding. Both children would appear to be old enough for their views on their schooling to carry considerable weight with the court, though Edwina may be too ill to be able to properly express her wishes and feelings. The court would consider each child's physical, emotional and educational needs. I note that David prefers a strict boarding school. This may provide a higher standard of education but may be detrimental to the children's emotional needs if they are used to attending a day school with a less strict regime. Given Edwina's physical and emotional problems the kind of schooling she receives must take these into account. A strict boarding school could make her problems worse. The court would also consider the likely effect on each child of a change in his or her circumstances. Edwina and Fred will already be used to a particular school and type of schooling. They may

117

have particular friends at those schools. If their schooling and their family life is suddenly changed by having to attend a boarding school any benefits of that change might be outweighed by the upset and confusion of the change. The courts recognise that children are often best served by stability in their lives particularly when there are difficulties in the relationship of their parents. The court will consider each child's age, sex, background and any other relevant characteristics. It will consider any harm each child has suffered or is at risk of suffering. Edwina's depression and anorexia nervosa will again be considered under this heading as would any harm to Fred of a change of schooling at this stage of his education. The court will consider how capable Edwina and David are of meeting each child's needs. I note that David appears to have played little part in the care of the children while Camilla cared for them until they were of school age. David may not be as capable of understanding and meeting the needs of his children as Camilla and hence his ideas as to their schooling may not be in their best interests. The court will also consider its full range of powers which means that it can make what order it sees fit as opposed to just the kind of order applied for. The court cannot make any order unless it is satisfied that to make an order would positively benefit each child (see s1(5) CA 1989). Since there is a clear parental dispute the need for an order seems clear.

In conclusion, the treatment of Edwina by Dr Hart is likely to continue in accordance with the doctor's instructions given David's consent. If Edwina's condition is serious the refusal of Camilla and Edwina is likely to carry even less weight. In relation to the dispute over schooling Edwina is advised to apply to the court for a prohibited steps order to prevent David suddenly changing the schools Fred and Edwina are currently attending.

QUESTION FOUR

Ursula and Vernon began living together in 1985. In 1987, they had a son, William. In December 1993 after fertility treatment at a clinic licensed under the Human Fertilisation and Embryology Act 1990, Ursula gave birth to a girl, Xanthe, who [was] registered as Vernon's child.

In December 1994, Ursula left Vernon, taking the children with her and went to live with Zack, a 20-year-old musician with whom she has been having an affair since January 1993. Ursula has refused to allow Vernon to see the children. She has told him that Xanthe is Zack's child and, although she will never allow Xanthe to be tested for the purposes of establishing her paternity, she will swear that Zack is her father in any legal proceedings. Ursula has also told Vernon that she intends to change the children's surname to that of Zack and to start a new life with him where Vernon will be unable to find them.

Advise Vernon.

University of London LLB Examination
(for External Students) Family Law June 1995 Q6

General Comment

The question deals with the status of children. The student is required to display knowledge of the legal status of an unmarried father in relation first to a child born naturally, and second to a child born after artificial insemination within an unmarried relationship. The student also has to show how an unmarried father can acquire legal rights over such children, and how a court can resolve a dispute over the parentage of a child. Finally, the legal position relating to a child's surname needs to be outlined together with advice on how a dispute over contact with the children can be resolved.

118

Skeleton Solution

- Status of William – child of unmarried parents – father lacks parental responsibility (s2(2) Children Act 1989) – application for parental responsibility (s4(1)(a) CA 1989).
- Status of Xanthe – licensed fertility treatment to Ursula while she was living with Vernon – Vernon is the legal father by s28(3) Human Fertilisation and Embryology Act 1990 (HFEA 1990).
- Dispute as to parentage of Xanthe – power to direct blood tests (s20 Family Law Reform Act 1969) – consequences of failure to comply with blood test direction (s23 FLRA 1969).
- Application for contact with children and principles to be applied (ss1, 8 and 10 CA 1989).
- Change of surname and move away – prohibited steps and specific issues order (ss1, 8 and 10 CA 1989), and case law on change of surname.

Suggested Solution

Vernon asks for advice in relation to his two children, William and Xanthe. The question suggests that he wishes to have contact with them, that he would like to confirm his status as their father and that he would wish to prevent Ursula changing the children's surname and taking them away from him in order to start a new life with Zack.

Ursula and Vernon lived together from 1985 to December 1994, namely for nine years. They did not marry. William was born in 1987 and lived with Ursula and Vernon for seven years until he left with his mother to live with Zack. Xanthe was born in December 1993 so only lived with Ursula and Vernon for a year before she left with her mother and brother to live with Zack. Vernon should first be advised about his legal status in relation to William. There appears to be no dispute that Vernon is his father. However Vernon, as an unmarried father, does not have parental responsibility for him (s2(2)(a) Children Act 1989 – hereinafter referred to as the CA 1989). Parental responsibility is entirely vested in Ursula. Parental responsibility means all the rights, duties, powers, responsibilities and authority which by law a parent of a child has in relation to that child and his or her property (see s3(1) CA 1989). It would include the right to be consulted on major decisions concerning William (eg, about his health or his schooling) though it would not give Vernon the right to interfere in day-to-day decisions (see *Re P (a minor) (parental responsibility order)* (1994)). Vernon should take action to acquire parental responsibility by way of an application to the court for a parental responsibility order (see s4(1)(a) CA 1989). It is possible for him to sign a parental responsibility agreement with Ursula, giving him parental responsibility, but given her present stance this does not appear to be a viable option (see s4(1)(b) CA 1989). In order to succeed in an application for parental responsibility he must satisfy the court of various matters. He must demonstrate to the court that he has shown commitment to William and that he has a good relationship with him. He must also show that his application is motivated by a concern for William's welfare and to be involved in his life (and is not motivated by malice against Ursula and with a wish to use William to interfere with her life) (see *Re C (minors)* (1992)). Given the fact that William lived with Vernon for some seven years, this appears to demonstrate that Vernon is committed to William's welfare, that they have a relationship and that he does wish to be involved in important decisions in relation to William's life. Vernon appears to have a strong case should he apply for parental responsibility.

In relation to Xanthe, she appears to have been conceived as a result of fertility treatment at a clinic licensed under the Human Fertilisation and Embryology Act 1990 (hereinafter referred to as the HFEA 1990). It is assumed that this was with Vernon's consent and support since

119

Vernon was registered as Xanthe's father. If Vernon's sperm was used in the treatment he will be treated as the biological and legal father. If his sperm was not used, but the treatment can be said to have been provided for Ursula and Vernon together, then Vernon is treated as being the legal father of Xanthe (see s28(3) HFEA 1990). No other man can then be treated as Xanthe's father (see s28(4) HFEA 1990). In particular, if Ursula was inseminated by sperm from an anonymous donor then that donor is specifically excluded from being Xanthe's father (see s28(6) HFEA 1990). Vernon would have the status of an unmarried father in relation to Xanthe so all the comments in relation to parental responsibility for William and how it can be acquired apply equally to her as they do to William. Vernon appears to have a weaker case if he applies to the court for parental responsibility in relation to Xanthe since she only lived with him and Ursula for a year before Ursula left with her. However, he may still be able to demonstrate sufficient commitment and a sufficient relationship to be successful in such an application.

Ursula now states that Xanthe was conceived as a result of an affair with Zack which started in January 1993. As has been outlined above, Vernon appears to have the legal status of father in relation to Xanthe. If he applies for a parental responsibility order (and for contact and a prohibited steps order) in relation to his two children no doubt she will challenge his status in relation to Xanthe. The court may then be called upon to make a declaration as to Xanthe's parentage before proceeding with the applications. Whether the court will give any credence to Ursula's claim will depend on the circumstances. If she and Vernon received fertility treatment as a result of problems with her ability to conceive a child then any claim that these difficulties suddenly ceased when she started her affair with Zack may lack any credibility. If the treatment was provided as a result of Vernon being unable to provide suitable sperm then her claim may have more validity. More information is required on the nature of Vernon's and Ursula's problems in conceiving a child and in relation to the treatment they received. The fact that she presumably agreed to register Vernon as Xanthe's father will weaken her claim. If the court does give credence to Ursula's claim it may direct of its own motion (or at Vernon's request) that blood tests be carried out to establish Xanthe's paternity (see s20 Family Law Reform Act 1969 – hereinafter referred to as the FLRA 1969). The court is likely to direct that DNA tests be carried out since these conclusively establish paternity. Blood samples would be required from Xanthe (with her mother's consent), from Ursula, from Vernon (unless it is accepted that he cannot be the biological father because of the nature of the fertility treatment) and from Zack. The DNA from these samples would analysed to show conclusively whether Zack is or is not the father of Xanthe (and if appropriate to show that Vernon is Xanthe's biological father). The taking of blood samples is voluntary so Ursula could refuse to allow samples to be taken from her and from Xanthe. However, the court could then draw such inferences from that refusal as appear proper in the circumstances (see s23(1) FLRA 1969). Such an inference could be that Ursula knows that Zack is not Xanthe's biological father and is afraid that the truth will be revealed by the tests (see *McVeigh* v *Beattie* (1988) and *Re A (a minor) (paternity: refusal of blood test)* (1994)). The courts have held that it is in the child's best interests for the truth of his/her parentage to be established, so Ursula is unlikely to be able to persuade a court that there is good reason for her failure to comply with any blood test direction.

As the children's father (with or without parental responsibility) Vernon can apply to the court for a contact order, namely an order requiring Ursula to allow the children to visit or stay with him or for Vernon and the children to otherwise have contact with each other (see ss8(1) and s10 CA 1989). He can also apply for a prohibited steps order prohibiting the children from being known by a different surname and prohibiting Ursula from moving without notifying Vernon, so that he knows where the children are (see ss8(1) and 10 CA 1989). He can make these applications at the same time as any applications for parental responsibility. In deciding whether to grant the applications the court will treat the welfare of William and Xanthe as paramount (see s1(1) CA 1989). This means that their welfare will determine the decision to be made, as opposed to what either parent may consider fair or just (see *J* v *C* (1969)). The court will also assume that any delay in deciding on the issues affecting the children is likely to prejudice their welfare. As a result, the court is likely to lay down a timetable for hearing the applications before it and ensure that the parties stick to the timetable (see ss1(2) and 11 CA 1989). The court can also not make any order relating to the children unless it is satisfied that making that order would be better for the children than making no order at all (see s1(5) CA 1989). Vernon must show that any orders he seeks will positively benefit the children.

In relation to the applications for contact or prohibited steps, assuming that Ursula opposes them, the court will have regard to particular considerations (see s1(3),(4) CA 1989). The court will consider the ascertainable wishes and feelings of each child considered in the light of his or her age and understanding (see s1(3)(a) CA 1989). Xanthe is too young to express her wishes and feelings. William is aged seven or eight years and may well be old and mature enough to make his views clear. Though he is too young for his views to be decisive with the court, they are likely to carry great weight. If he wishes to keep in touch with his father and wishes to retain his surname then this will greatly strengthen Vernon's case. The court is likely to order that a welfare report be prepared by a welfare officer so that he or she can independently ascertain William's views rather than rely on whatever Ursula or Vernon say William's wishes and feelings are. The court will consider the children's physical, emotional and educational needs (see s1(3)(b) CA 1989). This will include each child's emotional need to know their father. The court will also consider the likely effect on each child of a change in his or her circumstances (see s1(3)(c) CA 1989). The court may ask whether Ursula's planned change of surname and breaking off of contact between the children and their father is likely to harm them. The court will also consider the age, sex, background and characteristics of the children aswell as any harm they have suffered or are at risk of suffering (eg by a loss of contact with their father and/or a change of surname) (see s1(3)(d) and (e) CA 1989). The court will also consider how capable Vernon and Ursula (and, if appropriate, Zack) are of meeting the children's needs as well as its full range of powers (see s1(3)(f) and (g) CA 1989).

In relation to Vernon's application for contact, it has been stated that no court should deprive a child of contact with either parent unless it is wholly satisfied that it is in the child's interests that there should be no contact. This is a conclusion which courts are generally extremely slow to arrive at. The courts have recognised the long-term advantages of a child keeping in touch with the absent parent after a family breakdown. To deprive a child of contact with such a parent may deprive the child of an important contribution to his/her emotional welfare (see *Re H (minors) (access)* (1992) and *Re M (contact: welfare test)* (1995)). Unless Ursula can demonstrate that the children will be harmed by contact with Vernon, he is likely to have a strong case for the making of a contact order and for a prohibited steps order preventing Ursula from moving without telling him.

In relation to the children's surname, Vernon should be advised that the existing case law is not always consistent and was mostly decided before the Children Act 1989 came into force. However, the weight of the authorities suggest that if Vernon has played and will continue to play an important part in the lives of the children then the court will not permit a change in surname (see *L* v *F* (1978), *W* v *A (child: surname)* (1981) and *Re F (child: surname)* (1994)). The use of Vernon's surname will preserve the link with him. This may outweigh any embarrassment which may be caused should Ursula and Zack marry or otherwise by Ursula taking a different surname.

9 Adoption

9.1 Introduction

Adoption was introduced in 1926. It is now governed by the Adoption Act (AA) 1976 which came into force in 1988 (and replaced previous provisions in the Children Act 1975 and the Adoption Act 1958). An adoption order ends the legal relationship between a child and his or her natural parents and creates a new and exclusive relationship between the child and the adopters. It gives the applicants parental responsibility for the child and extinguishes the parental responsibility of the birth parents (see s12(1) and (3) AA 1976).

Applications for adoption have fallen dramatically in recent years. In 1994 there were 6,326 adoptions (nearly half of them being applications by a natural parent and a step-parent) compared with 22,500 in 1974.

9.2 Key points

a) *Who can apply for an adoption order?*

A married couple may apply for an adoption order. Each partner should be at least 21 years of age but if the husband or wife is the father or mother of the child and is at least 18 years of age and his or her spouse is at least 21 years of age then application can be made (see s14(1) and (1A) AA 1976).

Under s15(1) AA 1976 a single person may apply for an adoption order if he or she is at least 21 years of age. He or she must be unmarried or if he or she is married the court must be satisfied that:

i)   his or her spouse cannot be found; or

ii) that they have separated and are living apart and the separation is likely to be permanent; or

iii) the spouse is incapable of making an application for an adoption by reason of physical or mental ill-health.

Under s15(3) AA 1976 if the single applicant is the mother or father of the child the court cannot make an adoption order unless it is satisfied that:

i)   the other parent is dead or cannot be found; or

ii) there is some other reason justifying the exclusion of the other natural parent.

These provisions do not allow an unmarried couple to apply for an adoption order.

However, it is possible for one partner to apply for adoption and, if an adoption order is made, for a joint residence order to be made whereby the other partner acquires parental responsibility for the child (see *Re AB (adoption: joint residence)* [1996] 1 FLR 27).

b) *The child must live with the applicant(s) before the making of the application*

If the applicant, or one of the applicants is a parent, step-parent or relative of the child (or the child was placed with the applicants by an adoption agency or by the High Court) the child must be at least 19 weeks old and must have had his or her home with the applicant(s) or one of them for at least 13 weeks preceding the making of the application (see s13(1) AA 1976).

If the applicant or one of the applicants is not so related to the child, the child must be at least twelve months old and have had his or her home with the applicant(s) or one of them for at least the 12 months preceding the making of the application (see s13(2) AA 1976).

The applicant(s) must notify the local authority of the application. The local authority prepares a report (called a 'Schedule II' report) which assists the court in making its decision.

c) *What the court must consider*

In reaching any decision relating to the adoption of a child the court must have regard to all the circumstances, first consideration being given to the need to safeguard and promote the welfare of the child throughout his/her childhood and shall give due consideration to the child's wishes and feelings having regard to his/her age and understanding (see s6 AA 1976). It is important to note that this is not the same test as that applied in s1(1) Children Act 1989. 'All the circumstances' include the interests of the natural parents. While the welfare of the child is the single most important factor it does necessarily outweigh all other circumstances such as the wish of the natural parents to retain links with their child (see *Re W (an infant)* [1971] 2 WLR 1011).

The delay principle in s1(2) CA 1989 applies so the court must assume that any delay in deciding upon the adoption is likely to prejudice the child's welfare.

d) *The need for parental consent*

An adoption order cannot be made unless the child has been freed for adoption, or in the case of each parent or guardian of the child the court is satisfied that the parent or guardian freely and with full understanding of what is involved agrees unconditionally to the making of an adoption order or that agreement has been dispensed with (see s16(1) and (2) AA 1976).

The mother cannot give agreement until at least six weeks after the child's birth (to avoid any immediate post-natal depression which might influence a mother's wishes – see s16(4) AA 1976).

A parent for these purposes does not include an unmarried father unless he has obtained parental responsibility for the child under s4 Children Act 1989, or has a residence order in his favour (see s72 AA 1976 and *Re C (adoption: parties)* [1995] 2 FLR 483).

An adoption question is likely to focus on the grounds for dispensing with consent:

i) Has persistently failed without reasonable cause to discharge his/her parental responsibility for the child (s16(2)(c)).

ii) Has abandoned or neglected the child (s16(2)(d)).

iii) Has persistently ill-treated the child or has seriously ill-treated the child (and because of that ill-treatment or for other reasons the rehabilitation of the child within the household of the parent is unlikely) (see s16(2)(e) and (f) and s16(5)).

iv) Is withholding agreement unreasonably (see s16(2)(b)).

Students will be expected to be aware of the main cases dealing with these grounds. These cases include:

i) *Re D (minors) (adoption by parent)* [1973] 3 WLR 595 on the s16(2)(c) ground where it was said that the failure had not only to be culpable to a high degree but also so grave and complete that the child would derive no advantage from maintaining contact with the natural parent – a temporary withdrawal or drifting apart would not suffice.

ii) *Watson v Nickolaisen* [1955] 2 WLR 1187 on the s16(2)(d) ground where it was held that abandoning a child had to be wilful or in a manner likely to cause suffering – a mother who placed her child in the hands of a couple in whom she had confidence could not be said to have abandoned the child.

The most difficult of the grounds is that of withholding agreement unreasonably. Leading cases on this ground include:

i) *Re W (an infant)* [1971] 2 WLR 1011 where it was held that the court judged the situation as at the date of the hearing, and applied the test objectively – namely would a reasonable parent withhold agreement in all the circumstances? The welfare of the child was not paramount. The parent has legitimate rights to veto the adoption – adoption could not be granted simply because the child's welfare suggested it. In judging reasonableness a reasonable parent gives great weight to what is better for the child and does not ignore any risk or ill likely to be avoided by the adoption or the loss of some appreciable benefit likely to be gained by an adoption order. There is no need to establish culpability on the parent's behalf.

ii) *Re H(B) (an infant) and W(N) (an infant)* (1983) 4 FLR 614 – there was room for reasonable withholding of consent; even those responsible for the child's welfare held an acceptable view that the child's welfare demanded adoption. Where the natural parent presented him/herself at the time of the hearing as someone capable of caring for the child that was a relevant factor. Where there was an inherent defect in the parent which was likely to persist that was also important. But where the unsuitability only related to past history unless the past history was likely to influence the future position then it should carry little weight in the mind of the hypothetical reasonable parent. The chances of a successful reintroduction to, or continuation of contact with, the natural parent was a critical factor.

e) *Orders which can be made*

If an adoption order is made it may contain such terms and conditions as the court thinks fit (see s12(6) AA 1976). In particular, an adoption order can include a condition allowing contact between the child and his/her natural family. In normal circumstances such a condition is not appropriate because it is desirable that there be a complete break with the natural family on adoption. If the applicants agree to contact, and this is in the interests of the child, then a condition of contact can be made. There would have to be exceptional circumstances before a court would impose such a condition without the agreement of the adoptive parents (see *Re C (a minor)(adoption: conditions)* [1988] 1 All ER 705).

Adoptions have come to be classified as 'closed adoptions' (where there is no contact between the child and his/her natural family) and 'open adoptions' (where members of the child's natural family continue to have contact after the adoption order has been made). 'Open adoptions' are only practicable if the adoptive parents agree to it (see *Re C* (above), *Re GR (adoption: access)* [1985] FLR 643 and *Re T (adoption: contact)* [1995] 2 FLR 251). If the adoptive parents agree to contact, but then renege on that agreement, a member of the child's natural family could then apply for leave to apply for a contact order (see *Re T (minors) (adopted children: contact)* [1995] 3 WLR 793).

It is rare for any other kind of condition to be attached to an adoption order. The court disapproved of a condition obliging adoptive parents (who were Jehovah's Witnesses) to co-operate with a blood transfusion if the child required one. Since there were established procedures to deal with such a situation there was no need for such a condition (see *Re S (a minor) (blood transfusion: adoption order: condition)* [1995] 2 All ER 122).

Adoption proceedings are family proceedings (see s8(4) CA 1989). The court can therefore make a s8 order on application or of its own motion. The court could make a residence order and contact order instead of an adoption order. Third parties (eg grandparents) could apply for leave to intervene in the proceedings. The court has the flexibility in finding an alternative to adoption if that is appropriate.

f) *Prohibition on private placements and payments for adoption*

A person other than an adoption agency shall not make arrangements for the adoption of a child or place a child for adoption unless the proposed adopter is a relative of the child or he/she is acting in pursuance of an order of the High Court (see s11(1) AA 1976). Contravention of this provision is a criminal offence.

It is also unlawful to make or give to any person any payment or reward for or in consideration of the adoption by that person of a child, including payment to obtain agreement or consent to the adoption (see s57(1) AA 1976). Again contravention of this provision is a criminal offence.

The s57(1) prohibition does not apply to payments of reasonable expenses of an adoption agency or to payment authorised by the court to which the adoption application is made (see s57(3) AA 1976). Such authorisation can be done retrospectively, thus allowing an adoption preceded by an unauthorised payment to be granted (see *Re Adoption Application (surrogacy)* [1987] 2 All ER 826).

Contravention of the ss11 and 57 prohibitions does not prevent an adoption order being made if this is clearly in the child's interests (see *Re ZHH (adoption application)* [1993] 1 FLR 83 and *Re MW (adoption: surrogacy)* [1995] 2 FLR 759).

9.3 Recent cases

Re G (adoption: freeing order) [1997] 2 WLR 747

Re W (a minor) (adoption: homosexual adopter) [1997] 2 FLR 406

9.4 Analysis of questions

Adoption is a popular University of London LLB examination topic. Questions are invariably problem type questions. Occasionally the area is examined on its own but it is often included with another topic (eg children in local authority care). Questions often focus on the issue of parental consent.

9.5 Questions

QUESTION ONE

Andrea and Bart were married in 1988. Bart often works abroad, and during one of Bart's absences in 1992 Andrea began an affair with Kevin. In early 1993, Andrea discovered she was pregnant and decided to end the affair, telling Kevin never to contact her again. Later that year, Andrea gave birth to a girl, Imogen. Imogen was a lovely child and Bart became very attached to her. During 1995, Kevin found out about Imogen and told Bart about the affair he had had with Andrea and that he suspected that Imogen was his, not Bart's, child. Bart was devastated and began divorce proceedings. Overcome with guilt, Andrea entered a religious order, leaving Imogen with her sister and brother-in-law, the Smiths, who have long wanted, but have been unable to have, children.

Andrea has decided to remain in the religious order and wants the Smiths to adopt Imogen. Advise the Smiths who tell you that both Bart and Kevin are adamantly opposed to the adoption and will employ every legal means necessary to prevent its occurrence.

University of London LLB Examination
(for External Students) Family Law June 1996 Q7

General Comment

The question combines the subjects of a child's status with the various considerations in an adoption application. The parentage of the child is in issue since two men claim to be the child's father. Resolving this issue requires a discussion of the presumption of legitimacy and how this may be rebutted by evidence of 'non-access' or via blood tests. Once this issue is determined then the need for consent in adoption needs to be outlined. One potential father would be an unmarried father so he would lack parental responsibility and have no standing in the adoption. Because of this an outline of the law on obtaining parental responsibility is required. Finally, the grounds for dispensing with consent need to be given, along with an indication of how they might apply in the circumstances of this case.

Skeleton Solution

• Qualifying to apply for adoption: ss11, 13 and 14 AA 1976.
• Need for consent by parents (s16 AA 1976) – need to establish paternity of child.
• Presumption of legitimacy and how it may be rebutted – rebuttal by 'non-access' – rebuttal using blood tests – whether blood tests would be directed.
• Status of unmarried father – application for parental responsibility.
• Dispensing with consent – application of grounds: s16(2) AA 1976.

Family Law

Suggested Solution

Mr and Mrs Smith ask for advice in relation to their application to adopt Imogen in light of the opposition of Bart and Kevin. It is assumed that Mr and Mrs Smith are married and at least 21 years of age and so qualify to adopt Imogen: see s14 Adoption Act 1976 – hereinafter referred to as the AA 1976. It is also assumed that Imogen has lived with Mr and Mrs Smith for at least 13 weeks which is the minimum period of residence for adoption: see s13 AA 1976. They must also inform the local authority within whose area they reside so that the local authority can investigate the application and prepare the necessary report. Since Mrs. Smith is Imogen's aunt they can make their own arrangements to adopt Imogen and do not need to go through an adoption agency: see s11 AA 1976.

Assuming that the adoption application proceeds Mr and Mrs Smith should be advised that the court has the duty to have regard to all the circumstances, the primary consideration being given to the need to safeguard and promote the welfare of Imogen throughout her childhood, and shall take into account her wishes and feelings regarding the decision and give due consideration to them, having regard to her age and understanding: see s6 AA 1976. Since Imogen is so young it is unlikely that her wishes and feelings will carry much weight with the court.

An adoption order cannot be made unless each of Imogen's parents freely and with full understanding of what is involved agrees unconditionally to the making of the adoption order (whether or not the parents know the identity of the applicants, which can be kept secret if Mr and Mrs Smith so wish), or the agreement of the parent has been dispensed with on a specified ground: see s16(1) AA 1976. It is clear that Andrea is Imogen's mother and that she will consent to the adoption. The difficulty is in identifying Imogen's father. If Bart is her father his consent must be obtained or be dispensed with. If Kevin is her father his consent is not required because he is an unmarried father. He does not have parental responsibility for her and is not therefore a parent for the purposes of the Adoption Act 1976: see s72 AA 1976 and *Re L (a minor) (adoption: procedure)* (1991); *Re C (adoption: parties)* (1995). He cannot play any part in the adoption proceedings unless he takes steps to acquire parental responsibility. Advice on this point will be given later. It is therefore important to give advice on how the court is likely to resolve any dispute as to who is the father of Imogen. Since Andrea and Bart were married when Imogen was born then there is a common law presumption that Bart is her father. If Kevin were to try to establish that he was the father he would had to overcome this presumption. He may adduce evidence to rebut the presumption on a balance of probabilities: see s26 Family Law Reform Act 1969. However, the courts have considered the status of a child to be a grave matter and the burden of proof is more than a narrow balance of probabilities: see *W* v *K* (1988); *Serio* v *Serio* (1983). Kevin may be able to persuade the court that he is the father if he can show that Bart must have been absent at the time of Imogen's conception: see *Preston-Jones* v *Preston-Jones* (1951). The court will apply existing medical knowledge in determining the dates between which Imogen must have been conceived and then discover whether Bart was absent so that he could not be her father. It is assumed that this is unlikely since Bart accepted Imogen as his child. This implies that he believed that he was responsible for her conception so was present within the likely dates for conception.

Alternatively, Kevin can ask that there be blood tests to ascertain Imogen's paternity: see s20 Family Law Reform Act 1969. If the blood samples are tested using DNA techniques then this normally produces certain proof of paternity: see *Re A (a minor) (paternity: refusal of blood test)* (1994). Normally the court considers that a child should know the truth of her paternity and will direct that there be blood tests (a position recently restated in *Re H (a minor) (blood tests: parental rights)* (1996)). The courts take the view that normally adults should establish the truth of their relationship with a child rather than rely on what they wish the situation was. A blood test direction could be made even if Andrea refused to comply with the direction. However, if the blood test is designed to establish the status needed to make an application to the court, but that application is unlikely to be successful, then the court may refuse to direct the blood test: see *Re F (a minor) (blood tests: paternity rights)* (1993). The purpose of Kevin asking for blood tests would be to establish that he is the father of Imogen and then for him to apply for a parental responsibility order in order to give him the locus standi to oppose the adoption. If a blood test did establish that he was the father what would be his prospects of success in applying for parental responsibility?

Kevin would make his application under s4 Children Act 1989. In considering such an application the court would ask three questions. First, it would ask what degree of commitment he had shown to Imogen? Second, it would ask what degree of attachment there was between him and Imogen? Finally, it would ask why he was applying for parental responsibility: see *Re H (minors) (parental responsibility)* (1993). Kevin appears to have left when Andrea became pregnant and decided to end the affair. He does not appear to have had any opportunity to demonstrate any commitment towards Imogen. He does not appear to have any relationship with her since he has not had any contact with her. His motive in applying for parental responsibility appears to be one of frustrating the adoption. If the court takes the view that the chance of him obtaining parental responsibility is remote it may take the view that to disturb the present situation would be wrong. This in turn may depend on how well settled Imogen is with Mr and Mrs Smith following her mother's departure to the religious order. If she is well settled the court may not wish to disturb Imogen's stability, upon which her physical and emotional welfare depend.

If Kevin is able to establish that he is the father of Imogen and is then able to apply for parental responsibility then he acquires the status of a parent and his consent must be given or be dispensed with. If he fails to establish that he is the father then Bart will be considered to be Imogen's father and his consent must be given or dispensed with. Mr and Mrs Smith therefore need to be advised on the grounds which can be used for dispensing with the consent of a parent. The first ground is that the parent cannot be found or is incapable of giving agreement: see s16(2)(a) AA 1976. This does not appear to apply to either Bart or Kevin. The second ground is that Bart or Kevin is withholding his consent unreasonably: see s16(2)(b) AA 1976. This is an objective test based on whether a reasonable parent would withhold agreement. The welfare of Imogen is not the first consideration in answering the question since a parent has legitimate rights which would be extinguished by an adoption and so the parent is able legitimately to veto the adoption to preserve those rights. However, in judging whether a parent was unreasonably withholding his consent, that decision is compared to what a reasonable parent, considering the welfare of his child and the benefits which an adoption would bring, would decide: see *Re W (an infant)* (1971). The court recognises the anguish of a parent but it must nevertheless see what a reasonable parent would do in Bart's or Kevin's place in all the circumstances of the case. In the case of Bart he became very attached to Imogen and presumably acted as a loving father to her from her birth in 1993 up until the divorce proceedings in 1995. It may therefore be difficult to say that his refusal to consent is unreasonable if he has established a relationship with his daughter and wishes to preserve that relationship. Much will depend on his decision to divorce Andrea and how he treated his daughter after she and Andrea left and Imogen went to live with Mr and Mrs Smith. If he behaved particularly badly (eg specifically disowned or rejected her) it may be that his consent could be dispensed with on this ground. In the case of Kevin his apparent lack of any link with Imogen may suggest that he has little prospect of providing a home for her so that his refusal to consent may be deemed unreasonable. The third ground is that the parent has persistently failed without reasonable cause to discharge his parental responsibility for Imogen: see s16(2)(c) AA 1976. It appears difficult to apply this to Bart given his attachment to Imogen for the first two years of her life. It may apply to Kevin given his apparent lack of dealings with Imogen. The court applies a high standard to this ground. Mr and Mrs Smith would have to show a high degree of culpability and a 'permanent failure' rather than a temporary withdrawal or drifting apart due to the breakdown of family relationships: see *Re D (minors) (adoption by parent)* (1973). The fourth ground is that the parent has abandoned or neglected the child: see s16(2)(d) AA 1976. Again it seems difficult to suggest that this applies to Bart given his care of Imogen. When he divorced Andrea he may well have left her in the capable hands of her mother which falls far short of abandoning her. It is also difficult to say that Kevin abandoned Imogen since Andrea told him to have nothing to do with her when she ended the affair. There is no suggestion of neglect in either case. The remaining grounds only apply if Imogen has been ill-treated by either Bart or Kevin and, since there is no suggestion of this, they cannot apply: see s16(2)(e) and (f) AA 1976.

In conclusion, Mr and Mrs Smith can be advised that Bart will be presumed to be the father unless Kevin can persuade the court otherwise. If he fails to do this then he will have no standing and cannot oppose the adoption. In these circumstances Bart must agree to the adoption or have his consent dispensed with. As discussed above this may prove difficult given his apparent close relationship with Imogen for the first two years of his life. The chances of successfully dispensing with his consent may depend on the circumstances of the divorce and how he behaved towards Imogen from that date. If Kevin is able to establish that he is the father he would still lack the status to oppose the adoption since he has no parental responsibility for Imogen (as an unmarried father). He would have to apply successfully for a parental responsibility order. As discussed above, his chances of doing so are not good. If he was successful, then Mr and Mrs Smith could apply to dispense with his consent. They would have a greater chance of success in doing this given Kevin's lack of any relationship with Imogen. If Mr and Mrs Smith are unable to obtain an adoption order the court may make a residence order in their favour whereby Imogen lives with them. This would give them parental responsibility for her but would preserve the parental responsibility of Andrea and Bart (or possibly Kevin). This could allow Andrea and Bart (or Kevin) to maintain links with Imogen (eg the right to have contact with her).

QUESTION TWO

Nora and Oswald, who are 35 and 40 respectively, are married and unable to have children. In January 1992 Oswald, who works as a social worker, met Pippa, who was 15 and pregnant.

Conscious that he and Nora were possibly too old to be considered appropriate to adopt a baby, and aware that Nora's chronic asthma might also affect their chances of success as applicants, he, Nora and Pippa agreed that as soon as Pippa's baby was born, she would hand it over to the couple, so that they could apply to adopt it. Oswald and Nora also agreed to pay her £700 per month during her pregnancy, any medical and hospital bills and £3,000 when the baby was delivered, which they described as an 'adjustment allowance'.

The baby, called Quentin, was born in June 1992. Pippa immediately handed him over to Nora and Oswald. However, she began to regret giving up the baby and repeatedly, but unsuccessfully, demanded his return. In May 1993 Nora and Oswald made a formal application to adopt Quentin.

Advise Pippa.

University of London LLB Examination
(for External Students) Family Law June 1993 Q7

General Comment

This question deals with an adoption application made by a couple who have privately arranged to have the child placed with them and have made payments to the surrogate mother in consideration of the adoption. The legality of such a private placement and of such payments needs to be considered. The mother requires advice on her legal status and the likelihood of an adoption being granted. This will require discussion of the principles behind adoption and in particular the need for parental consent. Finally the mother will need to be advised as to how she can secure the return of the child using a residence order under the Children Act 1989.

Skeleton Solution

- Prohibition on private placements for adoption (s11(1) Adoption Act 1976).
- Prohibition of payments in consideration of adoption and possible exceptions (s57 Adoption Act 1976).
- Requirements as to the making of an adoption order – in particular the need for parental consent.
- The likelihood of an adoption order being made.
- Obtaining a residence order to gain the return of the baby (applying the principles of the Children Act 1989).

Suggested Solution

Pippa needs advice on how she can oppose the adoption application made by Nora and Oswald and how she can obtain the return of Quentin.

Firstly Pippa should be advised that there is a legal prohibition on private placements for adoption unless the proposed adopter is a relative of the child or the placement is pursuant to a high Court order (see s11(1) Adoption Act (AA) 1976). It appears that Nora and Oswald have committed an offence punishable with imprisonment and/or a fine by arranging for Pippa to hand her baby over so that they could apply to adopt it (see ss11(3) and 72(3) AA 1976). Pippa would also be guilty of such an offence by being party to the agreement. However, given her age and the probable 'undue influence' of Oswald (who may possibly have been her social worker and in some other position of trust with her) and Nora it is unlikely that Pippa would be prosecuted or, if prosecuted, punished in any substantial way for her part in the agreement which she now regrets ever having made.

Pippa should also be advised that it is not lawful to give any person any payment or reward for or in consideration of an adoption or to gain a parent's agreement or in order to persuade a person to hand over a child with a view to adoption or to make any arrangements for adoption (see s57(1) AA 1976). It appears that Nora and Oswald have committed an offence, again punishable by a fine and imprisonment, by paying Pippa during her pregnancy, plus her

131

medical bills and the £3,000 adjustment allowance (see s57(3) AA 1976). Pippa may also have committed an offence by receiving the money but she is unlikely to be prosecuted or substantially punished for the reasons already outlined. Nora and Oswald may try to argue that the payments to Pippa involved no profit or reward to her. If such financial arrangements are sincere and there is no profit motive then a court may either treat the payments as lawful or retrospectively authorise them (see s57(3) and *Adoption Application (surrogacy)* (1987)). This could be the position in Pippa's case if, for example, the £700 a month represented lost wages and the £3,000 lost employment opportunities. Given Pippa's age this does not seem probable and the payments are likely to be held to be unlawful. Given these breaches of the law Nora and Oswald's adoption application is so tinged with illegality as to have little prospect of success.

Pippa should also be advised as the requirements Nora and Oswald have to meet in making an adoption application. As a married couple of sufficient age Nora and Oswald can apply for adoption (see s14 AA 1976). Since neither are related to the baby and the placement has not been arranged through an adoption agency or by order of the High Court the baby must be at least 12 months old and have lived with them for at least a year preceding the making of the application (see s13(2) AA 1976). This latter condition is likely to invalidate Nora and Oswald's application since they have only had Quentin since June, 1992 yet have made the application in May, 1993, some 11 months afterwards.

In reaching a decision about whether the baby should be adopted the court must have regard to all the circumstances giving first consideration to the need to safeguard and promote the welfare of the child throughout his childhood and to ascertain the child's wishes and feelings and give due consideration to them (see s6 AA 1976). This means that the child's welfare is not paramount and does not outweigh all other considerations but is of the first importance (see *Re D (an infant) (adoption: parent's consent)* (1977)). Pippa must give her unconditional consent to the adoption with full understanding of what is involved or have her consent dispensed with by the court (see s16 AA 1976). Since Pippa clearly does not want Quentin adopted Nora and Oswald would have to persuade the court to dispense with her consent. They could argue that Pippa is withholding her consent unreasonably, or has persistently failed without reasonable excuse to discharge her parental responsibilities for her baby or that she had abandoned Quentin (see s16(2)(b), (c) and (d) AA 1976). It is difficult to see how a court could be satisfied as to any of these grounds. Pippa cannot be said to have 'abandoned' Quentin because she left the baby with people she presumably trusted would provide for him and has asked for his return (see *Watson v Nickolaisen* (1955)). She could not be said to have persistently failed to discharge her parental responsibilities for Quentin since she has not actually had the opportunity to look after him and has repeatedly asked for his return. Whether Pippa could be held to be withholding consent unreasonably is an objective test judged at the date of the hearing of the application. The court would ask itself what a reasonable parent would do taking into account the welfare of the child (see *Re W (an infant)* (1971)). In a similar case to Pippa's, a mother handed a child over to a couple for adoption under pressure and when she never wanted the child adopted. It was held that she withheld agreement reasonably in the circumstances since she reasonably hoped to provide a secure home for the child in the future. The upset of moving the child in that case (who had only lived with the applicants for a year) would be temporary. It was held that the child would benefit from the care of her natural mother (see *Re PA (an infant)* (1971)). If Pippa's circumstances are such that she could not reasonably expect to provide for Quentin while Norma and Oswald could provide a warm and secure home then her consent might be dispensed with (see *Re P (an infant) (adoption: parental consent)* (1976)). The prospects of Pippa caring for Quentin properly would be crucial to how the court regarded her withholding of consent.

Since the adoption application would be opposed by Pippa the court would appoint a guardian ad litem (an independent social worker) to investigate the case on Quentin's behalf. Both the guardian and the local authority would prepare reports for the court. One matter which would be investigated is the health of the applicants. Norma and Oswald would have to provide medical reports about their health. Nora's chronic asthma would be revealed to the court and is likely to be an important factor in determining Quentin's long term future.

In all the circumstances of the apparent illegality of the arrangements for the adoption and the payments made and in all the other circumstances outlined above a court is likely to refuse the adoption application made by Nora and Oswald. Pippa should be made aware that she has sole parental responsibility for Quentin as an unmarried mother (see s2(2)(a) Children Act (CA) 1989 – assuming that she has not subsequently married the father). Norma and Oswald have no parental responsibility for Quentin unless they obtain a court order giving them that responsibility (which an adoption order would to the exclusion of Pippa). Pippa is entitled to the return of Quentin. If Norma and Oswald refuse to return him Pippa would be advised to make her own application for a residence order whereby the court orders that Quentin reside with her (see ss8 and 10 CA 1989) though the court has the power to make such an order of its own motion when dealing with the adoption application. When determining with whom Quentin should reside his welfare is the paramount consideration outweighing all others (see s1(1) CA 1989). The court will consider particular matters including the child's wishes and feelings (though Quentin is too young to be able to express these), his physical, emotional and educational needs, the likely effect on him of changing his residence from Nora and Oswald, and how capable Pippa is of meeting his needs as well as Nora and Oswald's capabilities in this respect (see s1(3), (4) CA 1989). The courts have assumed that a young child, especially a baby, is best brought up by his mother (see *Re W (a minor) (residence order)* (1992)). The courts have also assumed that a child is best brought up by his natural parents rather than by third parties (see *Re KD (a minor) (ward: termination of access)* (1988)). Quentin is unlikely to be upset at being moved to live with his mother having regard to his age. His mother is able to provide him with all the advantages of a young natural mother whereas Norma and Oswald have the disadvantage of being a lot older, having no genetic ties with Quentin and, in the case of Norma, health problems. Given Quentin's long term interests and the fact that his welfare is paramount it is likely that a residence order would be made in Pippa's favour (unless she is clearly incapable of providing for him).

QUESTION THREE

Maria and Nicholas began cohabiting in 1986 and have two children, Oliver and Pam, who are now four and two. Shortly after Pam was born, Maria and Nicholas separated. The children remained with Maria, but the couple agreed that Nicholas would have extensive contact with them. In May 1993, Maria married Quentin, a man Nicholas dislikes. Since that time, Nicholas has had little contact with Oliver and Pam, although he has sent them cards and presents through the post. The children have little memory of Nicholas and regard Quentin as their father. Maria and Quentin have decided that they would like to adopt Oliver and Pam in order to provide them with a sense of security.

Nicholas, who is opposed to the plans for adoption and would like his contact with the children formalised, seeks your advice. He also tells you that his mother, Ruth, would like to be able to see Oliver and Pam.

Advise Nicholas and Ruth.

University of London LLB Examination
(for External Students) Family Law June 1994 Q6

General Comment

This question deals with the relationship between an unmarried father and his two children from whom he is separated. There is a possibility of adoption by the children's mother and her new husband. How an unmarried father can oppose such an adoption application needs to be outlined. He has not had contact with his children. How he could apply for contact and the considerations the court would take into account under the Children Act 1989 need to be discussed. The children's paternal grandmother also wishes to apply for contact. She will need to obtain leave to make such an application and the provisions relating to obtaining leave need to be described.

Skeleton Solution

- Application for adoption order by Maria and Quentin – the need for parental consent – the position of an unmarried father – dispensing with parental consent (Adoption Act 1976).
- Application by Nicholas for a contact order under s8 of the Children Act 1989 – considerations under s1 and case law in deciding how his application would be determined.
- Application for leave by grandparent to apply for contact – provisions governing leave under s10(9) of the Children Act 1989.

Suggested Solution

Nicholas is opposed to the plans by Maria and Quentin to adopt his two children. If Maria and Quentin are successful in their application to adopt Oliver and Pam then they will acquire sole parental responsibility for the two children to the exclusion of Nicholas and in effect end his status as the children's parent (see s12 Adoption Act (AA) 1976). An adoption order also would extinguish any order made for contact under the Children Act (CA) 1989. In effect Nicholas would be deprived of any right to have contact with his children. It would be most unusual for him to be able to apply for contact after the making of an adoption order (see *Re C (a minor) (adopted child: contact)* (1993)). An adoption order can contain a condition allowing contact but given Maria and Quentin's opposition to Nicholas having contact such a condition would be unlikely to be made (see *Re C (a minor) (adoption: conditions)* (1988)).

How could Nicholas oppose an application by Maria and Quentin for adoption? Nicholas has the status of an unmarried father in relation to his children. This means that he does not have parental responsibility for them and that Maria has sole parental responsibility for them (see s2(2) CA 1989). This means that though he would be informed of the adoption application and be able to make representations about it he would be in a weak legal position to prevent the adoption. Before an adoption order can be made the parents of the children must freely and with full understanding agree unconditionally to the making of the adoption order or have their consent dispensed with (see s16(1) AA 1976). A parent for these purposes is a parent with parental responsibility (see s72 AA 1976). Therefore Nicholas's consent to the adoption would not be required unless he obtained parental responsibility. In order to obtain parental responsibility he would either have to enter into a parental responsibility agreement with Maria (which is unlikely given her views) or apply to the court for a parental responsibility order under s4 CA 1989. If he does apply for a parental responsibility order the welfare of the two children will be treated as paramount (see s1(1) CA 1989). The court will have regard to the degree of commitment he has shown to his children, the degree of attachment between him and his children and the reason(s) he wants parental responsibility for them (see *Re C (minors)* (1992)). In this case Nicholas helped bring up Oliver for two years. After the separation he had extensive contact with both children up until a year ago. Even after contact ceased he displayed commitment to them by sending cards and presents in the post. His application for parental responsibility would be motivated by concern for the children rather than interfering with their lives. Even though the children may have little memory of Nicholas, and even though Maria and Nicholas would be opposed to such an application and prevent any contact, the courts have stated that parental responsibility should be conferred in similar circumstances. This gives the father a status and 'rights in waiting' which may become relevant should there be an adoption application or should something happen to Maria or Quentin (see *Re H (minors) (parental responsibility)* (1993) and *Re A (minors) (parental responsibility)* (1993)).

Assuming Nicholas obtains parental responsibility his consent would then be required for the adoption unless his consent was dispensed with by the court. A court could only dispense with his agreement on certain grounds (see s16(2) AA 1976). There appear to be only two grounds which could be applied in these circumstances – namely, that Nicholas has persistently failed without reasonable cause to discharge his parental responsibility for the children; or that he is withholding his consent unreasonably (see s16(2)(b) and (c) AA 1976). It would be difficult for the first ground to be made out since he appears to have made every effort to discharge his parental responsibilities despite Maria and Quentin's opposition. In relation to whether he could be said to be withholding his consent unreasonably the court would apply an objective test – would a reasonable parent in these circumstances withhold agreement? A reasonable parent would give great weight to what is best for the children. A reasonable parent would not ignore any risk or ill likely to be avoided by adoption or some appreciable benefit likely to accrue from adoption. In deciding whether to dispense with consent the welfare of the children would not be paramount since Nicholas has legitimate rights which would be extinguished by adoption and so has a right to veto it. The children would not be adopted simply because their welfare suggests it (see *Re W (an infant)* (1971)). In these circumstances Nicholas appears to have a strong case in arguing that his consent should not be dispensed with. He appears to have good reasons to maintain his legal status with regard to his children which should not be extinguished by adoption.

Assuming the children are not adopted Nicholas could apply for a contact order to formalise contact arrangements with his children (see s8 CA 1989). He could apply for such an order whether or not he had parental responsibility for them. In deciding whether or not to grant his application the welfare of Oliver and Pam would be paramount (see s1(1) CA 1989). This means their welfare would outweigh the wishes of Nicholas or of Maria and Quentin. The court would assume that any delay in hearing the application would be harmful to the children so would wish to proceed with the application quickly (see s1(2) CA 1989). Assuming that the application was opposed the court would have regard to a number of particular considerations (see ss1(3),(4) CA 1989). It would take into account the ascertainable wishes and feelings of each child considered in the light of their age and understanding. Oliver and Pam are too young for their wishes and feelings to carry great weight with a court. It would consider their physical, emotional and educational needs and the likely effect on them of any change in their circumstances. This could include any harm or benefits of being reintroduced to their father. Their age, sex, background and any other relevant characteristics would be considered as would any harm they have suffered or would be at risk of suffering. The capability of Nicholas and of Maria and Quentin in meeting each child's needs would be considered. For example, if Maria and Quentin are opposed to Nicholas having contact more because of their feelings towards him rather than what they know is best for the children this will stand against them. The court will also consider its full range of powers. The court will not make any order unless the order will bring positive benefits for the children (see s1(5) CA 1989). In considering applications by fathers for contact it has been held that a court should not deprive any child of contact with either parent unless it was wholly satisfied that it was in the interests of the child that there should be no contact. This is a conclusion at which courts are extremely slow to arrive because of the long-term benefits of children keeping in contact with both parents. Save in exceptional cases to deprive a child of contact was to deprive a child of an important contribution to the child's emotional and material growing up in the long term (see *Re H (minors) (access)* (1992)). Unless Maria and Quentin can show that the children will be harmed by contact, or that contact will so destabilise Maria and Quentin's family as to outweigh the benefits of contact, then Nicholas is likely to have a strong case. If contact is ordered it may be in the form of direct contact such as visits to or by the children and/or indirect contact by letters or telephone calls.

Since Ruth is not a parent of Pam and Oliver she cannot apply as of right for contact. She must apply for leave in order to make an application (see s10(9) CA 1989). In considering whether to grant leave the court will consider the nature of her application, her connection with the children and any risk there might be of her proposed application disrupting each child's life to such an extent that the child would be harmed by it. The welfare of the children would not be paramount in considering whether to grant leave (see *Re A and Others (minors) (residence order)* (1992)). Whether leave would be granted will depend on Ruth's previous relationship with her grandchildren and their relationship with her. The court will be concerned to stop Ruth's application if it appears to unwarranted interference in the children's lives. If leave is granted then the court would apply similar considerations as in Nicholas's case, though there would not be the same presumption in favour of contact as there is for a parent seeking contact.

QUESTION FOUR

Paula and Quentin began living together in 1992. In August 1993, Paula discovered that she was pregnant. Both Paula and Quentin were pleased that they were going to have a child and, although they talked of marriage, decided that the child would be sufficient evidence of commitment between them. In May 1994, Paula gave birth to Rebecca. It was a difficult birth and Paula suffered a long and serious period of post-natal depression, during which time she was unable to look after Rebecca. Quentin took leave from his job as a university lecturer to care for Paula and Rebecca and developed a close bond with the child. Paula's depression continued into 1995 and Quentin, deciding that the relationship had no future, left her to live with Silvia, one of his students. At the suggestion of Paula's psychiatrist, Rebecca was placed in the care of the local authority with a view to adoption in 1995. The local authority placed Rebecca with Mr and Mrs Tomkins, professionals in their late twenties, who wished to adopt her.

In May 1995, Mr and Mrs Tomkins, with the support of the local authority applied to adopt

Rebecca. Paula, although still ill, decided that she wanted to have an opportunity to care for her daughter and wishes to oppose the adoption. Quentin, who has now married Silvia, considers that Rebecca should live with him or, if that is not possible, he should be able to maintain close contact with her.

Advise Paula and Quentin.

University of London LLB Examination
(for External Students) Family Law June 1995 Q7

General Comment

The question deals with the rights of a mother to oppose an adoption and the possible grounds for dispensing with her consent. In particular, the authorities concerning whether she is withholding her consent 'unreasonably' need to be discussed. The position of an unmarried father then needs to be outlined in relation to the adoption and in relation to his rights to apply for orders concerning his daughter. The interplay between applications under the Adoption Act 1976 and the Children Act 1989 is a particular feature of this question. The student is asked to demonstrate a sound knowledge of the different principles which apply to each type of application.

Skeleton Solution

- Position of mother in relation to proposed adoption – need for her consent (s16 Adoption Act 1976).
- Status of child with local authority – right of mother to ask for her return (s20 Children Act 1989).
- Dispensing with her consent (s16(2) AA 1976) – the relevant grounds – in particular whether she is withholding her consent unreasonably.
- Position of unmarried father in relation to adoption – his lack of status (s72 AA 1976).
- Right of unmarried father to apply for a residence order and principles to be applied (ss1, 8 and 10 CA 1989).

Suggested Solution

Paula should first be advised that at present she appears to have sole parental responsibility for Rebecca (see s2(2) Children Act 1989 – hereinafter referred to as the CA 1989). She has asked the local authority to look after her daughter. It is not clear on what basis Rebecca is in the care of the local authority. If the local authority have obtained a care order then it shares parental responsibility for Rebecca with Paula but can prevent Rebecca from being returned to her (see s33 CA 1989) If Rebecca is accommodated by the local authority purely on a voluntary basis (eg, because Paula cannot cope) she has the right to require Rebecca to be returned to her at any time (see s20(8) CA 1989). Therefore, she may be able to prevent the adoption by asking that Rebecca be returned to her. However, this may not be appropriate if Paula is still ill. If she asks for Rebecca to be returned to her the local authority is liable to take immediate action to prevent this by applying for an emergency protection order and starting care proceedings so that Rebecca is placed compulsorily in their care (see ss31 and 44 CA 1989). The court would grant an emergency protection order if it was satisfied that there is reasonable cause to believe that Rebecca is likely to suffer significant harm if removed from Mr and Mrs Tomkins (see s44(1)(a) CA 1989). If such an order were granted then it would last for up to eight days but could be extended by a further seven days. Only one day's notice would be required to be given to Paula. At the same time, the local authority is likely to start care proceedings and ask the court to make an interim care order. The court could only make such an order if it was satisfied that there were reasonable grounds to believe that Rebecca is likely to suffer significant harm if removed by Paula, as a result of the lack of reasonable care given to her by Paula (see s38(2) CA 1989). Such an order if granted could last up to eight weeks and could be renewed at up to four weekly intervals until either the care proceedings were heard or the court made an adoption order.

In order to obtain an adoption order Mr and Mrs Tomkins must satisfy the court of certain requirements. At least one of them must be over 21 years of age and they must be married (see ss14 and 14A AA 1976). Rebecca must be at least 12 months old and have had her home with Mr and Mrs Tomkins for at least 12 months preceding the application (see s13(2) AA 1976). Assuming that these criteria have been satisfied the court will apply a two-fold test in deciding whether an adoption order should be made in Mr and Mrs Tomkins' favour. First, the court must give first consideration to the need to safeguard and promote Rebecca's welfare throughout her childhood (see s6 AA 1976). It must have regard to her wishes and feelings regarding the decision in light of her age and understanding. Given her age, this will not be practicable. The court must be satisfied that an adoption order would be in Rebecca's best long-term interests. Second, the court must be satisfied that either Paula consents to the adoption or that her consent can be dispensed with (see s16(1) AA 1976). Since Paula does not agree to the adoption then she will need to be advised as to the grounds on which her consent can be dispensed with.

First the court can dispense with her consent on the basis that she is incapable of giving agreement (see s16(2)(a) AA 1976). Her illness does not suggest that she is incapable of making a rational decision so this ground does not appear to apply. Second the court can dispense with her consent on the ground that she is withholding her agreement unreasonably (see s16(2)(b) AA 1976). If Mr and Mrs Tomkins ask the court to dispense with Paula's agreement on this ground the court will make its decision on the available information and evidence at the date of the hearing. It will apply an objective test, namely, would a reasonable parent, knowing all the circumstances, withhold her agreement? In applying this test Rebecca's welfare is not paramount. Paula has a legitimate right of veto which must be respected even if the adoption might be the best decision in Rebecca's interests. A reasonable parent would take into account the welfare of her child and would place great weight on what is best for that child. Such a parent would not ignore any risk or ill which might be avoided by the adoption or any appreciable benefit which might be provided by the adoption. The court would understand Paula's anguish in refusing to give consent but would ask itself what a reasonable parent in her place would do in all the circumstances (see *Re W (an infant)* (1971)). The court will ask what kind of future Paula can offer Rebecca should the adoption not be granted. This will depend on the extent of her illness and whether she has any relationship with her daughter or can re-establish such a relationship. If the court decides that there are serious doubts that she could cope with her daughter and that her refusal to consent is motivated by feelings of guilt and/or sentimentality then it is likely her consent would be dispensed with, particularly if Rebecca has settled well with Mr and Mrs Tomkins. If the court decides that she is well enough to provide a good home for Rebecca then it may refuse to dispense with her consent (see *Re PA (an infant)* (1971) and *Re H(B) and W(N)* (1983)).

Another ground for dispensing with Paula's consent would be that she has persistently failed without reasonable cause to discharge her parental responsibility for Rebecca (see s16(2)(c)

AA 1976). This ground may be difficult to satisfy since Paula appears to have acted quite responsibly in giving up the care of her daughter given her illness, particularly if she has also made efforts to keep in touch with Rebecca (see *Re D (minors) (adoption by parent)* (1973)). Similarly, she can hardly be said to have abandoned the child (another ground for dispensing with consent) if she took steps to ensure that Rebecca was properly looked after when she could not cope (see s16(2)(d) AA 1976 and *Watson v Nikolaisen* (1955)). Since there is no suggestion that she has ill-treated the child then none of the other grounds for dispensing with her consent will apply.

If the court grants the adoption then Paula's parental responsibility for Rebecca is extinguished and vests entirely with Mr and Mrs Tomkins (see s12 AA 1976). If the court refuses to make an adoption order it may make a residence order instead whereby Rebecca lives with Mr and Mrs Tomkins. Paula would retain her parental responsibility and share it with Mr and Mrs Tomkins, though she could not remove Rebecca in breach of the residence order (see s2(5), (7) and (8) CA 1989). It would also be possible for the court to make a residence order whereby Rebecca lives with Paula. This does not seem a likely option given her illness. However, the criteria for making such an order are outlined in the advice given to Quentin which equally applies should Rebecca apply for a residence order or the court consider making such an order of its own motion.

Quentin did not marry Paula so has the status of an unmarried father in relation to Rebecca. He therefore has no parental responsibility for her unless he takes action to acquire it (see s2(2) CA 1989). Since he does not have parental responsibility his consent is not required for the adoption and indeed he would not even be a party to the adoption application (see s72 AA 1976 – meaning of 'parent'). He wishes to either have Rebecca with him or maintain close contact with her. He may make application to the court for a number of orders to achieve these wishes. First. he may apply to the court for a parental responsibility order giving him parental responsibility for Rebecca (see s4(1)(a) CA 1989). In order to obtain such an order he would have to show that he has demonstrated commitment towards her, has established a close relationship with her and that his application is motivated out of genuine concern for her welfare rather than as a way of getting at either Paula or Mr and Mrs Tomkins (see *Re C (minors)* (1992)). Since Quentin took leave from his work to look after Rebecca and developed a close bond with her he appears to have a good case. It is not clear whether he has kept in close touch with her after he left Paula. If he did this will further strengthen his case. If he does obtain parental responsibility he will then become a party to the adoption, and his consent must be given for the adoption, or his consent dispensed with on one or more of the same grounds already discussed in relation to Paula. It is also possible for him to obtain parental responsibility by signing a written parental responsibility agreement with Paula (see s4(1)(b) CA 1989). This would be an easier way of obtaining parental responsibility, if Paula would agree to such a course.

In addition he may apply to the court for a residence order or a contact order (see ss8 and 10 CA 1989). A residence order would be an order that Rebecca live with him. A contact order would be an order requiring whomever Rebecca was living with to allow Rebecca to visit her father or to otherwise have contact with him. If a residence order was made in his favour the court would be obliged to make a parental responsibility order at the same time (see s12(1) CA 1989). In considering applications for parental responsibility, residence or contact the court would have regard to a number of principles. First, it would treat Rebecca's welfare as the paramount consideration (see s1(1) CA 1989). This means that her welfare would determine the course to be followed, as opposed to what any of the adults thought was fair or just (see *J* v

C (1969)). Second, the court would try to deal with any application as quickly as possible since it must assume that any delay in making a decision is likely to be prejudicial to Rebecca's welfare (see s1(2) CA 1989). The court would lay down a timetable for the application(s) and ensure that the parties stuck to it (see s11 CA 1989). Third, the court would not make any order unless it would be better for Rebecca than making no order at all (see s1(5) CA 1989). Quentin would have to demonstrate that any order he seeks would provide a positive benefit for Rebecca. Fourth, in considering any applications for a residence or contact order which was opposed the court would have regard to certain matters (see s1(3), (4) CA 1989).

The court would first have regard to Rebecca's ascertainable wishes and feelings in light of her age and understanding (see s1(3)(a) CA 1989). Since she is so young these are not likely to be ascertainable. The court would then consider her physical, educational and emotional needs as well as her age, sex and characteristics (see s1(3)(b) and (d) CA 1989). Rebecca will have the needs of a one-year-old baby. She needs security and safety. She requires good housing and sustenance. She needs a good emotional bond with her carers. The court will consider the likely effect on her of any change in her circumstances (see s1(3)(c) CA 1989). If she has been living with Mr and Mrs Tomkins for a year, would she be harmed if she was moved to live with Paula or with Quentin and his wife? If either Quentin or Paula have kept in touch with Rebecca any change may be less upsetting than if they have become strangers to her. The court would consider any harm which Rebecca has suffered or is at risk of suffering, as well as the capabilities of Paula, of Quentin and Silvia and of Mr and Mrs Tomkins in meeting her needs (see s1(3)(e) and (f) CA 1989). Paula's illness will be relevant here insofar as it affects her ability to care for her daughter. The court is likely to favour whomever can provide full-time care for Rebecca, as opposed to the use of babysitters while the adults are at work. Finally, the court would consider its full range of powers (see s1(3)(g) CA 1989).

Much will depend on the court's decision in relation to the adoption. If the adoption is granted Paula and Quentin (if he has acquired parental responsibility) will lose their parental responsibility. They will lose any rights in relation to Rebecca, including the right to see her. While it is possible for an adoption order to contain a condition that Mr and Mrs Tomkins allow either or both parents to see Rebecca, such a condition is unlikely to be imposed unless Mr and Mrs Tomkins agree to it and if the court finds exceptional circumstances to justify it (see *Re C (a minor) (adoption: conditions)* (1988)). If the adoption application fails (eg, because the court refuses to dispense with parental consent) then the court could make a residence order in favour of the Tomkins with or without contact orders in favour of Quentin and Paula. Alternatively, a residence order could be made in Quentin and Sylvia's favour with contact to Paula (and Mr and Mrs Tomkins, if the court considered that appropriate). There is also the possibility of a residence order in Paula's favour with contact orders for Quentin (and Mr and Mrs Tomkins). This will depend on how the court balances the strengths and weaknesses of the competing claims. Both Paula and Quentin should be advised that the court will be assisted in its deliberations by a report prepared by the local authority concerning the adoption and also by a report prepared by a guardian ad litem. The guardian ad litem would be an independent person who, where an adoption is contested, investigates the case from the child's point of view. Such reports carry weight with the court so Paula and Quentin are advised to co-operate in its preparation.

10 Local Authority Powers to Protect Children

10.1 Introduction

10.2 Key points

10.3 Analysis of questions

10.4 Questions

10.1 Introduction

During the last thirty years the State, through local authorities, has increasingly played a role in, providing for children in need and protecting children from abusive parents. Local authority powers and duties are contained in the Children Act (CA) 1989 which seeks to strike a balance between the rights of parents and giving powers to a local authority to intervene to protect a child.

10.2 Key points

a) *Accommodating children*

The student must understand the distinction between the local authority *accommodating* children at the request of their parents (which is a voluntary arrangement) and the local authority taking children into care through *care proceedings* (which allows the local authority to compel the parents to hand over care of the child to the authority).

Every local authority has a general duty to safeguard and promote the welfare of the children in their area who are in need and so far as is consistent with that duty to promote the upbringing of such children by their families (see s17 Children Act 1989).

As required by s20(1) CA 1989, every local authority must provide accommodation for any child in need within their area who appears to them to require accommodation as a result of:

i)   there being no person who has parental responsibility for the child;

ii) the child being lost or having been abandoned; or

iii) the person who has been caring for the child being prevented (whether or not permanently and for whatever reason) from providing the child with suitable accommodation or care.

A local authority may not provide such accommodation if any person who has parental responsibility for the child and is willing and able to provide or arrange accommodation for the child objects (see s20(7) CA 1989). Any person with parental responsibility for a child may at any time remove the child from such accommodation (see s20(8) CA 1989). There is no need for written notice or otherwise. If the local authority wishes to prevent the child's removal it will have to apply for compulsory powers using the emergency protection order and care proceedings.

b) *Significant harm*

Where a child is suffering or is likely to suffer significant harm due to a lack of reasonable parental care a local authority can take action to compulsorily remove the child. The key phrase is 'significant harm'. There is no definition of this important phrase. 'Harm' includes ill-treatment or impairment of health or development. Ill-treatment includes sexual and emotional abuse. Development includes physical, intellectual, emotional, social and behavioural development. Health includes physical or mental health (see s31(9) CA 1989). In deciding whether any harm is 'significant' the court can compare the child's health and development against what would be reasonably expected of a similar child (see s31(10) CA 1989). 'Similar' child' means a child of equivalent intellectual and social development not merely an average child of that age (see *Re O (a minor) (care proceedings: education)* [1992] 1 WLR 912).

One definition of 'significant harm' is that it is any harm which the court should take into account in considering a child's future (see *Humberside County Council* v *B* [1993] 1 FLR 257).

c) *Emergency protection order, police protection and child assessment orders*

If there is an emergency the local authority can apply for an emergency protection order (see s44 CA 1989). Application would be made to the local family proceedings court and could be made ex parte with the permission of the justices' clerk. In order to obtain an emergency protection order the local authority would have to satisfy the court that there is reasonable cause to believe that the child is likely to suffer significant harm if he/she is not removed to local authority accommodation or does not remain where he/she is then being accommodated (see s44(1)(a)). There is a second ground, namely that enquiries made by the local authority are being frustrated by access to the child being unreasonably refused and the local authority has reasonable cause to believe that access to the child is required as a matter of urgency (see s44(1)(b)).

If the emergency protection order is granted it operates as a direction to produce the child to the local authority and authorises the child's removal to local authority accommodation or prevents the child's removal from where he/she is presently accommodated (eg a hospital). It also gives the local authority parental responsibility for the child (see s44(4)).

An emergency protection order can only last for up to eight days. It can be renewed once for a further seven days (see s45 CA 1989). The local authority must decide within that time whether to apply for a care order. The child's parents can apply to discharge the order 72 hours after it was made (see s45(8) and (9)). If the order was made ex parte it must be served on the parents within 48 hours of being made.

An alternative to the emergency protection order is for the police to take the child into police protection. This can be done where a police constable has reasonable cause to believe that the child would be likely to suffer significant harm if he/she did not remove the child to suitable accommodation or prevent the removal of the child from his/her present accommodation. A child may only be kept in police protection for up to 72 hours (see s46 CA 1989).

If the situation is not so serious that it requires an emergency protection order or police protection, the local authority can apply for a child assessment order. It must satisfy the court that it has reasonable cause to suspect that the child is suffering or is likely to suffer significant harm, and an assessment of the child is required to enable the local authority to determine whether or not the child is so suffering or likely to so suffer and it is unlikely that such an assessment will be made (or be satisfactory) without a child assessment order being made (see s43(1) CA 1989). If made the order lasts for seven days and obliges any person named in the order to produce the child for the assessment or otherwise comply with the order. If the court believes the situation to be more serious it can treat the application as one for an emergency protection order.

d) *Applying for a care or supervision order – the threshold criteria*

Under s31(2) CA 1989 the local authority can apply for a care or supervision order if it can satisfy the court that:

i)   the child is suffering significant harm or is likely to suffer significant harm; and

ii) the harm or likelihood of harm is attributable to –

- the care given to the child being not what would be reasonable to expect a parent to given to his or her child (or the care likely to be given to the child falling below that standard); or
- the child being beyond parental control.

This single ground is called the *threshold criteria*.

The phrase *is suffering significant harm* means that where a child has suffered significant harm but arrangements have been made to protect the child (eg via an emergency protection order and interim care orders), and those arrangements have continuously been in place up to the date when the court was deciding whether s31(2) is satisfied, the relevant date is the date when the local authority initiated its child protection procedures. If, after initiating child protection procedures the need for them ended (eg the child was returned to the parents) then the court could not look back to the date when child protection procedures first started but has to be satisfied that the child *is suffering significant harm* on the date it considered whether s31(2) had been satisfied (see *Re M (a minor) (care order: threshold conditions)* [1994] 3 WLR 558).

The phrase *is likely to suffer significant harm* was defined in *Re H and R (child sexual abuse: standard of proof)* [1996] 1 FLR 80. The word *likely* means a real possibility. The standard of proof is on a balance of probabilities. The court has to decide how highly it evaluates the risk of significant harm befalling the child on the basis of facts either admitted or proved on the balance of probabilities. A care order could not be made on the basis of suspicions.

e) *Applying for a care or supervision order – the second stage*

If the threshold criteria is satisfied the court has to consider the no order principle and the welfare checklist in deciding what order (if any) to make (see s1(3), (4) and (5) CA 1989).

In particular the court must consider its full range of powers (eg making a residence order instead of a care or supervision order) (see s1(3)(g) CA 1989 and *Humberside County Council v B* (above)).

f) *Miscellaneous matters*

The court will appoint a guardian ad litem to investigate the case from the child's point of view (see s41 CA 1989). The guardian will appoint a solicitor to act for the child. The court will also lay down a timetable for hearing the application and will direct that each party serves its evidence in the form of written statements on the court and the other parties. Since it is likely to take some time before the final hearing can be arranged the local authority can ask the court to make an interim care or supervision order during the period of an adjournment. The court can only make an interim care or supervision order if it is satisfied that there are reasonable grounds for believing that the circumstances with the respect to the child satisfy the threshold criteria (see s38 CA 1989).

If a care order is made it gives parental responsibility for the child to the local authority. The parents share parental responsibility with the local authority but the parent's parental responsibility is limited by the care order and may be limited by the local authority (see s33(3) and (4) CA 1989). Before making a care order the court must consider what arrangements will be made to allow contact between the child and his/her parents (see s34(11) Children Act 1989). There is a presumption of reasonable contact between the child and his/her parents unless the court orders otherwise (see s34(1) and (2) CA 1989).

A supervision order gives the local authority the duty to advise, assist and befriend the supervised child (see s35(1) CA 1989). The order can only be made for one year though it can be renewed for up to three years.

g) *Role of unmarried father*

An unmarried father has no party status in care proceedings. As a result he may not be able to play any part in those proceedings unless he acquires parental responsibility or is made a party to the proceedings by the court.

h) *Limitations on local authority applying for s8 orders*

A local authority cannot apply for a residence order and a court cannot make a residence order in favour of a local authority (see s9(2) CA 1989). A local authority is also prohibited from applying for a contact order (see s9(2) CA 1989). A local authority cannot apply for a prohibited steps or specific issues order with a view to achieving a result which could be achieved by making a residence or contact order (see s9(5) CA 1989 and *Nottinghamshire County Council v P* [1993] 3 All ER 815).

i) *Family Law Act 1996*

The Family Law Act 1996 provides a solution to a problem identified in *Nottinghamshire County Council v P (No 2)* [1993] 2 FLR 134, whereby a local authority was prevented from applying for a prohibited steps order to exclude an abuser from the family home. An attempt by a local authority to apply for an ouster order under the inherent jurisdiction of the court failed (see *Re S (minors) (inherent jurisdiction: ouster)* [1994] 1 FLR 623. The same restriction applies in private law situations (see *Re M (minors) (disclosure of evidence)* [1994] 1 FLR 760). The court may, when making an emergency protection order or interim care order, make an 'exclusion requirement' requiring a named individual to leave the home in which he or she is living with the child or to prevent him or her from entering the home in which the child lives. The court must be satisfied that: (i) there is reasonable cause to believe that if the person is excluded the child would cease to suffer or cease to be likely to suffer significant harm; and (ii) the caring parent remaining in the home can provide reasonable care and consents to the inclusion of the exclusion requirement. The court can attach a power of arrest or accept undertakings in place of the exclusion requirement.

The court may also be able to make a non-molestation order either on application or of its own motion (see s42(2) and (3) FLA 1996).

j) *Wardship*

The use of wardship is now more restricted. A local authority cannot use wardship as an alternative to care proceedings (see s100 CA 1989). If a local authority wishes to apply to make a child a ward of court it must obtain leave. Leave may only be granted if the High Court is satisfied that the result which the local authority wishes to achieve could not be achieved in other way open to the local authority, and there is reasonable cause to believe that if the child is not made a ward of court the child is likely to suffer significant harm (see s100(4) and (5) CA 1989).

An example of where leave was granted is *Devon County Council* v *S* [1995] 1 All ER 243 where children were made wards of court to protect them from a potential abuser, Y, married to the eldest child. Care proceedings were not appropriate because the mother's care of the children was good, though she did not appreciate the risk posed by Y.

A person cannot use wardship to challenge the decisions of a local authority (see *A* v *Liverpool City Council* [1981] 2 WLR 948).

Otherwise wardship can be used to make important and difficult decisions concerning a child (eg whether or not to provide medical treatment for a profoundly handicapped child as in *Re Baby J* [1990] 3 All ER 930).

10.3 Analysis of questions

Questions on this area have traditionally been problem questions. They often involve more than one area (eg including an adoption or s8 order aspect to the question). The student may be asked to advise a local authority social worker on his or her powers to protect children, or to advise parents on what powers are available to a local authority to remove the children or otherwise interfere in their family life.

10.4 Questions

QUESTION ONE

Sarah, whose husband Tim died in 1990, has two daughters, Ursula and Veronica, who were born in 1982 and 1987 respectively. Sarah's boyfriend, William, who is unemployed, moved in with the family in 1994. Since early 1995, Ursula has been a regular school truant and has been cautioned by the police for shop-lifting on more than one occasion. In September 1995, Veronica complained to her teacher that William had been sexually abusing her. Her teacher alerted Zoe, a social worker at the Grantchester Local Authority, of Veronica's allegation and investigations followed which revealed that William had been convicted ten years previously of a sexual offence involving a young boy. Sarah assured the local authority that William had left the house and that she would not have him back. Criminal charges were brought against him in respect of Veronica, but were later dropped.

Zoe has recently been told that contrary to Sarah's assurances, William regularly visits Sarah and the children and that he and Ursula spend a great deal of time together. Ursula has denied that she is in contact with William, but she has not attended school for the last month and has begun to behave in a disturbed manner. Zoe has recently learned that Sarah is two months pregnant.

Advise Zoe, who is concerned about the welfare of Ursula and Veronica, of the steps she can take to protect them. Are there any steps that she may take to protect Sarah's unborn child?

University of London LLB Examination
(for External Students) Family Law June 1996 Q6

General Comment

The question is timely in light of the recent House of Lords judgment in *Re H and R (child sexual abuse: standard of proof)* (1996) which dealt with a not dissimilar situation to the facts in the question. The student is given the opportunity to apply the decision to these facts and explain how a court is likely to approach an unproved complaint of sexual abuse in asking whether the threshold criteria in s31(2) Children Act 1989 is satisfied. The questions also allows an outline of local authority powers to protect children to be given and the various factors a court is likely to consider in determining any applications made to it. Finally, the status of an unborn child must be explained.

Skeleton Solution

- Definition of phrase 'significant harm'.
- Application for emergency protection orders (s44 CA 1989) or child assessment orders (s43 CA 1989) to meet the immediate situation.
- Application for care orders:
  – the threshold criteria in s31(2) CA 1989;
  – meaning of 'suffering significant harm';
  – meaning of 'is likely to suffer significant harm'.
- No order principle (s1(5) CA 1989) and welfare checklist (s1(3) and (4) CA 1989).
- Exclusion requirement (ss38A and 44A CA 1989).
- Alternatives to care proceedings through prohibited steps order or wardship.
- Status of unborn child.

Suggested Solution

Zoe seeks advice on what steps she can take to protect Ursula and Veronica and whether there are any steps she can take to protect Sarah's unborn child. Her concerns in relation to Ursula, who is now aged 14 years, can be summarised as the regular truancy from school since early 1995, her cautions for theft and the fact that she spends a lot time with her mother's boyfriend, William, who has a previous conviction for a sexual offence on a young boy and against whom her sister has made a complaint of sexual abuse. This has led to further truancy and disturbed behaviour. Zoe's concerns about Veronica are centred on Veronica's complaint of sexual abuse by William. It is noted that criminal proceedings in relation to her complaint were dropped but that William continues to spend time with both children. It is also noted that the children's mother, Sarah, does not appear to be co-operating with Zoe and that Zoe may have to resort to statutory intervention to protect the children.

Zoe can be advised in relation to Ursula and Veronica that she could apply to her local magistrates' court for emergency protection orders to authorise the removal of them from the family home to local authority accommodation. She can ask the clerk to the justices at the court for permission to make the application ex parte (ie without informing Sarah). If permission is not given, she must serve application forms on the court and at least one day's notice must be given to Sarah of the applications. At the hearing Zoe would have to satisfy the court that there is reasonable cause to believe that each child is likely to suffer significant harm if each child is not removed to local authority accommodation: see s44(1)(a) Children Act 1989 – hereinafter referred to as CA 1989. Zoe can be advised that 'harm' means ill-treatment or the impairment of health or development and that 'development' means physical, intellectual, emotional, social or behavioural development. 'Health' means physical or mental health and 'ill-treatment' includes sexual abuse and forms of ill-treatment which are not physical. Where the question of whether harm suffered by a child is significant depends on the child's health or development, her health or development shall be compared with that which could reasonably be expected of a similar child: see s31(9) CA 1989. 'A similar child' means a child of equivalent intellectual and social development: see *Re O (a minor) (care proceedings: education)* (1992). This means that in terms of Ursula's truanting the court may compare her with a girl of equivalent intellectual and development who is attending school as opposed to an average child of her age who may or may not have gone to school. If the court grants the emergency protection orders then they can only last for a maximum of eight days (with an single option to extend them for a further seven days): see s45 CA 1989. On the information given, Zoe appears to have a strong case for the grant of emergency protection orders.

Alternatively, Zoe could apply for child assessment orders with respect to the two girls. Such orders would allow the girls to be assessed (eg to see if they had been sexually abused by William) rather than being removed from the family home. To obtain child assessment orders, Zoe would have to satisfy the court that she had reasonable cause to suspect that each child is suffering or is likely to suffer significant harm, and that an assessment of the state of each child's health or development or the way in which each child is being treated is required to enable Zoe to determine whether or not each child is suffering or is likely to suffer significant harm, and it is unlikely that such an assessment will be made or be satisfactory in the absence of an order: see s43 CA 1989. It is not clear whether Sarah has been asked to co-operate with such an assessment or what her attitude would be if this was suggested. This may have to be explored with her before Zoe could make applications for child assessment orders. The circumstances of the girls suggests that they are in real danger of harm so Zoe may be better advised to apply for emergency protection orders.

The above applications deal with the immediate situation. In the long term Zoe would be advised that she may have to apply to the court for care or supervision orders to be made. Such proceedings would take some time to reach a final hearing so her initial applications would be for interim care or supervision orders. Interim care orders would mean that the local authority maintained parental responsibility for the girls alongside Sarah and maintained control over where the girls lived. Interim supervision orders would only provide for Zoe advising and assisting Sarah and the children. The court could only make such interim orders if it was satisfied that there are reasonable grounds for believing that the circumstances with respect to each child satisfied the 'threshold criteria' in s31(2) CA 1989. The court would be concerned to deal with the applications with the minimum delay since it has to assume that delay in dealing with them is likely to be prejudicial to each child's welfare: see s1(2) CA 1989. It will lay down a timetable for the filing of evidence and for the final hearing which all the parties will be expected to comply with. It will also appoint a guardian ad litem (an independent social worker) to investigate the applications from the children's point of view. The children will also be separately legally represented so that their point of view can be put before the court.

The key to whether care or supervision orders would be made at the final hearing would be whether the threshold criteria in s31(2) CA 1989 were satisfied. The court must be satisfied that each child is suffering or is likely to suffer significant harm and that the harm of likelihood of harm is attributable to a lack of reasonable parental care or each child's being beyond parental control. As to whether the court was satisfied that either child 'is suffering significant harm', if the child concerned had been constantly subject to local authority protective procedures since the start of the applications (eg emergency protection order and interim care orders) then the court would look back at the time when those emergency measures were first applied for. If such protective procedures had not applied for all of the period up to the final hearing (eg the children had remained or been returned home without interim orders being made) the court would look at the situation as it was at the date of the final hearing: see *Re M (a minor) (care order: threshold conditions)* (1994). In interpreting the phrase 'is likely to suffer significant harm' the court would have to find that there was a real possibility of the child suffering significant harm based on admitted facts or on facts proved on the balance of probabilities: see *Re H and R (child sexual abuse: standard of proof)* (1996). This may pose difficulties for Zoe. She can seek to rely on the fact of William's previous conviction to persuade the court that there is a real possibility that he will harm both girls by sexually abusing them. However, that conviction was ten years ago and involved a young boy. She could seek to rely on Veronica's recent complaint even though criminal charges for that were dropped. If she considers that there is good evidence to substantiate her complaint she may seek to prove sexual abuse on a balance of probabilities (bearing in mind that this is a lower standard than the criminal standard of proof beyond reasonable doubt). However, if she fails to establish the fact of abuse the court may not be able to find a likelihood of harm even though it may be more than a little suspicious of William. Having said that, Ursula's persistent truanting for over a year, her offending and now her disturbed behaviour, coupled with her association with a known sexual offender, amount to a strong case that she is suffering significant harm. Veronica's case may be less strong. However, the proof of the harm which her older sister is suffering may be sufficient to persuade the court that Veronica is likely to suffer significant harm even if it finds it is not satisfied of the truth of her complaint against William in September 1995. If the court makes such findings it is also likely to find that Sarah has not provided reasonable care for her daughters, and in particular has failed to protect them from William despite being warned and despite agreeing with Zoe to do so.

If the court does find that the threshold criteria are satisfied it must consider a number of other matters before deciding whether to make care or supervision orders. It must treat the welfare of each girl as the paramount consideration outweighing all other considerations: see s1(1) CA 1989. It must consider that making any orders would be better than making no orders at all (ie that the orders will improve the girls' lives): see s1(5) CA 1989. Given the girls' circumstances it is likely to assume that orders should be made. It must also consider the welfare checklist: see s1(3) and (4) CA 1989. This includes the ascertainable wishes and feelings of each child considered in the light of her age and understanding: see s1(3)(a). Since Ursula is aged 14 her wishes and feelings are likely to carry weight with the court, though not if it is clear that she does not recognise the harm being done to her. Veronica is nine years old so may not be sufficiently mature for her wishes and feelings to carry great weight with the court. The court must also consider each child's physical, emotional and educational needs and must consider their sex, ages, background and other relevant characteristics: see s1(3)(b) and (d). It must also consider the likely effect on each child of any change in her circumstances: see s1(3)(c). If the children are to be removed from their home, and possibly from their mother, the consequences of this must be considered along with the harm they have suffered or are at risk of suffering: see s1(3)(e). The court must consider Sarah's capabilities as a mother (see s1(3)(f)) and its full range of powers: see s1(3)(g). In considering the orders available to it the court will take into account that only a care order gives the local authority the power to control the children's lives should Sarah choose not to co-operate with or try to deceive Zoe. This may persuade the court that a supervision order or any other orders which do not give the local authority such powers do not meet the needs of the case. In addition, the court must consider the recommendations of the guardian ad litem and the care plan provided by the local authority mapping out the children's future.

Zoe can also be advised that she can ask the court to make an exclusion requirement as part of an emergency protection order or interim care order whereby William is excluded from entering the children's home. Such a requirement can only be made if the court finds that there is cause to believe that if William is excluded either child will cease to be likely to suffer significant harm (see ss38A and 44A CA 1989). However, the court would also have to be satisfied that Sarah is able and willing to give the children reasonable care and agrees to William being excluded. Given Sarah's apparent lack of co-operation and lack of reasonable care for the children, the court may feel unable to make an exclusion requirement.

Zoe should be advised that there is an alternative to taking care proceedings but that this approach has not found favour with the courts, so cannot be recommended. This would involve the local authority not applying for care proceedings but applying for a prohibited steps order (under ss8 and 10 CA 1989), which is an order prohibiting William from having contact with the girls. The courts disapprove of such an application being used instead of care proceedings since it does not give the local authority any powers to deal with the situation and prevents it from having the powers and discretion conferred by a care order: see *Nottinghamshire County Council* v *P* (1993). If Zoe does not want to bring care proceedings because she considers this would do more harm than good there is the possibility of her applying to make the children wards of court. This is only likely if Zoe is satisfied that Sarah's care of the girls is otherwise good and the local authority do not wish to invade her parental responsibility and risk destabilising the children's care. The court would only allow the children to be made wards if it accepted that there were valid reasons why care proceedings were not appropriate and if it was satisfied that was reasonable cause to believe that if the court's powers were not exercised the children would suffer significant harm: see s100 CA 1989 and *Devon County Council* v *S* (1995). Since Sarah's care of the children does not appear to fall into this category this does not seem to be a likely option.

In relation to Sarah's unborn child Zoe can be advised that no statutory proceedings can be taken to protect the unborn child since he or she is not treated as having a separate existence to Sarah: see *Re F* (1988). Proceedings could be started as soon as the child was born on the basis of likelihood of significant harm if Zoe was able to satisfy the court that the harm caused to the baby's half sisters was sufficient to show that there was a real possibility that the baby would suffer significant harm.

QUESTION TWO

Rosemary and Simon, who are unmarried, have two children, Tim aged 14 and Ursula aged four. In January 1993 Rosemary, a television presenter, who was then three months pregnant, lost her job. Since that time, the family have found it increasingly difficult to live on Simon's salary and the couple have often argued, sometimes in front of the children. Simon began to drink heavily and has assaulted Rosemary.

In May 1993 Rosemary, who has become increasingly worried about the tension in the household and particularly concerned about the welfare of her unborn child, sought the assistance of the Helpful Local Authority social worker, Miss Vane.

Miss Vane, who visits regularly, has become aware that Tim rarely attends school, although his parents do insist that he does so, and that Ursula is withdrawn and tense. She has noted that Ursula appears particularly upset during the frequent visits of her 16 year old cousin, Wilfred.

Advise Miss Vane of the procedures she can invoke to address the problems of Tim, Ursula and the unborn child.

University of London LLB Examination
(for External Students) Family Law June 1993 Q8

General Comment

The Children Act 1989 provides the framework for social work intervention where children are experiencing problems in families. The difficulties in this family centre around a truanting teenager and possible abuse of a four year old child. In the case of truanting application may be made for an education supervision order or, if the circumstances are sufficiently serious, for a care order. In the case of the younger child more information is needed before decisions can be taken about future action. An application for a child assessment order appears to be the appropriate course. If that reveals 'significant harm' then an emergency protection order application followed by care proceedings may be required. Finally advice has to be given about safeguarding the unborn child eg by an application for an emergency protection order as soon as the child is born.

Skeleton Solution

- Application for education supervision order with respect to truanting child (s36 Children Act 1989).
- Application for care order if circumstances sufficiently grave to show 'significant harm' (s31 CA 1989).
- Application for child assessment order in relation to younger child (s43 CA 1989) and subsequent application for emergency protection order (s44 CA 1989) and care proceedings if 'significant harm' revealed, and use of exclusion requirement (ss38A and 44A CA 1989).
- Protection for unborn child only after child's birth (eg via emergency protection order).

Suggested Solution

Miss Vane asks for advice on the procedures she can invoke to address the problems of Tim, Ursula and the unborn child.

In relation to Tim the problem appears to be one of truanting from school. The clearest procedure to follow in this case would be the making of an application to the local family proceedings court for an education supervision order. The application must be made by the local education authority so Miss Vane should ask them to consider taking proceedings. Application for such an order may be made on the ground that Tim is of compulsory school age and is not being properly educated (ie he is not receiving efficient full time education suitable to his age, ability and aptitude) (see s36 Children Act (CA) 1989). This is assumed to be the case if he is a registered pupil at a school which he is not attending regularly. If an education supervision order is granted then a duty is placed on a supervisor to advise, assist and befriend Tim and give him and his parents directions in order to secure his proper education, after consulting Tim and his parents' wishes (see Sched 3, Part III CA 1989). The supervision may help to resolve the problems caused to Tim by the tension in the household. Such an order would only last one year though it could be extended for up to three years. There is an alternative or additional procedure via the criminal courts which the local education authority can proceed with. They can take Tim's parents before the local magistrates' court for the offence of failing to secure Tim's attendance at school (see s39 Education Act (EA) 1944). If found guilty the parents could be fined and the court could direct that the local education authority apply for an education supervision order (see s40 EA 1944). This procedure is perhaps least helpful if Miss Vane wishes to retain the parents' co-operation.

If, after considering the option of an education supervision order, Miss Vane considers that numerous attempts have already been made by the local education authority to advise, assist and befriend Tim in order to get him to school and that Tim's problems are now too serious to be dealt with in this way, then she can recommend that application be made for Tim to be taken into care. This might be the only option if the parents refuse to recognise Tim's problems and refuse to co-operate with any offers of assistance whether on a voluntary basis or under an education supervision order. A court could only make a care order if it is satisfied that Tim is suffering significant harm or is likely to suffer significant harm and that harm or likelihood of harm is attributable to the care given to him not being what would be expected of a reasonable parent or the child being beyond parental control. Harm is given a wide meaning to include impairment of intellectual, emotional, social and behavioural development (see s31 CA 1989). The court can judge Tim's development against what would be reasonably expected of a similar child of Tim's age and capabilities who had been attending school (see s31(10) CA 1989 and *Re O (a minor) (care proceedings: education)* (1992)). If, as a result of his truanting and the tensions in the family, Tim cannot cope with boundaries and the difficulties of adult life and has a lack of commitment then a care order could be made (see *Re O*). This procedure is a drastic one and Miss Vane should consider what more work could be done with the parents before application is made to take Tim into care.

Miss Vane does not seem to know why Ursula is withdrawn and tense. She has noticed Ursula's reaction when Wilfred visits. This may indicate possible abuse on Wilfred's part, whether physical, emotional or sexual. Miss Vane should seek the parents' co-operation in having Ursula assessed by an expert in order to discover if she is being abused. Rosemary seems willing to co-operate. She can act independently of Simon in allowing Ursula to be assessed (see s2(7) CA 1989). If both parents will not co-operate in such an assessment Miss Vane may then apply to the local family proceedings court for a child assessment order. This is an order requiring Ursula's parents to produce the child for assessment or allow her to be visited at home for assessment so that the local authority can decide if she is suffering from significant harm (see s43 CA 1989). At least seven days' notice of such an application must be given to the parents (see s43(11) CA 1989 and r4 and Sched 1 Family Proceedings Courts (Children Act 1989) Rules 1991). The court must be satisfied that the applicant has reasonable cause to suspect that Ursula is suffering, or is likely to suffer, from significant harm and an assessment is required to enable the applicant to determine whether or not the child is suffering, or is likely to suffer, significant harm and it is unlikely that such an assessment will be made, or be satisfactory, in the absence of the order (see s43(1) CA 1989). In determining the application the court will treat Ursula's welfare as the paramount consideration and can only make an order if it is satisfied that it would be better than making no order at all (see s1(1) and (5) CA 1989). Miss Vane must be able to show that the parents are unreasonably refusing to allow Ursula to be assessed and that such an assessment will improve things for her. A child assessment order will take effect for a maximum of seven days. Once Ursula has been assessed then, if significant harm is revealed, consideration can be given to applying for a care order or supervision order using the grounds already discussed.

If Ursula's situation constitutes an emergency or the parents refuse to comply with the child assessment order the application can be made for an emergency protection order (see s44 CA 1989). Such an application may be made with one day's notice or, with the leave of the justices' clerk of the family proceedings court, ex parte (see r4 1991 Rules). She would have to satisfy a single magistrate or a family proceedings court either that there is reasonable cause to believe that Ursula is likely to suffer significant harm if she is not removed to local authority care or that the local authority reasonably suspects that Ursula is suffering or is likely to suffer significant harm but its enquiries are being frustrated by access to her being unreasonably refused and access to her is required as a matter of urgency. If an emergency protection order is granted it will only last a maximum of eight days during which application can be made for a care or supervision order (which requires at least three days' notice – r4 and Sched 1 1991 Rules).

The court has the additional power to make an exclusion requirement attached to an emergency protection or interim care order whereby Wilfred is excluded from coming to the children's home. Such a requirement could only be made if the court is satisfied that there is reasonable cause to believe that if Wilfred is excluded from coming to the home Ursula is likely to cease from being at significant risk and that her parents are able and willing to give her reasonable care and agree to the exclusion requirement. If the above criteria can be satisfied Ursula could be left in her family home and the possible source of harm, Wilfred, removed.

In relation to the unborn child Miss Vane can be advised that no application can be made with respect to the child until it is born (see *Re F* (1988)). As soon as the child is born an application can be made for an emergency protection order (if the grounds as outlined above apply) and/or for a care or supervision order on the basis of the likelihood of future harm. If Miss Vane is able to work with Rosemary and the threat to the unborn child is the violence of Simon against Rosemary then Miss Vane may be able to persuade Rosemary to seek a non-molestation injunction and exclusion order against him. If the source of the violence is removed this may ameliorate the danger to the unborn child and the tension caused to Ursula and Tim.

QUESTION THREE

Vernon and Wendy married in 1991 when they were both 18 years of age. Twin girls, Xanthe and Yota, were born in January 1993. Because they were born prematurely and were thus very small, the girls needed to stay in hospital for a month after their birth. When the twins came home, Wendy, who suffered from post-natal depression, found it difficult to cope. Accordingly, Wendy's mother, Zoe, who is in her early forties, moved into the house with Wendy and Vernon to help with the children.

Since March 1994, both Xanthe and Yota have suffered illnesses which have led to their overnight hospitalisation three times. On each occasion, Zoe has brought the children to hospital in a state of unconsciousness and on each occasion they have quickly recovered and been released. Medical staff have been unable to determine the cause of these events. Angela, a social worker for Doogood Local Authority, is concerned that the illnesses may be induced in some way by Wendy, who is now pregnant again, and she seeks your advice as to how she can protect the twins and Wendy's unborn child.

Advise Angela.

University of London LLB Examination
(for External Students) Family Law June 1994 Q8

General Comment

The question deals with the provisions available to local authorities under the Children Act 1989 for protecting children. Such provisions include child assessment orders, emergency protection orders and applying for care or supervision orders. The procedure and principles for each kind of application need to be outlined. The spirit behind the Children Act 1989 is one of co-operation with parents and so consideration should be given to this before more formal proceedings are instituted. The status of an unborn child in this context needs to be defined.

Skeleton Solution

- Investigation with the parents.
- If parents fail to cooperate make application for child assessment orders under s43 Children Act 1989 – criteria to be applied.
- If children suffering or at risk of significant harm make application for emergency protection orders under s44 Children Act 1989 – criteria to be applied.
- Application for care or supervision order under s31 Children Act 1989 – the threshold criteria and considerations under s1.

Suggested Solution

Angela is concerned for Xanthe and Yota and for Wendy's unborn baby. Before describing the procedures open to her under the Children Act (CA) 1989 she should remind herself that the Act encourages local authorities to work with parents before resorting to court proceedings. Though the local authority has a general duty to safeguard and promote the welfare of children in their area who are in need, part of that duty is to promote the upbringing of such children in their families so far as this is consistent with the duty to safeguard and promote welfare (see s17(1) CA 1989). Angela should satisfy herself that she has considered and, if appropriate, commenced an investigation with the parents and the medical authorities before instituting court proceedings. It may be that such an investigation involving Vernon and Wendy may answer the concerns she has. Wendy's difficulties may only be temporary and the children could be protected by Zoe and Vernon with the assistance of the local authority. The local authority does have a duty to investigate whenever it has reasonable cause to suspect that the children are suffering or are likely to suffer significant harm (see s47 CA 1989).

If Vernon and Wendy refuse to co-operate with her enquiries Angela may apply to the court for child assessment orders with respect to the two children (see s43 CA 1989). She would have to satisfy the court that she had reasonable cause to suspect that each child is suffering or is likely to suffer significant harm and that an assessment of the state of each child's health and development is required to enable Angela to determine whether or not each child is suffering or is likely to suffer significant harm and that it is unlikely that such assessments will be made or be satisfactory without the making of child assessment orders (see s43(1) CA 1989). 'Harm' means ill-treatment or the impairment of health or development; 'development' means physical, emotional, social or behavioural development; 'health' means physical or mental health; and 'ill-treatment' includes sexual abuse and forms of ill-treatment which are not physical (see s31(9) CA 1989). Where the question of whether harm suffered by a child is significant turns on a child's health or development, that child's health or development shall be compared with that which could reasonably be expected of a similar child (see s31(10) CA 1989). 'Significant harm' means harm which a court considers sufficiently serious to affect decisions about a child's future (see *Humberside County Council* v *B* (1993)). The illnesses which have afflicted the two children have clearly been serious. If the parents refuse to allow the children to be assessed it would appear that s43 would be likely to be satisfied and child assessment orders made. The court would specify when the children are to be assessed and by whom. The orders would require Vernon and Wendy to produce the children to the person named in the orders and to comply with the assessment and such directions as the court specified in the orders. The orders could allow the children to be kept away from home (eg at a hospital), but only in accordance with the terms of the order and only if it is necessary in order to carry out the assessment and only for such period or periods as specified in the order (see s43(9) CA 1989). Vernon and Wendy could visit their children in accordance with the directions as to contact given by the court in the orders.

Angela would make application to the family proceedings court of the magistrates' court using a special application form. Seven days' notice of the application would have to be served on Vernon and Wendy and on Zoe (since she is living in the house with the children) (see s43 and Schedule 2 Family Proceedings Courts (Children Act 1989) Rules (FPC(CA 1989)R) 1991).

If an emergency situation arises or the parents refuse to comply with the child assessment orders Angela may apply to the court for emergency protection orders to remove the children from the parents to the hospital or local authority accommodation or to keep them at hospital against the wishes of the parents (see s44 CA 1989). Indeed, if the magistrates considering applications for child assessment orders consider that the criteria for making emergency protection orders are made out then such orders will be made in any event (see s43(4) CA 1989). Angela would have to satisfy the family proceedings court that there is reasonable cause to believe that each child is likely to suffer significant harm if he or she is not removed to accommodation provided by or on behalf of the local authority or not kept in the place in which he or she is then being accommodated. Alternatively if the court is satisfied that there is reasonable cause to believe that the children are suffering or are likely to suffer significant harm, and the enquiries made by Angela are being frustrated by access to the children being unreasonably refused, the court can make the orders (see s44(1)(a) and (b) CA 1991). Angela can ask the justices' clerk of the family proceedings court to make the applications ex parte if the children were in imminent danger (see r4 FPC(CA 1989)R 1991) otherwise one day's notice would have to be served on Vernon and Wendy and Zoe. If emergency protection orders were granted they would last up to eight days and be capable of being renewed, on Angela's application to the court, for up to seven days (see s45(1) and (5) CA 1989). The parents could apply to discharge the orders once 72 hours had elapsed from when they were made. Within the period of the emergency protection orders the local authority would have to decide whether to initiate care proceedings in order to enable it to keep the children for longer periods against the will of the parents.

Should Angela wish to commence care proceedings she must serve three days notice on both parents and Zoe (see Schedule 2 FPC(CA 1989)R 1991). She would have to satisfy the court that each child was suffering or is likely to suffer significant harm and that the harm or likelihood of harm is attributable to the care given to each child, or likely to be given if orders were not made, not being what it would be reasonable to expect a parent to give to each child (see s31(2) CA 1989). Since the court would require a thorough investigation the case may take some time before it reaches a final hearing. The court will assume that any delay in reaching its decision is likely to be harmful to the children's welfare (see s1(2) CA 1989) so will set down a timetable to make sure that the case is heard as quickly as possible. It may make interim care orders to keep the children in the interim care of the local authority if it is satisfied that there are reasonable grounds for believing that the circumstances are as in s31(2) (see s38 CA 1989). It will appoint a guardian ad litem to separately investigate the case on the children's behalf and the guardian will instruct a solicitor to act for them (see s41 CA 1989). It will give directions on what contact the parents should have with the children if interim care orders are made. Once the case reaches a full hearing the court would have to be satisfied that each child 'is suffering significant harm' or was likely to so suffer. In this context 'is suffering significant harm' could refer to the time when Angela first took action to protect the children provided the children continued to be protected by the local authority right up to the final hearing. However, if the children had been returned to the parents or to Zoe at any time the court could only look at the situation at the time of the full hearing (see *Re M (a minor) (care order: threshold conditions)* (1994)). If the court is satisfied that the threshold criteria in s31(2) is satisfied it will then go on to consider what orders, if any, it will make. It must be satisfied that to make orders would be better for the children than making no orders at all (see s1(5) CA 1989). It must treat the welfare of each child as paramount (see s1(1) CA 1989). It must have regard to a number of particular considerations (see s1(3),(4) CA 1989) which include each child's individual circumstances, any harm which may be caused to them by a change in their circumstances (eg being removed from their parents) and the capabilities of each parent and of Zoe in meeting each child's needs, as well as its full range of powers (which would include making supervision orders).

In relation to Wendy's unborn child no proceedings can be taken until the child is born (see *Re F* (1988)). Once the child is born then Angela can apply for an emergency protection order if she is concerned that Wendy will harm the new born baby and the grounds for making such an order can be satisfied. An emergency protection would safeguard the baby until an application for a care order could be made if that was appropriate.

QUESTION FOUR

'Since the decision of the House of Lords in *Re M (a minor)*, the meaning of the threshold criteria in section 31 of the Children Act 1989 is now clear.'

Discuss.

University of London LLB Examination
(for External Students) Family Law June 1995 Q4

General Comment

The Children Act 1989 introduced major reforms for care proceedings (amongst other areas of family law). In particular, it replaced a series of grounds for the making of a care order in the Children and Young Persons Act 1969 (and in some other statutes) with a single ground – called the threshold criteria (contained in s31(2) Children Act 1989). In the four years since this change there have been relatively few decided cases on the threshold criteria since they appear to be reasonably easy to interpret. However, one part of the threshold criteria did cause problems, namely the phrase 'is suffering significant harm'. Did this mean suffering significant harm at the time of the court hearing or at the time when the child was first subject to action by the local authority? The House of Lords' decision in *Re M (a minor)* sought to resolve that difficulty. The question invites discussion of s31(2), how it has been interpreted and whether following *Re M* the meaning of the threshold criteria is now clear.

Skeleton Solution

• The reforms introduced by the Children Act 1989 in relation to the grounds for care proceedings.
• The threshold criteria in s31(2) Children Act 1989 – the meaning of 'significant harm'.
• The difficulty in interpreting the phrase 'is suffering significant harm'.
• The solution provided in *Re M (a minor)*.

Suggested Solution

In October 1991 the Children Act 1989 came into force and made sweeping changes to family law. One of the Act's most fundamental changes was in relation to the grounds for care proceedings. Before the Children Act 1989 there were a number of varied grounds, one or more of which had to be satisfied before a court could order that a child be taken into the care of the local authority (see s1 Children and Young Persons Act 1969). There were also various other powers to make a care order scattered amongst other statutes. It was accepted that this old law was not clear or coherent. The Children Act 1989 swept all the grounds and powers away and replaced them with a single ground for the making of a care or supervision order. Under s31(2) CA 1989, a court must be satisfied that:

'(a) that the child concerned is suffering, or is likely to suffer, significant harm; and

(b) that the harm, or likelihood of harm, is attributable to –

  (i) the care given to the child, or likely to be given to him if the order were not made, not being what it would be reasonable to expect a parent to give to him; or

  (ii) the child's being beyond parental control.'

This ground is referred to as the 'threshold criteria'. The meaning of parts of s31(2) is provided in the statute. The meaning of 'harm' is given as 'ill-treatment or the impairment of health or development'. 'Development' is defined as 'physical, intellectual, emotional, social and behavioural development'. 'Health' means 'physical or mental health'. 'Ill-treatment' is defined as including 'sexual abuse and forms of ill-treatment which are not physical' (see s31(9) Children Act 1989). The word 'significant' is not defined. However, some assistance is provided for courts in s31(10) Children Act 1989, which provides that where the question of whether harm suffered by a child is significant harm turns on the child's health or development, his health or development must be compared with that which could reasonably be expected of a similar child. One question which did arise was whether 'similar child' meant a child of general ability of a similar age and sex or a child of a similar age and sex and with similar abilities and attributes to the child concerned. This question was answered in *Re O (a minor) (care proceedings: education)* (1992) when it was held that a similar child meant a child of equivalent intellectual and social development who had gone to school (as compared to the child in question who had truanted from school), and not merely an average child who had or had not gone to school. In other respects the phrase 'significant harm' does not appear to have caused undue difficulties for the courts. One comment was that the phrase was like 'an elephant', namely difficult to describe but one knew what it was when one saw it. Another view can be found in *Humberside County Council* v *B* (1993) which defined 'significant harm' as any harm which the court should take into account in considering a child's future.

Judging from these few cases in the six years since the Act came into force the threshold criteria appear to have been reasonably free from interpretation difficulties. However, one aspect of the threshold criteria did cause confusion and it was this aspect which the House of Lords dealt with in *Re M (a minor) (care order: threshold conditions)* (1994). The difficulty was the phrase 'is suffering' significant harm. Did this refer to the time when the child was first taken into local authority protection (whether via an emergency protection order, or through police protection, or through the making of an interim care order), or did it refer to the time of the final hearing of the care proceedings when the court made its decision as to whether the threshold criteria is satisfied? The final hearing is usually many months after the first emergency protection measures have been taken. During that time many assessments may have been carried out and much changed in the child's life. The child may have started out as clearly suffering significant harm, but by the time of the final hearing may have ceased to suffer significant harm. Did this prevent a care order from being made (assuming that the 'likely to suffer significant harm' part of the criteria was not satisfied)?

The dilemma was well illustrated by the facts of *Re M* where the child's mother was savagely murdered by the child's father in front of the him and his half-siblings. This was not only profoundly emotionally harmful to the child, M, but deprived him of both his parents (since his father was taken into custody and eventually sentenced to life imprisonment). He was placed with foster parents. When M was taken into local authority care he was clearly suffering significant harm. Care proceedings were started. The deceased mother had a cousin, W. She took M's half-siblings into her household to live with her but she thought that she could not cope with M (who was the youngest child). He remained in local authority care. She then changed her mind and asked that M be allowed to live with her. At the final hearing of the application for a care order it was difficult to argue that M was at that time suffering significant harm because of the progress he had made, and the fact that a home was being offered to him. The court decided that it could look back to the situation when he was first taken into care and that the phrase 'is suffering significant harm' referred to that date. A care order was made. On appeal the Court of Appeal discharged the care order, holding that the phrase could only refer to the time when the final hearing was held. The other part of the threshold criteria 'is likely to suffer significant harm' could not apply since M's father was in prison and W was offering him a home with his half-siblings. In those circumstances it could not be said that the threshold criteria was satisfied. A residence order was made in W's favour.

M's father appealed to the House of Lords. By the time of the hearing before their Lordships, M had gone to live with W, had settled with her and was making good progress. Their Lordships ruled that the phrase 'is suffering significant harm' could refer to one of two moments in time. It could refer to the time when the local authority first took emergency action to protect the child (whether by an emergency protection order or by an interim care order) and started the proceedings which became the care proceedings. This could only apply if the child remained in the care of the local authority under the terms of interim care orders throughout the care proceedings and up to the final hearing date. Provided there was this continuous protective regime, the clock was frozen so that 'is suffering' could refer to that time when the protection was first initiated. To decide otherwise would be to deprive a local authority of the ability to obtain a care order. However, if at any time during the proceedings the child ceased to be subject to protective orders because his welfare was otherwise satisfactorily safeguarded (eg, he was returned to the parents or another person) the clock became 'unfrozen' and 'is suffering' could only refer to the time when the court made its decision at the final hearing. In M's case the threshold criteria had been satisfied and the care order was restored. However, it was understood by all concerned that he was not to be removed from his aunt's household given the progress he was making there.

Following the decision in *Re M* it can be said that the meaning of the threshold criteria is now clear. The House of Lords produced a workable interpretation of the phrase 'is suffering significant harm' which can be readily applied. In any event the second limb of 'likelihood of harm' is often open for the court to consider in care proceedings, circumventing any problems in the phrase 'is suffering significant harm'. Given the apparent lack of problems of interpretation of the other parts of s31(2), courts now have a foundation to apply the law to the distressing facts which so often apply to the children cases brought before them by local authorities (or the NSPCC) in care proceedings.

11 Property Disputes between Unmarried Couples (or Married Couples Who Are Not Divorcing)

11.1   Introduction

11.2   Key points

11.3   Recent cases

11.4   Analysis of questions

11.5   Questions

11.1 Introduction

The incidence of cohabitation outside marriage is increasing, as is the number of children born to cohabiting couples. Traditionally the English and Welsh legal system only acknowledged rights as existing within marriage. This has led to problems for unmarried couples. In particular, an unmarried 'wife' may be left in a much worse position on the breakdown of the relationship than would be the case if the parties were married. The classic example of this is *Burns* v *Burns* [1984] Ch 317 in which a woman who had given over 20 years of her life to her partner and the three children of the relationship received nothing on the breakdown of the relationship. Had she been married it is probable that she would have been granted a sufficiently large lump sum to enable her to purchase suitable alternative accommodation for herself. The student must be aware of what remedies are available to an unmarried couple in resolving property disputes.

A spouse may also have a need to resolve property disputes outside the scope of divorce or other statutory provisions. For example, if one spouse is made bankrupt the other spouse may need to establish his/her property rights against the trustee of bankruptcy. Such a spouse may need to use the same remedies as the unmarried partner.

11.2 Key points

a) *Establishing property rights*

Courts have a wide discretion to make orders concerning the matrimonial home in divorce proceedings pursuant to the Matrimonial Causes Act (MCA) 1973. The courts can make orders which are just and reasonable in light of the particular considerations in ss25, 25A–25D of the 1973 Act. Where the 1973 Act does not apply (eg where a couple are not married) the main remedy is to ask the courts to declare property rights in accordance with strict property law principles. Where a couple is married but does not wish to make use of the Matrimonial Causes Act 1973 either spouse can apply for an order under s17 Married Women's Property Act (MWPA) 1882, whereupon the court can consider any question as to the title or possession of property and make such order with respect to the property in dispute as it thinks fit.

An application for a declaration or for an order under s17 MWPA 1882 only allows the court to declare what property rights exist under property law – the court is not allowed to give title which does not already exist. It is not allowed to make orders as it considers just and reasonable but must declare property rights as it finds them (see *Pettitt* v *Pettitt* [1969] 2 WLR 966 and *Gissing* v *Gissing* [1970] 3 WLR 255).

b) *The conveyance*

All conveyances of land or any interest in land must be by way of deed (see s52 Law of Property Act (LPA) 1925). A declaration in a conveyance as to the beneficial interests of the parties is conclusive evidence of ownership unless the conveyance can be set aside on the grounds of fraud or mistake (see *Goodman* v *Gallant* [1986] 1 All ER 311 and *Turton* v *Turton* [1987] 2 All ER 641).

An unsigned deed or conveyance may be used to decide interests (see *Re Gorman* [1990] 2 FLR 284, but contrast *Huntingford* v *Hobbs* [1993] 1 FLR 736).

c) *By written document*

An equitable interest may be evidenced by a document in writing (see s53(1)(b) Law of Property Act 1925). From 27 September 1989 such an interest can only be created by a written contract incorporating all the terms which the parties have expressly agreed to and which must be signed by or on behalf of each party (see ss2(1) and 3 Law of Property (Miscellaneous Provisions) Act (LP(MP)A) 1989).

d) *By resulting, implied or constructive trust*

In everyday life spouses or unmarried couples often fail to comply with the strict requirements of s52 LPA 1925 or s53(1)(b) LPA 1925 or ss2(1) and 3 LP(MP)A 1989). As a result s53(2) LPA 1925 and s2(5) LP(MP)A 1989 allow a person who cannot establish his or her interest in the home by the conveyance or by a written and signed contract to nevertheless ask the court to declare his or her interest under a resulting, implied or constructive trust. The court will not therefore allow one party with the legal interest to stand on his or her strict legal rights when it is clear that the other party has a beneficial interest.

A resulting or constructive trusts requires:

i)   Clear evidence of a common intention between the parties that at the time of the purchase of the property (or exceptionally some time after the purchase) though one party has the legal title to the property *both* parties clearly intended that the other party has a beneficial interest in the property; and

ii) the other party has acted to his or her detriment based on that common intention.

In practice there now appear to be only two ways to satisfy these requirements:

i)   the other party making direct financial contributions towards the purchase of the property (where there is an obvious inference that there must have been a common intention between the parties that the contributing party should acquire a beneficial interest) – this gives rise to a presumption of *resulting trust*; or

ii) clear evidence of conversations between the parties showing that they formed a common intention that the party without legal title has a beneficial interest and that party acting to his or her detriment based on that common intention – this gives rise to a *constructive trust*.

See *Lloyds Bank* v *Rosset* [1990] 2 WLR 867.

The courts are likely to refuse to infer any common intention based on how the parties behaved towards each other if there is no evidence of direct financial contributions or no evidence of direct conversations establishing a common intention. An uncommunicated belief by one party that there is a common intention is insufficient (see *Springette* v *Defoe* [1992] 2 FLR 437).

If a common intention is established by constructive trust the courts appear to give themselves a broad discretion to determine the shares under that trust on the basis of inferences as to the parties' common understanding about the ownership. The court may not limit itself to the direct contributions made (see *Midland Bank* v *Cooke* [1995] 4 All ER 562 and *Drake* v *Whipp* [1996] 1 FLR 826). However, this broad approach to quantifying shares under a resulting or constructive approach may not be in keeping with earlier authorities and with the spirit of *Lloyds Bank* v *Rosset*, so it remains to be seen whether this approach will continue.

e) *Contractual licence*

A lesser form of protection of property rights is the contractual licence. Where no resulting or constructive trust exists a partner may have a right of occupation protected by contractual licence, namely a contract giving him or her a licence to remain in occupation which, if breached, gives rise to a claim for damages. In order for a contractual licence to exist there must be an intention to create a legally binding contract and the claimant must show he or she has provided consideration for the contract (see *Tanner* v *Tanner* [1975] 1 WLR 1346 and *Hardwick* v *Johnson* [1978] 1 WLR 683).

f) *Proprietary estoppel*

Where one person has acted to his or her detriment in reliance on a belief, which was known of and encouraged by another person, that he or she has or is going to be given a right in or over the other person's property, the other person cannot insist on his or her strict legal rights if to do so would be inconsistent with the person's belief. The other person would be 'estopped' from relying on his or her strict legal rights (see *Re Basham* [1986] 1 WLR 1498).

This is similar to a constructive trust but there is no need to establish a common intention, only that the claimant has been misled in the manner described above. Examples of proprietary estoppel can be found in *Maharaj* v *Chand* [1986] 3 All ER 107, *Matharu* v *Matharu* [1994] 2 FLR 597, *Wayling* v *Jones* [1995] 2 FLR 1030 and *Gillett* v *Holt* [1998] 3 All ER 917.

g) *Equitable accounting*

After one party has left the other party may remain in the home. The party in the home may continue to pay the mortgage and make improvements to the property and may ask the court to take these payments into account. The other party may argue that the party in occupation has enjoyed the occupation of the property while he or she has had to find alternative accommodation and that this should be taken into account. The court can adjust the shares of the parties to take these factors into account. This is called *equitable accounting*.

Credit can be given for the capital element of mortgage payments paid by the party in occupation. The court will credit one-half of those repayments to the party in occupation who paid them (see *Cracknell* v *Cracknell* [1971] 3 WLR 490 and *Leake* v *Bruzzi* [1974] 1 WLR 1528). Mortgage payments relating to interest may not be credited, though they can be counted towards occupation rent (see below) (see *Suttill* v *Graham* [1977] 1 WLR 819).

If one party leaves voluntarily then the occupying party is not expected to pay occupation rent to the other party to reflect the benefit of occupation. However, if one party is forced to leave then the occupying party can be liable to pay occupation rent to the party who was forced to leave (see *Dennis* v *MacDonald* [1982] 2 WLR 275 and *Re Pavlou (a bankrupt)* [1993] 3 All ER 955). Interest only mortgage payments can be taken into account in deciding on occupation rent.

Improvements by the occupying party after the other party has left will also be taken into account (see *Re Pavlou* (above)).

h) *Improvements to the property*

There is a special provision for married people whereby a contribution in money or money's worth by a spouse to the improvement of real or personal property shall, if the contribution is of a substantial nature and subject to any contrary intention, be taken to increase the beneficial interest of that spouse in such amount as agreed between the spouses or, in the absence of such agreement, as may seem just in all the circumstances to the court (see s37 Matrimonial Proceedings and Property Act 1970).

Any improvement must be of a substantial nature (see *Re Nicholson (deceased)* [1974] 1 WLR 476). Minor improvements of a DIY nature are unlikely to suffice (see *Pettitt* v *Pettitt* (above) and *Gissing* v *Gissing* (above)).

i) *Allowances for housekeeping and maintenance*

In the absence of any agreement any allowance made by the husband for the expenses of a matrimonial home, or for similar purposes or any property acquired out of such money, shall be treated as belonging to them in equal shares (see s1 Married Women's Property Act 1964).

j) *Bank accounts*

Ownership of money in a joint bank account and property bought therewith depends on the intention of the parties and, in particular, where there is an established common purse. If a bank account is regarded as for their joint use then, regardless of who puts money into it, the parties are entitled to it equally and to any investments bought using money from the account equally (see *Jones* v *Maynard* [1951] 1 All ER 802). However, in *Re Bishop (deceased)* [1965] 2 WLR 188 a contrary view was taken in relation to property bought using money from the joint account. The spouse who bought the chattel or investment in his or her own name owns that chattel or investment.

k) *Engaged couples*

Engaged couples may use s17 MWPA 1882 to resolve property disputes (see s1 Law Reform (Miscellaneous Provisions) Act 1970 and *Shaw* v *Fitzgerald* [1992] 1 FLR 357).

l) *Protection of overriding interests against third parties*

A person with an overriding interest who is in 'actual occupation' of the property can protect his/her interest against a claim for possession by a third party (eg a bank) because the interest is an overriding interest under s70(1)(g) Land Registration Act 1925 (see *William & Glyn's Bank Limited* v *Boland* [1980] 2 All ER 408). This applies to registered land, but the situation appears to be the same for unregistered land (see *Kingsnorth Finance Co Ltd* v *Tizard* [1986] 1 WLR 783).

For there to be an overriding interest the person has to show that he/she has a beneficial interest in the property and that he/she was in actual occupation of the property before the charge to the third party took effect and that he/she was unaware of the charge (eg had been deceived by his/her spouse or partner). If the claimant was aware of the charge before it took effect then it is not an overriding interest (see *Bristol & West Building Society* v *Henning* [1985] 2 All ER 606). It also does not apply if the house has been conveyed into two names and the claimant is a third person. See *City of London Building Society* v *Flegg* [1987] 3 All ER 435 where the house was in the names of a husband and wife. The wife's parents had a beneficial interest. The spouses mortgaged the house to a bank without the knowledge of the parents. The parents could not claim an overriding interest because there were two trustees, namely the spouses.

In other cases a spouse or partner can have a charge set aside because the document on which it was based was signed by him/her under duress, undue influence or misrepresentation. This is because it is recognised that a spouse or partner is likely to have an emotional involvement with the debtor (normally the husband) which makes her vulnerable. Any lending situation is expected to take reasonable steps to satisfy itself that the spouse/partner entered into the obligation freely and in knowledge of the true facts. The lending institution should warn the spouse/partner in the absence of the principal debtor of the consequences of the liability and advise her to take independent legal advice. If the bank fails to take such steps it will be fixed with constructive notice of the duress, undue influence or misrepresentation (see *Barclays Bank* v *O'Brien* [1993] 3 WLR 786 and *CIBC Mortgages* v *Pitt* [1993] 3 WLR 802).

11.3 Recent cases

Bank of Baroda v *Dhillon* [1998] 1 FLR 524

Gillett v *Holt* [1998] 3 All ER 917

Judd v *Brown* [1998] 2 FLR 360

Royal Bank of Scotland v *Etridge (No 2)* [1998] 2 FLR 843

11.4 Analysis of questions

Questions on property rights for unmarried couples are fairly frequent. Sometimes the question is framed from the point of view of a married couple who do not wish to divorce. Questions tend to be of the problem format. This area of the law is uncertain and is not always subject to consistent decisions from the courts. Students will need to be aware of the up-to-date leading cases.

11.5 Questions

QUESTION ONE

When Ivan and Jane became engaged in 1980 they exchanged rings. Ivan presented Jane with a ring worn by his late grandmother during her fifty year marriage: Jane gave Ivan a gold signet ring that she had bought for him. Ivan purchased a small bungalow in his name. He paid the deposit, and the mortgage instalments were paid from his earnings as a merchant banker. Jane rewired the house and repaired the roof.

They married in June 1983 shortly after Jane had become pregnant. She gave up her career and was paid an allowance by Ivan which was used to pay for food, clothes and to pay off the fuel bills. Jane was able to save enough from the allowance to buy a second-hand car and a number of expensive dresses and coats. She gave birth to Karen in February 1984.

In January 1988 Jane confessed to Ivan that he was not Karen's father and that the plumber, Len, was the true father. Ivan immediately left her.

Jane does not want a divorce and hopes that she and Ivan may eventually become reconciled.

Advise Jane who wishes to know:

a) who is entitled to the rings they exchanged at the time of their engagement;

b) whether she has a property interest in the bungalow purchased by Ivan;

c) whether the car, dresses and coats bought from savings made from her allowance belong to her.

> Adapted from University of London LLB Examination
> (for External Students) Family Law June 1988 Q4

General Comment

This is a fairly typical though wide ranging question in property and maintenance rights in a non-divorce situation. The question is relatively straightforward, but it is long and candidates will have to pay close attention to time to ensure that all parts of the question are answered adequately. Not all parts of the question will necessarily carry equal marks. On the whole this is not a difficult question for the well prepared candidate. Note that the issues raised in (b) are the same as those relevant in a property dispute between cohabitees. Section 20(1) Law Reform (Miscellaneous Provisions) Act 1970 is a relevant consideration in the case of cohabiting couples of course if the dispute arises before marriage – see *Bernard* v *Josephs* (1982).

Skeleton Solution

a) • Discuss application of Law Reform (Miscellaneous Provisions) Act 1970 to the dispute over the rings, and explain the principle to be applied distinguishing between engagement rings and other gifts which may still be of some assistance in determining the intentions of the parties.

   • Consider whether the grandmother's ring is an heirloom, as evidence of whether it was a conditional gift. With regard to the signet ring consider whether it is an absolute or conditional gift. Consider also whether it is an engagement ring.

   • Refer to an application under s17 MWPA 1882 to resolve the dispute.

b) • Explain the use of a s17 MWPA application to resolve the dispute over the bungalow.

- Explain the general principles of equity and property law to be applied to establish the existence of a trust – direct/indirect contributions to the purchase price should be considered but may not apply on the facts.
- Consider MPPA 1970 which applies also to improvements made during an engagement (s20(1) Law Reform (Miscellaneous Provisions) Act 1970), in detail, with particular reference to the distinction to be made between works of maintenance and works of improvement.

c) • Consider s1 MWPA 1964 – savings made from a housekeeping allowance and items purchased therefrom – with regard to the clothes, consider whether an agreement can be implied that they belong to the wife absolutely in view of the personal nature of those items.

- Consider also the presumption of advancement in relation to the clothes in view of the intended use of the allowance monies.

Suggested Solution

a) As Jane does not wish to divorce Ivan and therefore will not be in a position to invoke the Matrimonial Causes Act 1973 to resolve her property interests, the ownership of the items in dispute will be determined in accordance with the general principles of property law. In the particular case of the rings exchanged at the time of the engagement, however, reference must also be made to the provision of the Law Reform (Miscellaneous Provisions) Act 1970 which deals specifically with engagement rings.

Jane will be able to make an application under s17 Married Women's Property Act 1882 (hereinafter s17 MWPA 1882) for a declaration as to the ownership of all the property in dispute, including the rings. Section 17 provides that in any question between a husband and wife as to the title to or possession of property, either party may apply to any judge and the judge may make such order with respect to the property as he thinks fit. In deciding the question of the ownership of the rings the principles of the Law Reform (Miscellaneous Provisions) Act 1970 will be of some assistance to the court although its provisions were intended to be applied in cases of engagements which had been terminated, that is to resolve property disputes between formerly engaged couples. Here, Ivan and Jane did marry and so normally the ordinary principles of property law would be applied in any application under s17 MWPA 1882 to resolve their disputes. In the case of the rings however references to the 1970 Act will be of assistance to determine the intentions of the parties.

The 1970 Act makes a distinction between engagement rings and other gifts made between engaged couples. In the case of an engagement ring there is a rebuttable presumption that is was an absolute gift and therefore that it may be retained by the donee. The presumption can be rebutted by evidence that the ring was given subject to a condition, express or implied, that the ring should be returned if the marriage did not take place: s3(2) Law Reform (Miscellaneous Provision) Act 1970.

There is no doubt that the ring, given by Ivan to Jane would fall under the classification of an engagement ring. However it is questionable whether the ring given by Jane to Ivan will fall into the same category. If it does not, then, as with other gifts, the general law must be referred to in order to decide if the gift is conditional or absolute.

With regard to the ring given by Ivan to Jane we can assume that it was an absolute gift even though it did belong to his grandmother, and may therefore have taken on something of the character of an heirloom. The presumption that it was an absolute gift should apply here because even if Ivan was interested in retaining it in his family, the condition referred to in s3(2) of the 1970 Act which may rebut the presumption of an absolute gift, has been complied with, that is Ivan and Jane did marry. So we would have to look for further evidence of an intention that the ring was given to her as Ivan's spouse only if the return of the ring to Ivan is to be considered.

This same principle will apply to the ring given by Jane to Ivan. Normally, property intended to become part of the matrimonial home or assets will be deemed to be conditional. The test is, was the gift made to the donee as an individual or solely as the donor's spouse. If the gift is given to the donee as the donor's spouse then the gift is conditional; if however it is given to the donee as an individual, it will be deemed to be absolute and will be recoverable only in the circumstances any other gift would be recoverable, that is, for example where fraud or undue influence can be shown.

In the case of these two rings, particularly because any condition (as to the marriage taking place) that could be implied has been fulfilled, it is suggested that they will be deemed to be absolute gifts. There is no evidence of any intentions of the parties that they should be returned to the donors in the event of a marital breakdown. This is clearly the case in respect of the signet ring by Jane to Ivan, and perhaps also applies in respect of Ivan's grandmother's ring. However if Ivan can show an intention that that ring be retained in his family, to be worn only by female members of it, then he may be able to recover it in any s17 MWPA 1882 proceedings.

b) The s17 MWPA 1882 application referred to in part (a) above will also include Jane's claim to an interest in the bungalow purchased by Ivan.

We are told that Ivan purchased the bungalow following his engagement to Jane and that he paid the deposit and the mortgage instalments. We can assume that the legal estate is vested in his sole name. Prima facie therefore he owns the legal estate absolutely and Jane has no interest in it. However, a proprietary interest may also exist in equity and the court may look behind the title deeds and may establish the existence of a trust in which case Ivan would be deemed to hold the property on trust for himself and Jane in the shares declared by the court. Under s17 MWPA 1882 the court cannot create an interest for Jane merely because it thinks it just to do so in view of her contribution to the marriage (*Burns* v *Burns* (1984)), it may only declare existing interests: *Pettitt* v *Pettitt* (1970).

The legal estate can be displaced where there is evidence of a contrary intention on the part of the spouses. If there is evidence of an intention of the parties at the date of the acquisition of the property, the court will give effect to it by imposing a trust in relation to the proceeds of sale in the shares agreed upon. Following *Lloyds Bank* v *Rosset* (1990) it appears that only express conversations between the parties about the ownership of the property or direct financial contributions to its purchase can give rise to an interest under a resulting or constructive trust.

In this case seemingly only Ivan has contributed directly to the acquisition of the property in that he paid the deposit, and the mortgage instalments were paid from his earnings. Until her marriage and pregnancy, Jane worked although no information is given as to how she expended her income after the purchase of the bungalow. Further it is not clear from the facts whether, after their engagement they cohabited at all prior to the marriage and Jane giving up her career. If they did cohabit and Jane used her income to pay household expenses she might be able to claim an indirect contribution to the acquisition costs if she could show that her contribution freed Ivan's own earnings and enabled him to pay the mortgage instalments (*Gordon* v *Douce* (1983)). However such a contribution must be substantial (*Gissing* v *Gissing* (1971)).

On these facts therefore it is uncertain whether Jane can claim any interest in the property by virtue of any indirect contribution to the mortgage instalments. However she may acquire, or increase an interest in the property by virtue of her work on the property in rewiring the house and repairing the roof. Section 37 Matrimonial Proceedings and Property Act 1970 (hereinafter MPPA 1970) provides that where a husband or wife contributes in money or monies worth to the improvement of real or personal property in which, or in the proceeds of sale which either or both of them has a beneficial interest, the husband or wife so contributing shall, if the contribution is of substantial nature, and subject to any agreement between them to the contrary, be treated as having acquired by virtue of his or her contribution, a share or an enlarged share, as the case may be, in that beneficial interest of such an extent as may then have been agreed, or in the absence of such agreement, as may seem just in all the circumstances of the case.

The contribution must be in money or monies worth. It is not clear whether Jane paid for the work to be done, or did it herself. However either form of contribution will suffice. The contribution must be of a substantial nature (*Re Nicholson* (1974)) and it must effect an improvement to the property as distinguished from merely maintaining it (*Pettitt* v *Pettitt* (1970)).

It is probable that the costs of rewiring the property and the roof repairs would be substantial. However it is not clear whether these works would be viewed as improvements rather than as maintenance. In *Re Nicholson* it was suggested that a 'replacement' may not consititute an improvement although Professor Cretney suggests that this must be a question of degree. However he also states in his book *Principles of Family Law* that it is unlikely that work such as rewiring the house or carrying out extensive roof repairs would be considered as anything other than maintenance work even though the value of the work may be substantial. Certainly such a view would seem to apply in this case with regard to the roof repairs which can be seen as maintenance work only. However it is submitted that the rewiring of the house should be viewed as an improvement although it is not certain that it will be so viewed.

It may be the case therefore that unless Jane can show that she made an indirect contribution to the mortgage repayments she will have no interest in the bungalow at all because it is perhaps doubtful whether the work she carried out on the property, or paid to be carried out, will be viewed as improvements.

It should be noted that although the possible contributions discussed above were made before the marriage, the same principles will be applied in assessing interests in property of cohabitees (*Bernard* v *Josephs* (1982)) although the nature of the relationship between the parties will be an important factor when deciding what inferences can be drawn from their conduct. Further, s20(1) Law Reform (Miscellaneous Provisions) Act 1970 provides that s37 MPPA 1970 shall apply to contributions made by a party to an engagement in the same way as it applies to spouses.

c)   At common law if a husband provided an allowance out of his income to his wife to pay housekeeping expenses, any sums not spent for that purpose, prima facie remained his and he would be entitled to any property purchased with any such savings (*Blackwell* v *Blackwell* (1943)). This principle was altered by s1 Married Women's Property Act 1964

167

(hereinafter MWPA 1964) which provides that where 'any question arises as to the right of a husband or wife to money derived from any allowance made by the husband for the expenses of the matrimonial home or for similar purposes, or any property acquired out of such money, the money or property shall, in the absence of any agreement between them to the contrary, be treated as belonging to the husband and wife in equal shares'.

Expenses of the matrimonial home will involve money spent in running the home and so the fact that Ivan paid the allowance to Jane to purchase food and pay the fuel bills will mean that it falls within the category of matrimonial home expenses even if it may be debatable whether the purchase of clothes would do so.

It seems therefore that any savings made by Jane out of the housekeeping allowance, or property purchased out of them will on an application of s1 MWPA 1964, belong to Jane and Ivan equally unless there is evidence of any agreement to the contrary between them. On the facts there is no evidence of any express agreement to the contrary unless it could be argued, in respect of the clothes that as Ivan paid the allowance specifically to include the purchase of clothes the presumption of advancement in respect of the clothes would apply and so they would be deemed to be a gift from Ivan to Jane and she would be entitled to them absolutely. If this is not the case it would seem that the car and the clothes belong to the parties equally. It is not clear whether the courts would be prepared to infer an implied agreement between the parties to the contrary where the circumstances would seem to demand it as for example in this case with regard to the dresses and coats which Jane bought. One can see the logic of deciding that Ivan should have an equal interest in the second hand car, but the clothes are such personal items which presumably Ivan would not be particularly interested in in any event, unless they are particularly valuable. It is suggested in Bromley's *Family Law* that in such circumstances it might be argued that there would be a tacit agreement that the whole should belong to the wife. If however the items of clothing are valuable, for example they include fur coats, then it would be difficult to argue such a tacit agreement and Ivan would be deemed to have a half interest in the clothes and Jane would have to account to him for half their value, or depending on the relative values of the car and clothes, agree to a distribution of these items on the lines that Ivan takes the car and she keeps the clothes.

QUESTION TWO

Imogen and Bruce were married in 1984. They have one child, Deborah, who was born in 1986 and Imogen is expecting a baby in August 1991. The matrimonial home, 'Misrule', which was purchased by Imogen out of funds provided by her parents, is registered in her name alone. Bruce, who is a builder, has been unemployed since December 1987, and since that time he has taken care of Deborah and carried out various improvements to the house which include the installation of central heating and an ornamental gas fire. In return, Imogen, who works as a doctor, has paid him a weekly allowance, some of which he has invested in a deposit account.

Unknown to Bruce, in 1988 Imogen borrowed £25,000 from the bank using the house as security, but she has been unable to keep up the repayments. The bank would like 'Misrule' to be sold so that it can recover the money. Further, Imogen and Bruce have been unhappy since January 1991, often arguing in front of Deborah. Imogen, who is concerned about Deborah and the effect the situation is having on the unborn child, has asked Bruce to leave 'Misrule'.

University of London LLB Examination
(for External Students) Family Law June 1991 Q4

General Comment

Note that the establishment of a beneficial interest in property by cohabitees is very similar in principle to a spouse establishing an interest under the Married Women's Property Act.

This question requires a long and detailed answer on ownership of the matrimonial home, applying the principles under s17 Married Women's Property Act 1882, and on protecting rights of occupation against the bank and the other spouse. The question raises issues which have been tested regularly in the past, so it should pose no real problems for the well prepared student.

Skeleton Solution

• Discuss ownership of the matrimonial home – s17 MWPA 1882. Have direct or indirect contributions towards the acquisition of the property been made?

• Consider s37 Matrimonial Proceedings and Property Act 1970; discount s1 MWPA 1964 in relation to the deposit account.

• Consider whether Bruce can resist the bank's claim – discuss the effect of the decision in *Williams and Glyn's Bank Ltd* v *Boland* – establish whether the conditions applicable under that case can be made out.

• In the event Bruce cannot establish an equitable interest, discuss s14 Trusts of Land and Appointment of Trustees Act 1996 application for sale – principles to be applied.

• Consider dispute over occupation with Imogen – s30 Family Law Act 1996 – right of occupation – application for occupation order (s33 FLA 1996).

Suggested Solution

Bruce requires advice as to his general position with regard to the property 'Misrule' in respect of ownership and his continued occupation of the same. The ownership of the deposit account must also be considered.

On the assumption that divorce proceedings are not contemplated at this time and therefore that the provisions of the Matrimonial Causes Act 1973 cannot be invoked to settle the dispute over the ownership of the property, the issue could be resolved by reference to s17 Married Women's Property Act 1882 (hereinafter MWPA 1882). Under s17 an application may be made by either a husband or wife to settle any question between them as to the title to or possession of property.

Under s17 MWPA 1882 the matter will be resolved by the application of general principles of property law. The legal estate in 'Misrule' is vested in Imogen's name and therefore, prima facie, the legal title is vested in her absolutely and Bruce has no interest in the property. However, a proprietary interest may exist in equity and the court may look behind the title deeds and may establish the existence of a trust, that is that Imogen holds the property on trust for herself and Bruce. Under s17 the court may not create an interest in the property because it considers it fair to do so; it may declare existing interests only (*Pettitt* v *Pettitt* (1970)).

The legal estate may be displaced where there is evidence of a contrary intention on the part of the spouses. If there is evidence of a contrary intention at the date of acquisition of the property the court will give effect to it by imposing a trust in the shares agreed upon. The court may draw inferences which a reasonable person would draw from the parties' conduct at the date of acquisition and subsequently and in *Gissing* v *Gissing* (1971) it was recognised that

169

the parties may have agreed to hold property jointly without having used express words to communicate that intention to each other.

In this case, 'Misrule' was purchased by Imogen out of funds provided by her parents. It is not clear when the property was purchased, that is, before or after the marriage, or whether the funds provided were a gift from Imogen's parents to her and intended to be used for the purchase of the house. If so the next question must be whether the gift of the money was intended for Imogen alone or for both herself and Bruce. If the funds were provided to Imogen to purchase a home for herself and Bruce then it is likely that Bruce would be deemed to have a joint interest in the property on that basis alone. However if the funds were provided for Imogen alone then Bruce will have to rely on agreements or conduct which took place subsequent to the acquisition of the property to establish the existence of a trust.

It can be inferred that the parties intended both to have an interest in the property conveyed to one of them if both contributed towards the acquisition of the property either directly (through payment of the deposit or mortgage repayments) or possibly indirectly (for example by meeting household expenses which the owner could not otherwise afford to make, although in *Lloyds Bank plc* v *Rosset* (1990) the House of Lords doubted the possibility of establishing a trust by indirect contributions.

There is no evidence of direct or indirect contributions of the nature referred to above having been made by Bruce. However he would acquire an interest in 'Misrule' by virtue of his works of improvement carried out at the property. Section 37 Matrimonial Proceedings and Property Act 1970 (hereinafter MPPA 1970), provides that where a husband or wife contributes in money or money's worth to the improvement of real or personal property in which, or in the proceeds of sale of which, either or both of them has or have a beneficial interest, the husband or wife so contributing shall, if the contribution is of a substantial nature, and subject to any agreement between them to the contrary, be treated as having acquired, by virtue of his or her contribution, a share or an enlarged share in that beneficial interest, of such an extent as may then have been agreed, or in the absence of such agreement, as may, in all the circumstances, seem just.

The contribution must be substantial and in money or money's worth. In this case Bruce carried out the work himself. Certainly the installation of the central heating will be considered a substantial improvement within the terms of s37 (*Re Nicholson* (1974)), but the installation of the ornamental gas fire will not be considered substantial enough. It is not clear what other improvements were carried out by Bruce. To come within the terms of s37 the contribution must effect an improvement to the property as distinguished from merely maintaining it (*Pettitt* v *Pettitt*), and so, depending on the nature and extent of those other improvements, Bruce may be deemed to have an interest in 'Misrule' by virtue of them as well as the installation of the central heating.

The next question to consider is whether there was any agreement between Imogen and Bruce as to an interest, if any, he was to have in the property by virtue of these improvements. We are told that 'in return' for the works carried out by Bruce, Imogen paid him a weekly allowance. Such an allowance would not come within the terms of s1 Married Women's Property Act 1964, which, in the absence of contrary agreement, establishes that where a husband pays a housekeeping allowance to a wife, it shall be treated as belonging to them equally. This payment by Imogen to Bruce may not be a housekeeping allowance and in any event the Act only covers payments made by a husband to a wife. Prima facie therefore monies paid by a wife to a husband as an allowance would remain the property of the wife unless a contrary intention could be established and so prima facie the deposit account would belong to Imogen.

If Imogen made the allowance to Bruce in payment for the works carried out at 'Misrule' and the intention was that he was not to take any interest in the property by virtue of these improvements, then the deposit account belongs to Bruce. However if the allowance was not intended for that purpose then Bruce will take an interest in the property but the deposit account is likely to be deemed to belong to Imogen. When deciding the extent of Bruce's interest, if any, in 'Misrule' the court will consider the increase in value attributable to the improvements and calculate Bruce's share accordingly.

The next problem to consider is whether the sale of the property, desired by the bank, can be prevented. It is not clear what Imogen's position with regard to such a sale would be. In the event of a dispute between Bruce and the bank as to whether the sale should take place, Bruce may be able to protect his occupation of 'Misrule' on the strength of his beneficial interest, if he has one.

Since Bruce is married he has a right of occupation by virtue of s30 Family Law Act 1996. This is a right not to be evicted if in occupation and if not in occupation a right to enter and occupy the dwelling-house by court order. This is a personal right which can be registered and if registered the right binds all subsequent purchasers. It is unlikely that Bruce has registered his right of occupation. However, even if this is the case there is the possibility that Bruce could resist the bank's claim in any event. It is clear that in 1988, when the mortgage came into effect, Bruce was in occupation so is likely to have an overriding interest under s70(1)(g) Land Registration Act 1925 (see *Lloyds Bank* v *Rosset* (1990)). This will depend on the matters referred to previously, such as the intention of Imogen's parents when they supplied the funds to purchase the home and whether Bruce's works of improvement give rise to an interest. If he can establish an equitable interest then, following *William and Glyn's Bank* v *Boland* (1981), it will mean that he can resist the bank's claim for possession. If he has no equitable interest he would be unable to resist the bank's claim (*Midland Bank* v *Dobson* (1986)). In this context the bank could obtain judgment against Imogen and then obtain a charging order on her interest in the property and apply for the house to be sold under the Trusts of Land and Appointment of Trustees Act 1996. Generally the bank's claim is likely to prevail, although in exceptional circumstances the court may delay sale to prevent hardship to the family.

If Imogen asks that he leave 'Misrule' because of their matrimonial difficulties and he refuses she can apply for an occupation order under s33 FLA 1996 requiring him to leave.

In deciding whether to make such an order the court would have regard to all the circumstances including particular matters (see s33(6) FLA 1996). The court would consider the housing needs and housing resources of each of the parties and Deborah as well as the financial resources of the parties. The financial position of the parties is not clear. Imogen and Deborah are likely to have greater housing needs than Bruce. The court will also consider the likely effect of an order on Bruce's health, safety or well-being and the likely effect of a refusal to make an order on the health, safety or well-being of Imogen and Deborah. The court will also consider the conduct of Bruce and Imogen in relation to each other and otherwise. If it appears to the court that Imogen and Deborah are likely to suffer significant harm attributable to Bruce's conduct if an exclusion order is not made the court must make the order, unless it appears to the court that Bruce is likely to suffer significant harm if the order is made and the harm he is likely to suffer is as great as or greater than the harm which Imogen and Deborah are likely to suffer if the order is not made (see s33(7) FLA 1996). It is noted that there are arguments which appear to be verbal rather than violent. It is not clear what effect the arguments have had on Deborah. As a result it is not clear whether the balance of harm test favours Imogen. In the absence of further evidence it seems doubtful that an occupation order would be made in Imogen's favour.

QUESTION THREE

See Question 1 in Chapter 7: *Domestic violence*.

QUESTION FOUR

In January 1990, on Francesca's 30th birthday, Francesca and Graham announced their engagement. Graham gave Francesca an emerald and diamond ring, now valued at £20,000, and a matching bracelet, valued at £10,000. They moved into a flat which was a birthday present from Francesca's grandmother. The flat, which was registered in Francesca's name alone, was dilapidated and required structural improvements and decoration.

Although Graham is a tax consultant, he is a competent builder and he devoted each weekend of 1990 to improving the flat. He installed central heating, rewired the flat and decorated it and in 1991 he completely replaced the bathroom with units that he and Francesca bought together out of a joint bank account. According to Francesca's brother, a property surveyor, the improvements effected by Graham doubled the value of the flat.

Francesca has now decided that she no longer wishes to marry Graham and has asked him to leave the flat.

Advise Graham who is curious to know if he has any interest in the flat and who would like the jewellery he gave to Francesca returned to him together with his share of the bank account.

University of London LLB Examination
(for External Students) Family Law June 1993 Q4

General Comment

This is a straightforward question about property disputes between an engaged couple. The provisions of the Law Reform (Miscellaneous Provisions) Act 1970 have to be discussed in relation to the engagement ring, the bracelet and the bank account. The property dispute requires discussion of s37 Matrimonial Proceedings and Property Act 1970 (which appears to provide the most direct answer to the consequences of the work Graham has done on the flat). Given s37 of the 1970 Act there appears to be no need to explore the uncertain world of resulting and constructive trusts.

Skeleton Solution

• Engagement ring is presumed to be an absolute gift (s3(2) LR(MP)A 1970).
• Bracelet may be an absolute gift or conditional on getting married.
• What was the intention of the parties in relation to the money in the joint bank account? Bank account may be held in equal shares but property bought with money from account may belong to individual.
• Application of s37 Matrimonial Proceedings and Property Act 1970 in terms of substantial improvements made to the flat.
• Application for declaration under s17 Married Women's Property Act 1882.

Suggested Solution

Graham asks for advice as to whether he has any interest in the flat. He also asks whether he is entitled to have the engagement ring and bracelet returned to him. He also wants the return of his share of the bank account.

In relation to the emerald and diamond ring it is assumed that this was an engagement ring. The engagement ring is presumed to be an absolute gift by Graham to Francesca (see s3(2) Law Reform (Miscellaneous Provisions) Act (LR(MP)A) 1970). Graham could seek to rebut that presumption by proof that the ring was given with a condition that it be returned should the engagement be broken off. For example if the ring was a family heirloom Graham might persuade a court that the ring was meant to be kept in his family and that on the breaking of the engagement it should be returned. There is no evidence suggesting that this is the case. In the absence of such evidence it would appear that Francesca is entitled to keep the ring.

Whether Francesca can keep the bracelet will depend on the circumstances of Graham giving it to her. If he intended it as an absolute gift Francesca may keep it. If he intended it as a gift conditional on the parties marrying then it should be returned to him. Since the bracelet matches the ring the fate of the ring is likely to determine that of the bracelet. Therefore it appears that Francesca is entitled to keep the bracelet.

Ownership of the money in the joint bank account will depend on the intention of Graham and Francesca. If the bank account was intended to be held equally and used as a common purse (as opposed to being held in the shares each contributed to it) then a court is likely to order that Francesca and Graham receive the money in the bank account in equal shares (even if Graham put in more money than Francesca or vice versa) (see *Jones* v *Maynard* (1951)). However, property bought by one party for his or her own benefit using money from the joint account may be held to belong to that party since a joint bank account not only allows one party to spend money for the mutual benefit of both parties, but also to spend money for the sole benefit of one party (see *Re Bishop* (1965)).

Graham can be advised that the work he has done in the flat is likely to have given him an interest in it. He has contributed in money and money's worth to the improvement of the flat by the work he has done for many weekends over 1990 to improve the flat. His contribution appears to be substantial. The installation of central heating has been held to be a substantial contribution in this context (see *Re Nicholson* (1974)). Rewiring the flat is also likely to have been a substantial contribution as was the replacement of the bathroom. The redecorating in itself may not amount to a substantial contribution since that may be likened to normal DIY work (see *Button* v *Button* (1968)) but taken in the context of the other work may become 'substantial'. The substantial nature of the work is underlined by the effect that the work has had on the value of the flat Unless there was an express or implied agreement between Graham and Francesca otherwise, Graham will be treated as having acquired a share in the beneficial interest of such an extent as seems just in all the circumstances (in default of any agreement between the parties as to the quantification of shares) (see s37 Matrimonial Proceedings and Property Act 1970). Since Graham's contribution appears to have doubled the value of the flat he is likely to be entitled to a one half beneficial interest in it. Graham can be advised that the work he has done to the flat may give rise to an interest under a resulting or constructive trust. However the law covering resulting or constructive trusts is not easy to apply and is not always clear. Unless there is clear evidence of a common intention between Francesca and Graham that Graham have a beneficial interest in the flat and that Graham acted to his detriment based on that common intention it is likely to be difficult for Graham to establish a beneficial interest in the property (see *Lloyds Bank* v *Rosset* (1990)). He has not made any financial contribution to its purchase which might give rise to a resulting trust. In a case concerning an unmarried couple one party did substantial work to improve a house. It was held that he had no beneficial interest in the property in the absence of an express agreement or common intention. Since the man did the work without a clear understanding as to the financial basis on which the work was done he did so at his own risk (see *Thomas* v *Fuller-Brown* (1988)). As Graham's position by virtue of the engagement appears to be covered by clear statutory provision there appears to be no need to advise him further with respect to this difficult area of trust law.

Graham can be advised that he may apply to the court under s17 Married Women's Property Act 1882 for a declaration as to his interests in the jewellery, the bank account and the flat, provided that he makes the application within three years of the termination of the engagement (see s2(2) LR(MP)A 1970).

12 University of London LLB (External) 1997 Questions and Suggested Solutions

UNIVERSITY OF LONDON
LLB EXAMINATIONS 1997
for External Students
PARTS I AND II EXAMINATIONS (Scheme A) and
THIRD AND FOURTH YEAR EXAMINATIONS (Scheme B)
GRADUATE ENTRY LEVEL II (Route A)
GRADUATE ENTRY THIRD YEAR EXAMINATIONS (Route B)

FAMILY LAW

Tuesday, 3 June: 2.30 pm to 5.30 pm

Answer *FOUR* of the following EIGHT questions

1 It is said that legal developments in relation to cohabitation are examples of interference with family autonomy. Those who exercise their right not to marry should not have the consequences of matrimony thrust upon them.

   What do you understand this to mean? Do you agree with the statement? Consider it with particular reference to financial provision and property entitlements and the status of children.

2 Alan was introduced to Bert by a mutual friend. Bert had been a member of an illegal organisation for gay rights in his own country and had come to England to escape from repression there. He offered Alan £5,000 to 'marry' him. Alan had incurred large debts and so reluctantly agreed. Although he was homosexual he did not intend to live with Bert; the 'marriage' would be in name only. Bert was anxious that his whereabouts might be traced and also wanted the 'marriage' to appear valid and so he disguised himself and gave a woman's name at the register office where they were to marry. Alan began to worry about the implication of the plan and shortly before the ceremony saw his doctor, who prescribed tranquillisers and advised him not to drink alcohol. He did, however, drink with friends on the night before the marriage and was in a confused state at the register office. A party was held after the ceremony at which he drank more alcohol. He awoke the next morning with Bert, remembering very little of the events. He then discovered that Bert was a woman. Since then they have not lived together, but Bertha, as he now knows her, has told him that she is expecting his child.

   Is the marriage valid? If it is valid, how can Alan end it?

3 The Law Commission has stated that the law of divorce is 'confusing, misleading, discriminatory and unjust'. What do you understand to be the reasons for the Law Commission's view? Are there any strengths in the present law of divorce? To what extent do you think that the Family Law Act 1996 will improve the law of divorce?

4   Abe and Beryl met in 1985 when she was working and he was a student. They lived
     together in her flat, and she supported him financially throughout the period of his training
     as an engineer. They married when he qualified in 1990. He soon obtained employment.
     She sold her flat for £70,000 and they bought a house for £100,000, which was conveyed
     into joint names and upon which they took a joint mortgage. After their first child was born
     in 1990, Beryl decided not to return to work, although Abe had said they could have
     afforded a nanny to look after the child, and he would have preferred Beryl to work. After
     their second child was born in 1994, Beryl suffered from serious post-natal depression.
     Abe had to spend increasing amounts of time away from work, helping in the home and
     caring for the children. In 1994 he was dismissed from his employment, with six months'
     salary in lieu of notice. Shortly afterwards he was able to find part-time work.

     Later in 1994 Beryl's health improved and she took greater charge of running the home and
     caring for the children. Abe, however, met Enid and in 1996 left home to live with her in
     rented accommodation. Enid is now expecting their child, and Abe has used the lump
     sum of £25,000 to start his own business.

     Beryl has now divorced Abe and seeks your advice on the upbringing of the children and
     financial and property matters. Advise her.

5   Ann and Bill began living together three years ago in a house they bought in joint names.
     Last year Ann's sister died and since then she and Bill have looked after her sister's two
     orphaned children. Bill had only reluctantly agreed to look after them, and their presence
     caused a rift between Ann and Bill. Their relationship deteriorated to the point where there
     was very little contact between them other than during day-to-day necessities. Bill
     developed a mental condition, one symptom of which was agoraphobia. His behaviour
     became very unpredictable. Ann showed no sympathy for or understanding of his condition
     and on one occasion, after accusing him of giving no help in running the home, she started
     to push him out into the street, telling him to go to the shops. He struck her several
     times, observed by the children, who became very upset by what they saw.

     Bill entered hospital for treatment for his condition two weeks ago. He made frequent
     telephone calls to Ann to apologise for his behaviour. On some occasions the telephone
     was answered by one of the children, who became very distressed on hearing Bill's voice.

     Bill is due to leave hospital in one week's time. Ann now feels that she needs breathing
     space to allow her and the children to recover, but if Bill's condition does not improve,
     she would not want him to return to the house.

     Advise Ann.

6   Linda and Matt have lived together for 16 years but they never married. They have two
     children: Nat who is 15 and Olivia who is 14.

     Nat has been unhappy at home for two years because he thinks his parents are too strict
     with him (Linda believes in corporal punishment but Matt does not). Nat has read that
     children can 'divorce' their parents and wishes to know how he can 'divorce' Linda and
     Matt. He wants to live with his 15-year-old girlfriend Kate and her parents, who have
     agreed that he can share Kate's self-contained apartment built on to their house. Nat
     knows that his parents will object.

     Olivia has recently become pregnant. She wishes to have an abortion but Matt, who is an active member of a pro-life movement, refuses to allow an abortion. Linda thinks that Olivia should decide.

Advise Nat and Olivia.

7   To what extent, in your opinion, has the Children Act 1989 achieved the aim of diminishing the powers of the state while asserting the autonomy of the family? What is the right balance? What part have the courts played in striking the appropriate balance?

8   Peter and Ruth, who are husband and wife, separated when Peter left England eight months ago to work abroad. He returned after Ruth wrote to him to say that she had given birth to a son, Simon, although she told Peter that he was not the father. Recently Ruth was badly injured when, after drinking alcohol, she crashed her car. She had experienced problems with alcohol in the past. Ruth's mother tried to care for Simon after the accident but had difficulties coping with him. Neighbours informed the local authority that they thought the child was being neglected. The local authority took over the care of Simon and placed him with foster-parents. Peter has tried to discover Simon's whereabouts and, if he succeeds, intends to take Simon abroad with him.

The local authority now has told the foster-parents to return Simon as it is concerned that Peter may discover Simon's whereabouts and take him away.

Consider the steps Peter may take to achieve what he thinks is best for Simon, and what steps the local authority may take to secure what it thinks is best for the child.

QUESTION ONE

It is said that legal developments in relation to cohabitation are examples of interference with family autonomy. Those who exercise their right not to marry should not have the consequences of matrimony thrust upon them.

What do you understand this to mean? Do you agree with the statement? Consider it with particular reference to financial provision and property entitlements and the status of children.

University of London LLB Examination
(for External Students) Family Law June 1997 Q1

General Comment

The question invites a comparison between the legal position of married and unmarried couples in relation to financial provision and property and in relation to the status of children. It also invites a discussion on how the law has developed in these areas and whether it can be said that such developments amount to interference with family autonomy.

Skeleton Solution

- Law relating to the financial provision between cohabitants.
- Financial provision of a child of an unmarried relationship – s15 and Schedule 1 Children Act 1989; Child Support Act 1991; Social Security and Administration Act 1992.
- Law relating to property entitlements between unmarried couples.
- Occupation of the family home by unmarried couple – Part IV Family Law Act 1996.
- Status of child of unmarried parents and status of unmarried father – Children Act 1989.

Suggested Solution

To answer the issues posed by this question one first has to identify what developments in the law in relation to cohabitation there have been with particular reference to financial provision and property entitlements and the status of children.

The law has not developed a great deal in relation to the financial provision between cohabitants. There still remains no statutory right for one cohabitant to apply for financial provision from another. This contrasts with the statutory framework dealing with the financial provision between married couples who divorce: see ss21–26 Matrimonial Causes Act (MCA) 1973. There are also provisions to allow for financial provision between married couples who separate: see s27 MCA 1973 and ss2, 6 or 7 Domestic Proceedings and Magistrates' Courts Act 1978. To this extent the consequences of matrimony have not been thrust on cohabiting couples.

The situation is different if there is a child of the unmarried couple. The cohabitant with whom the child is living can apply for financial provision from the other cohabitant for the child: see s15 and Sch 1 Children Act (CA) 1989. Such an application can be for maintenance or lump sum orders to the child, or to the applicant for the benefit of the child, or the transfer of property to the child, or to the applicant for the child's benefit. In deciding whether to make an order the court has to have regard to all the circumstances and to matters such as the income and outgoings of the parties, the financial needs and responsibilities of the parties and the child and certain other matters: see para 4(1), Sch 1 CA 1989. Of even greater importance is the Child Support Act (CSA) 1991, which now largely deals with the financial support of children when parents separate. Under the Act both married and unmarried parents are equally liable to be assessed for child support. The CSA 1991 emerged from a perceived failure of the courts to use their various powers to order reasonable financial provision for children – as a result the burden of financially supporting children fell largely to the state through benefits being paid to lone parents. The application of the CSA 1991 means that parents who choose not to marry cannot avoid the financial consequences of parenthood traditionally associated with the responsibilities of married parents. This development has long been part of the law. The Affiliation Proceedings Act 1957 and the Guardianship of Minors Act 1971 (both predecessors to the CA 1989 and then the CSA 1991) placed an obligation on the unmarried father to provide for a child of his unmarried relationship. This development has been partly 'child centred' (so that children are not brought up without the financial support of an absent parent) and partly 'state based' (trying to reduce the burden on the state of supporting children after parents have separated). Similar rules have applied in relation to social security legislation (see s26 Social Security Act 1986 and now s78(6) Social Security Administration Act 1992). This aspect of the law contradicts the assertion that those who exercise their right not to marry should not have the consequences of matrimony thrust upon them. There is a political imperative (to reduce the financial burden on the state) and a moral imperative (that unmarried parents should have the responsibility of financially supporting their children) which means that it is difficult to agree with the statement in the question.

The law relating to the property entitlements between cohabitants has not developed a great deal since the landmark decisions of *Pettitt* v *Pettitt* (1969) and *Gissing* v *Gissing* (1970). The courts still apply strict rules of property law when dealing with property disputes between unmarried cohabitants. There was a period when the courts appeared to adopt a more flexible approach to dealing with such property disputes, but the more strict approach was confirmed in *Lloyds Bank* v *Rosset* (1990). As a result unmarried couples must regulate their property interests either through the conveyance or by resulting, implied or constructive trust. Establishing an interest under a resulting, implied or constructive trust has proved difficult. In *Hammond* v *Mitchell* (1991) the difficulties were described as 'the judicial quest for the fugitive or phantom common intention' or as a 'detailed, time consuming and laborious' process. In *Midland Bank* v *Cooke* (1995) the difficulties in establishing property entitlements were such that the court called for law reform (as recommended by the Law Commission) to save a lot of human heartache and public expense. This situation sharply contrasts with married couples who can ask a divorce court to exercise a wide and generous discretion in allocating property as is fair and just following the marriage breakdown. To this extent the consequences of matrimony have not been thrust upon those who choose not to marry.

The law in relation to financial provision on death has developed in relation to unmarried couples. Under the rules of intestacy an unmarried partner is not entitled to any part of the estate of his/her partner if no valid will has been made. The law has developed to the extent of allowing an unmarried partner who immediately before the death of the deceased was wholly maintained, either wholly or in part by the deceased: see s1(1)(e) Inheritance (Provision for Family and Dependants) Act (I(PFD)A) 1975. More recently, the law has been changed where the deceased died on or after 1 January 1996. If during the whole of the period of two years before the deceased died the claimant lived with the deceased as his/her husband or wife then a claim can be made from the deceased's estate: see ss1(1)(ba) and 1A I(PFD)A 1975. This has partly thrust the consequences of matrimony on a person in an unmarried relationship who dies either intestate or makes no provision for the partner in his/her will.

Changes in taxation have tended to reduce the difference in the tax treatment of married and unmarried couples. However, such legal developments have largely affected the taxation of married couples rather than changing the taxation of an unmarried partner. It has been confirmed that an unmarried relationship cannot attract the married person's allowance: see *Rignell* v *Andrews* (1991).

Rights of occupation between unmarried couples have been codified in Part IV of the Family Law Act (FLA) 1996. The law in relation to unmarried couples has developed from the Domestic Violence and Matrimonial Proceedings Act 1976. This allowed an unmarried partner to apply to exclude his/her violent partner and apply for an order prohibiting further harassment. Section 33 FLA 1996 allows an unmarried partner who is entitled to occupy the home to apply for a occupation order to exclude the other partner. Section 36 FLA 1996 allows an unmarried partner with no right to occupy the home to apply for an occupation order against the partner who has a right to occupy, while s38 FLA 1996 allows an unmarried partner with no right to occupy for an occupation order against his/her partner also with no right to occupy. The considerations which apply differ according to the kind of application. In particular, a balance of harm test applies to a s33 occupation order whereby if it appears to the court that the applicant or any relevant child is likely to suffer greater significant harm (attributable to the respondent's conduct) if an occupation order is not made than any significant harm the respondent or any relevant child would suffer if an order was made, then the court must make an occupation order. This balance of harm test does not apply to s36 or s38 occupation orders. Also in considering the nature of an unmarried relationship the court must have regard to the fact that they have not given each other the commitment involved in marriage: s41 FLA 1996. A married partner is normally allowed to make a s33 application because s/he either is entitled to occupy or is given 'matrimonial home rights': see 30 FLA 1996. Therefore a married partner has greater scope for obtaining an occupation order than an unmarried partner. Despite this it could be said that some of the consequences of matrimony have been thrust upon unmarried couples in terms of regulating occupation of the home. Married couples and unmarried couples have the same right to apply to the courts for non-molestation orders: see s42 FLA 1996. This development in the law has been designed to protect the victims of domestic violence or other forms of unacceptable behaviour. As a result it is perceived as an acceptable development as opposed to an imposition of the consequences of matrimony on cohabitees.

The law has developed in relation to the status of children of unmarried parents. The main theme of these developments has been to reduce the legal consequences of the child being of unmarried parents when compared to the legal status of a child of married parents. Put in another way, the law has sought to reduce the consequences of birth outside marriage, particularly in the context of the growing number of children born to unmarried parents. Examples of such developments include s1 Family Law Reform Act 1987, whereby references to any relationship between two persons must be construed without regard to whether or not the father or mother of either or them, or the father and mother of any person through whom the relationship is deduced, have or have not been married. Rights of children under intestate succession have also been improved: see s18 FLRA 1987. The position of the unmarried father in relation to his child has improved. Before the Children Act 1989 the law left the unmarried father with a confused and unsatisfactory legal status – he was described by one commentator as a 'beached whale'. His position is now much clearer as a result of the Children Act 1989. He starts with no rights in relation to his child (ie he has no automatic parental responsibility, this vests exclusively in the mother: s2(2)(a) CA 1989). The father must acquire parental responsibility either by agreement with the mother or by a parental responsibility order or by obtaining a residence order. This legal position clearly distinguishes between a married father who automatically shares parental responsibility with his wife. The unmarried father must earn parental responsibility, eg by establishing a relationship with, and showing commitment to, his child: see *Re P (a minor) (parental responsibility order)* (1994).

In conclusion, it is difficult to agree with the statement posed by the question. The consequences of matrimony have been thrust on those who choose not to marry to a limited extent but only where there has been a clear moral or political imperative for this to be done. The financial obligations of supporting the children of an unmarried relationship are justified in terms of the moral judgment that parents, whether married or unmarried, should be responsible for the financial support of their children. There is also the political imperative that the state does not wish to bear a financial burden which parents should bear. Rights to regulate occupation have been extended to unmarried couples but this is so an unmarried partner can protect herself from violence. In other respects, such as the right to financial support from an unmarried partner and property entitlements on the breakdown of an unmarried relationship, the law has not developed and the consequences of matrimony have not been thrust upon cohabitees. This has left some unmarried partners in a weak and disadvantaged position compared to those who choose to get married. The position of the unmarried father remains a relatively disadvantaged one when compared to a married father. The unmarried father has to take steps to gain the status of a married father. Where the law has developed it is difficult to say this amounts to interference with family autonomy. The law has moved to provide protection and rights where a clear need has been identified (eg the need to protect the victims of domestic violence). Indeed the present law could well be criticised for not developing more to provide greater protection for unmarried partners, particularly in resolving property and maintenance matters following the breakdown of a relationship.

QUESTION TWO

Alan was introduced to Bert by a mutual friend. Bert had been a member of an illegal organisation for gay rights in his own country and had come to England to escape from repression there. He offered Alan £5,000 to 'marry' him. Alan had incurred large debts and so reluctantly agreed. Although he was homosexual he did not intend to live with Bert; the 'marriage' would be in name only. Bert was anxious that his whereabouts might be traced and also wanted the 'marriage' to appear valid and so he disguised himself and gave a woman's name at the register office where they were to marry. Alan began to worry about the implication of the plan and shortly before the ceremony saw his doctor, who prescribed tranquillisers and advised him not to drink alcohol. He did, however, drink with friends on the night before the marriage and was in a confused state at the register office. A party was held after the ceremony at which he drank more alcohol. He awoke the next morning with Bert, remembering very little of the events. He then discovered that Bert was a woman. Since then they have not lived together, but Bertha, as he now knows her, has told him that she is expecting his child.

Is the marriage valid? If it is valid, how can Alan end it?

University of London LLB Examination
(for External Students) Family Law June 1997 Q2

General Comment

The question puts forward an intriguing set of facts which require the student to explore the grounds for annulling marriage. In particular the grounds on which a marriage is void must be discussed. The legal status of transsexuals is one element of that discussion. In addition, the grounds on which a marriage is voidable may be relevant. Finally, the option of divorce must be mentioned.

Skeleton Solution

• Grounds for voiding the marriage:
  – parties are not respectively male and female (s11(c) MCA 1973) and the position of transsexuals;
  – disregard of marriage requirements (s11(a) MCA 1973).
• Grounds for marriage being voidable:
  – non-consummation (s12(a) and (b) MCA 1973);
  – lack of consent due to duress, mistake or unsoundness of mind (s12(c) MCA 1973).
• Petition for divorce on basis of irretrievable breakdown – fact of behaviour (s1(2)(b) MCA 1973).

Suggested Solution

Alan asks for advice on the validity of the marriage and, if the marriage is valid, how Alan can end it.

Firstly, Alan can be advised that if one or more of the grounds in s11 Matrimonial Causes Act (MCA) 1973 can be established then the marriage can be declared to be void. This would have the effect of the law treating the marriage as if it had never existed: see *De Reneville* v *De Reneville* (1948).

One possible ground is that the parties are not respectively male and female: s11(c) MCA 1973. Marriage is not allowed in English law between persons of the same sex. There may be some doubt as the status of Bertha, who was known as Bert. A person's sex is fixed at birth. Even if a subsequent operation or other change is such that a person claims to have changed sex this makes no difference: see *Corbett* v *Corbett* (1970). Though the law on transsexuals is developing at the same time as developments in the scientific understanding of sexuality the most recent cases confirm *Corbett* as representing the existing law: see *Cossey* v *UK* (1991) and *Re P and G (Transsexuals)* (1996). Alan will need to obtain evidence of Bertha's (or Bert's) sex at birth. If it was male then the marriage will be void. If it was female then this ground cannot apply. If Bertha is indeed expecting a child then it seems likely that she must have been female at the time of her birth so the likelihood of establishing this ground appears small.

A second possible grounds is that Alan and Bertha have intermarried in disregard of certain requirements as to the formation of marriage: s11(a)(iii) MCA 1973. It is noted that Bertha gave a false name and disguised him/herself at the register office. If the marriage was by way of superintendent registrar's certificate and licence then it has been decided that the object of the giving of names is not to achieve publicity. As a result a deliberate misdescription of Bertha will not invalidate the marriage: see *Puttick* v *Attorney-General* (1979) where a false name and particulars were given by one of the parties to the marriage but the marriage was held to be valid. The situation is likely to be different if the ceremony was a Church of England marriage, but the information supplied does not suggest this.

Alan can be advised that none of the other grounds voiding the marriage appear to apply. If neither of the above two grounds can be established then Alan can seek to establish that the marriage is voidable pursuant to one or more of the grounds set out in s12 MCA 1973. If the marriage is voidable Alan needs to obtain a decree to prove that the marriage is a nullity and it may be possible for Bertha to establish a defence under s13 MCA 1973. The first ground Alan may seek to establish is that the marriage has not been consummated, either due to the incapacity of either party or owing to the wilful refusal of Bertha: see s12(a) and (b) MCA 1973. It is difficult to see how Alan could establish non-consummation on the basis of Bertha's wilful refusal. There is no suggestion of such refusal on Bertha's part. It is likely to be difficult to establish an incapacity to consummate the marriage if Bertha is indeed a woman and is capable of 'ordinary and complete intercourse': see *D* v *A* (1845). If Bertha is not a woman then the marriage is void. Otherwise Alan would have to rely on medical evidence to show that she has a physical incapacity to consummate the marriage. He would also have to establish that such incapacity is either incapable of remedy or can only be cured by an operation which is either dangerous or has little chance of success, or that Bertha refuses to undergo the operation: see *S* v *S* (1954). In the absence of information suggesting an incapacity it is again difficult to see how this ground can be established.

A further ground is that Alan did not validly consent to the marriage, whether in consequence of duress, mistake, unsoundness of mind or otherwise: see s12(c) MCA 1973. It may be possible to say that Alan did not validly consent because he made a mistake as to identity of the person he was marrying – namely that Bertha was not a man but a woman. It has been held that a mistake as to the quality of the person is not sufficient: see *Moss* v *Moss* (1897) where the wife concealed that she was pregnant. A mistake as to the name would also not be sufficient to invalidate consent: see *Puttick* v *Attorney-General* (above). In addition, Alan appears to have been a party to any deception practised or, at least, aware of it. He appears to have been aware of the false name and that 'Bert' dressed up as a woman. In these circumstances he would not be advised to apply to the court on this basis.

Alan could seek to establish that he did not validly consent due to duress, namely he only agreed to the marriage because of his large debts. However, Alan should be advised that any duress must be so overbearing that the element of free consent is absent: *Szechter* v *Szechter* (1971). The court would ask whether Alan's will was overborne by a genuine and reasonably held fear caused by the threat of immediate danger (for which Alan is not responsible) to his life, limb or liberty so that the constraint destroyed the reality of consent. The facts do not suggest such duress. There may have been some pressure due to Alan's financial state whereby Alan 'reluctantly' agreed to the marriage, but this seems to fall far short of duress. Alan should also be advised that there is uncertainty about whether any fear must be a fear for which Alan is not responsible: contrast *Buckland* v *Buckland* (1967) with *Griffith* v *Griffith* (1944). If Alan has been responsible for his own debts this is likely to further weaken his case.

A further basis for lack of consent is unsoundness of mind. The combination of tranquillisers and drink may have been such that Alan was not aware of what was going on during the marriage ceremony. However, English law considers that marriage is a simple concept so no high degree of understanding is required: see *In the estate of Park* (1953) and *Re Roberts (deceased)* (1978). As a result it is likely to be difficult for Alan to establish this ground, particularly in the context of self-induced intoxication. The marriage could also be voidable if either party is suffering from a mental disorder (whether continuously or intermittently) within the meaning of the Mental Health Act 1983 so as to be unfitted for marriage: s12(d) MCA 1973. A temporary intoxication is unlikely to be classified as a mental disorder and is unlikely to be such that Alan is incapable of carrying out the ordinary duties and obligations of marriage. A temporary hysterical neurosis was insufficient in *Bennett* v *Bennett* (1969).

If Alan does establish that the marriage is voidable Bertha can seek to satisfy the court that Alan behaved in a way that led Bertha to believe that he would not seek to have the marriage annulled: see s13(1) MCA 1973. There does not appear to be anything to suggest that Bertha could satisfy the court as to the defence of 'approbation'.

If Alan is not able to satisfy the court that the marriage is void or voidable he could seek to petition for divorce. However, he would not be able to petition until one year had elapsed from the date of the marriage: see s3(1) MCA 1973. Once the year has elapsed then he could seek to establish, first, that the marriage had irretrievably broken down and, second, that one or more of five facts is established: see s1(1) and (2) MCA 1973. One fact is that Bertha has behaved in such a way that Alan cannot reasonably be expected to live with her: see s1(2)(b) MCA 1973. Bertha's deceitful behaviour may be sufficient to establish this fact, together with the fact that they have not lived together since the marriage. A second fact is that Bertha has deserted Alan for a continuous period of at least two years immediately preceding the presentation of the petition: see s1(2)(c) MCA 1973. Alan should be advised that this ground is not easy to establish. Alternatively, Alan could establish that he and Bertha have lived apart for a continuous period of at least two years and Bertha consents to the decree: see s1(2)(d) MCA 1973. The final fact is that the parties have lived apart continuously for a period of five years: see s1(2)(e) MCA 1973. Given the delay involved in establishing the facts in s1(2)(c), (d) and (e) it is assumed that Alan would seek to rely on s1(2)(b) should he fail to challenge the validity of the marriage.

QUESTION THREE

The Law Commission has stated that the law of divorce is 'confusing, misleading, discriminatory and unjust'. What do you understand to be the reasons for the Law Commission's view? Are there any strengths in the present law of divorce? To what extent do you think that the Family Law Act 1996 will improve the law of divorce?

University of London LLB Examination
(for External Students) Family Law June 1997 Q3

General Comment

This essay-style question invites the student to outline the background to the enactment of Parts I to III of the Family Law Act 1996. An understanding of the criticisms of the existing law needs to be demonstrated, together with a description of how the new law seeks to meet those criticisms. In conclusion, the student is required to give his/her view as to whether the Family Law Act 1996 is likely to succeed in improving on the existing law of divorce.

Skeleton Solution

• Existing law of divorce – the ground of irretrievable breakdown and the need to satisfy the court of one or more of five facts (s1(1) and (2) MCA 1973).

• The extensive use of the fault facts of adultery and behaviour and consequences of this – whether this amounts to the law being 'confusing, misleading, discriminatory and unjust'.

• Law Commission proposals for reform of divorce law.

- Government's approach to divorce law reform through Parts I to III Family Law Act 1996 – in particular the imposition of a period for reflection and to prepare for the consequences of the divorce – the use of mediation.
- Whether the Family Law Act 1996 meets the criticisms of the existing law and avoids confusion, discrimination and injustice.

Suggested Solution

The reform of divorce law enacted in the Family Law Act 1996 (but not substantially in force) has proved to be controversial. The new Act seeks to overcome the criticisms of the existing law but the new proposed framework has itself been subject to criticism.

It should be remembered that divorce law went through a similar period of reform in the 1950s and 1960s. A Royal Commission (the Morton Commission) published a report on divorce law reform in 1956. This was followed by a report from the Church of England called 'Putting Asunder' and a Law Commission report. The Law Commission report recommended that the aims of a good divorce law are to 'buttress, rather than undermine the stability of marriage, and when, regrettably, a marriage has irretrievably broken down, to enable the empty legal shell to be destroyed with the maximum fairness and the minimum bitterness, distress and humiliation.' The consequence was the passing of the Divorce Law Reform Act 1969. The existing law is contained in the Matrimonial Causes Act 1973 (which replaced the Divorce Reform Act 1969). This law replaced the notion of the matrimonial offence as being the basis for divorce with the notion of irretrievable breakdown of the marriage: see s1(1) Matrimonial Causes Act 1973 – hereinafter referred to as the MCA 1973. A petitioner has to establish that the marriage has broken down irretrievably. In addition, he or she must satisfy the court of one or more of five facts: see s1(2) MCA 1973. Three of these facts retain an element of fault. The first is that the respondent has committed adultery and that the petitioner finds it intolerable to live with the respondent: see s1(2)(a) MCA 1973. The second is that the respondent has behaved in such a way that the petitioner cannot be reasonably be expected to live with the respondent: see s1(2)(b) MCA 1973. The third is that the respondent has deserted the petitioner for a continuous period of at least two years immediately preceding the presentation of the divorce petition: see s1(2)(c) MCA 1973. The other two facts are not fault based. One is that the parties have lived apart for a continuous period of at least two years immediately preceding the presentation of the petition and the respondent consents to the decree being granted: see s1(2)(d) MCA 1973. The second is that the parties have lived apart for a continuous period of at least five years immediately preceding the presentation of the petition: see s1(2)(e) MCA 1973. There is protection for respondent spouses who would suffer grave financial or other hardship who can defend divorces based on five years living apart on the basis of such hardship: see s5 MCA 1973. There is a limited form of protection to safeguard other respondent spouses in divorces relying on s1(2)(d) and (e): see s10 MCA 1973. Petitions are barred within the first year of marriage: see s3 MCA 1973.

When the existing law was first proposed it was thought that the non-fault based facts would be relied upon in the majority of cases. In fact the fault based facts of adultery and behaviour are the most commonly used in divorce petitions. For example, the fact of adultery is used by female petitioners in 22 per cent of cases and by male petitioners in 37 per cent of cases. The fact of behaviour was used by female petitioners in 53 per cent of cases. The reason for the use of the fault based facts appears to be that this is the quickest way to obtain a divorce in many cases. As a result it was argued that petitioners were encouraged to make allegations (sometimes exaggerated) against their spouses in order to obtain a speedy divorce. This can lead to spouses taking up opposing situations from the beginning of the divorce process.

In May 1988 the Law Commission published a discussion paper 'Facing the Future' dealing with the possible reform of divorce law. In 1990 it published its report 'The Grounds for Divorce' which argued that the objectives of the law should be to support marriages which could be saved and to dissolve as painlessly as possible those marriages which could not be saved. These aims were the same as the previous report which led to the 1969 reforms. It also argued that divorce law should encourage parties to resolve issues relating to the children, the home and finance as amicably as possible, having regard to their responsibilities to their children and to each other. In particular, the law should aim to reduce the harm suffered by children at the time of divorce and afterwards, and to encourage the continued sharing of parental responsibilities towards the children. The existing law was criticised in the terms quoted in the question. The use of the fault based facts were said to encourage unnecessary hostility and bitterness. It argued that the law did little to save marriage, little to help the children and did not help the parties to consider the future in a calm and reasonable manner. The Commission argued that while irretrievable breakdown should remain the sole ground for divorce it should be proved by a single fact, namely the expiry of a minimum period of one year for the consideration of the practical consequences of the divorce and for reflection upon the possibility of reconciliation. In practice, this period would commence by either or both parties making a formal statement that the marriage had broken down and lodging that statement with the court. The court would then supply both parties with an information pack explaining the objectives of the ensuing one year period, the court's powers and about opportunities for reconciliation, counselling, mediation and conciliation. Within that year the court could make orders regarding the children, finance and property. Contested matters could be referred to conciliation before being determined by the court. After 11 months of the one-year period had elapsed either party could apply for a divorce order (or a separation order as judicial separation would be termed), and after one month had elapsed from the making of that application a divorce (or separation) order could be issued. These suggestions for reform came against a background of public concern about divorce and the number of divorcing couples. Great Britain has the highest divorce rate in Europe.

The Lord Chancellor published a Green Paper in December, 1993 called 'Facing the Future: Mediation and the Ground for Divorce' which followed the recommendations of the Law Commission. He proposed a no fault divorce after only one year of separation and focusing on mediation rather than the courts. Following consultation, a White Paper was published in 1995 detailing the decisions taken on divorce reform: this largely reflected the views of the Law Commission and the Green Paper. The single ground for divorce would be irretrievable breakdown which would be demonstrated by the passing of a one-year period for reflection and consideration, and for the parties to settle the arrangements for the children and financial provision. The petitioner would be obliged to attend an information-giving session, and the respondent would be encouraged to attend. At this session couples would be informed of the legal consequences of divorce and of options such as counselling and mediation. Local mediation services would be state funded. While supporting the objectives proposed by the Law Commission, the government was also concerned to minimise the cost to the taxpayer and to the parties of the existing divorce process. The government therefore proposed that legal aid would be limited in the new divorce process so that parties kept control of their own affairs, preferably through mediation rather than through lawyers. These provisions were then introduced to the 1995/96 Parliament in the Family Law Bill. They attracted considerable controversy and the passage through Parliament led to a number of amendments and concessions being made.

The Family Law Act 1996 has now been enacted. Part I, which deals with the general principles underlying the divorce reform, has been brought into force. However, the substantive provisions in Parts II and III are not likely to be brought into force until 1999 or 2000. Various pilot schemes have been set up, eg to pilot the effectiveness of information meetings.

The volume of divorce appears to be largely a product of wider historical and social forces (in particular the Second World War) rather than changes in the law. The attitude to divorce has changed considerably and religious attitudes have become far less rigid. There is an argument that reforms to divorce law follow social trends rather than shape them. Even with the extensive use of the existing fault based facts most divorces are undefended and amount to divorce by consent. One Member of Parliament put it this way: 'I am nervous about whether we in the House can pick up where 2,000 years of Judeao-Christian traditions appears to have failed to singly and, by the stroke of a legislative pen, safeguard marriage for the foreseeable future. That is wishful thinking.' The Family Law Act 1996 is designed to meet the principal criticisms of the existing law. The Act is designed to eliminate the unjust and arbitrary use of the fault facts which can engender bitterness. The Act seeks to eliminate fault altogether, concentrating on the consequences of divorce and encouraging spouses to prepare for them. The Act is laudable in these aims and objectives of making the end of marriage less painful. However, there is still an element of divorcing parties wishing to allocate blame for the failure of their marriage. The existing law allows parties to allocate that blame whereas the new law does not. There is the danger that the new provisions do not allow for a 'safety valve' in this respect and this may prove a weakness. Human nature may conspire to defeat the aims and objectives of the new law.

QUESTION FOUR

Abe and Beryl met in 1985 when she was working and he was a student. They lived together in her flat, and she supported him financially throughout the period of his training as an engineer. They married when he qualified in 1990. He soon obtained employment. She sold her flat for £70,000 and they bought a house for £100,000, which was conveyed into joint names and upon which they took a joint mortgage. After their first child was born in 1990, Beryl decided not to return to work, although Abe had said they could have afforded a nanny to look after the child, and he would have preferred Beryl to work. After their second child was born in 1994, Beryl suffered from serious post-natal depression. Abe had to spend increasing amounts of time away from work, helping in the home and caring for the children. In 1994 he was dismissed from his employment, with six months' salary in lieu of notice. Shortly afterwards he was able to find part-time work.

Later in 1994 Beryl's health improved and she took greater charge of running the home and caring for the children. Abe, however, met Enid and in 1996 left home to live with her in rented accommodation. Enid is now expecting their child, and Abe has used the lump sum of £25,000 to start his own business.

Beryl has now divorced Abe and seeks your advice on the upbringing of the children and financial and property matters. Advise her.

University of London LLB Examination
(for External Students) Family Law June 1997 Q4

General Comment

This is a standard question on ancillary relief after divorce. It involves a husband and a wife who are both of limited means and who have both made contributions to the family's welfare. The earning capacity of the respective parents is important. The involvement of the Child Support Agency is highly relevant. The questions also asks about resolving the upbringing of children following divorce.

Skeleton Solution

• Wide powers of the court under the MCA 1973 to make orders for financial consideration.

• Discretion to make orders as is just and reasonable but subject to certain considerations.

• Welfare of child of family is first consideration (s25(1) MCA 1973).

• Considerations under s25(2) MCA 1973:

    – income, property and earning capacity;

    – outgoings;

    – standard of living before marriage ended;

    – age of parties and duration of marriage;

    – contribution to welfare of family by looking after the home and child and contribution towards business;

    – relevance of conduct;

    – need to consider pension position.

• Clean break provisions under s25A MCA 1973 – whether this is feasible in this case.

• Financial support of the children – the Child Support Agency.

• Section 41 MCA 1973 and consideration of arrangements for children – orders under s8 Children Act 1989 to resolve any disputes.

• Conclusion – provision of accommodation for wife and child – maintenance for wife – child support for children – whether any application for residence/contact orders are needed with respect to the children.

Suggested Solution

Beryl should first be advised that the courts have wide powers to make orders for maintenance payments, lump sum orders and for the sale or settlement of property owned by either her or Abe: see ss23, 24 and 24A of the Matrimonial Causes Act 1973 – hereinafter referred to as the MCA 1973. The court has a wide discretion to make such orders as it considers just and reasonable, but must take into account particular considerations: see ss25 and 25A MCA 1973. Beryl can be advised that these particular considerations will have considerable influence on the likely financial provision for herself and their two children.

The court will give first consideration to the welfare of Beryl and Abe's two children: see s25(1) MCA 1973. This does not mean that their welfare will determine what orders are made, but the need for them to provided for, be properly housed and educated will be of the first importance: see *Suter* v *Suter and Jones* (1987). In deciding on financial provision for them the court will take into account their financial needs and any income, earning capacity, property and other financial resources they have. It will consider the manner in which they are being educated or trained, as well as the manner in which Beryl and Abe expected them to be educated or trained: see s23(3) MCA 1973.

The court will then go on to consider the income, earning capacity, property and other financial resources which each of Beryl and Abe has now or is likely to have in the foreseeable future, including any increase in earning capacity which it would be reasonable to expect either party to take steps to acquire: see s25(2)(a) MCA 1973. It is not clear if Beryl has any income of her own. Since their youngest child is only aged three years it is assumed that she is not working. It is also not clear whether she has any earning capacity. It is assumed that she had a reasonably paid job up to 1990 since she had a flat worth £70,000. However, she has now been out of employment for some seven years so it appears unlikely that she has much of a earning capacity, particularly with two young children to bring up. If she has any earning capacity she will be expected to take steps to realise it. Abe appears to have limited means in that he has only just started his own business. His income is unlikely to be augmented by Enid if she is expecting their child. The court will have to make an assessment of the earning capacity of the business in the foreseeable future. There do not appear to be any capital assets (given Abe's spending of his lump sum) apart from the home.

The court will then look at the financial needs, obligations and responsibilities which each of the parties has or is likely to have in the foreseeable future: see s25(2)(b) MCA 1973. Since Beryl appears to be continuing to care for the two children, this financial obligation and responsibility will be of first importance in the court's mind. She needs to be housed appropriately and to receive an appropriate income to live on. Abe can argue that he will have the obligation and responsibility for maintaining Enid and any child born to them. The court will also have regard to the standard of living enjoyed by the family before the breakdown of the marriage: see s25(2)(c) MCA 1973. It is assumed that Beryl and Abe had a limited lifestyle given Beryl's problems in 1994. The court will seek to ensure that Beryl does not suffer any further drop in her lifestyle or that at any drop is shared equitably between the parties. The court will have regard to the age of the parties and the duration of the marriage: see s25(2)(d) MCA 1973. The ages of the parties are not given. They may well be relatively young if they met as students in 1985. Both parties will be given credit for a marriage which has lasted seven years. The court may also have regard to the period before the marriage when they lived together. The courts do not normally have regard to a period of cohabitation before marriage since the commitment of marriage has not been entered into. However, Beryl's contribution in housing Abe and supporting him financially while he qualified could be included as part of the overall circumstances and should strengthen Beryl's claim: see *S v S (financial provision) (post-divorce cohabitation)* (1994).

The court will look at the contributions which each of the parties has made or is likely to make in the foreseeable future to the welfare of the family. This will include any contribution made by looking after the home or caring for the family: see s25(2)(f) MCA 1973. Beryl can be advised that this consideration is likely to be a significant factor since she gave up work to act as a mother. The court may have to make a judgment about whether this was reasonable in light of Abe's view that she should have stayed in work. Courts appear to accept as reasonable a mother's desire to give up work in order to care for very young children. Her future contribution in caring for the two children will also be noted by the court. Beryl can be advised that these factors are likely to increase any award for financial provision: see *Wachtel v Wachtel* (1973). Her contribution before the marriage may also be considered as outlined above. Abe's contribution in helping the family during Beryl's depression is likely to strengthen his case. His dismissal from his employment is difficult to criticise if it was as a result of him trying to help Beryl and the children. Beryl can be advised that the court is unlikely to consider the conduct of the parties unless that conduct is such that it would in the opinion of the court be inequitable to disregard it: see s25(2)(g) MCA 1973. The courts tend to treat financial provision as more of an arithmetical exercise than a moral one: see *Wachtel* v *Wachtel* and *Duxbury* v *Duxbury* (1987). The court may take both parties' positive conduct into account in their efforts to bring up the children despite all the difficulties.

The court will also consider the value of any benefit which each party will lose as a result of the divorce: see s25B–D MCA 1973. The question does not make it clear whether Beryl will lose any rights in any pension Abe may have. Given Abe's interrupted work history and likely age it seems unlikely that he will have built up much in the way of pension rights. The court is likely to be concerned that Beryl has some kind of provision for the future given her lack of any kind of cover in her own right. This includes the power to make a deferred pension order whereby when Abe's pensions come into effect provision can be made for Beryl.

The court will also consider whether it would appropriate to make orders whereby the financial obligations of Abe to Beryl will terminate as soon after the divorce decree as the court considers just and reasonable: see s25A(1) MCA 1973. If the court makes a maintenance order in her favour the court must consider whether it would be appropriate to limit the term of the order to such a term as would enable Beryl to adjust without undue hardship to the termination of her financial dependence on Abe: see s25A(2) MCA 1973. Beryl can be advised that the courts have shown some reluctance in imposing a clean break where a former wife is in a financially weak position, particularly where she may find it difficult to get back into the job market or to find any work with a reasonable income.

With regard to financial provision for the two children Beryl should be advised that jurisdiction now rests with the Child Support Agency: see s8 Child Support Act 1991. As a result she will have to make a separate application to the CSA should she wish to oblige Abe to provide for their two children. The CSA would assess child support on the basis of a fixed formula. The formula includes an assessment of the children's 'maintenance requirements' (which includes an element for Beryl), a calculation of the income of both Beryl and Abe, calculating a protected income for Abe and then reaching a final figure. As Beryl may be aware, child support assessments can be high (though recent changes aim to ensure that such an assessment would be no more than 30 per cent of Abe's income). Only a limited account would be taken of Enid and the forthcoming baby in assessing Abe's disposal income. Beryl may also be aware that the CSA has a backlog of work and may not be able to respond quickly to any application she makes. It is possible for Beryl and Abe to reach an agreement between themselves as to what Abe can afford to support the children. It would then be possible to incorporate such an agreement into a court order. Abe may be willing to consider this if the alternative of a child support assessment would work against him. If agreement is not possible then Beryl must approach the CSA and await their assessment of Abe. Given that Abe's income may be limited it may be that any child support is limited. If this is the case then Beryl may claim state benefit to make the difference. If she is already on benefit she is likely to be obliged to apply for child support or suffer a reduction in her benefit.

Beryl should be advised that the court is likely to provide her with accommodation suitable to her standard of living and suitable for the children. Given her contribution towards the purchase of the family home and the factors outlined above, it is likely that the court will transfer the home into her sole name. There is insufficient information to give clear advice on what financial support Abe can provide Beryl. The financial support of the children would be a matter for the Child Support Agency and again there is insufficient information to state what child support assessment is likely to be made.

With regard to the upbringing of the children, the divorce court would have considered the arrangements made for the children and asked whether it should exercise its powers under the Children Act 1989 before granting a decree absolute of divorce: see s41 MCA 1973. No disputes or difficulties over the arrangements for the children are revealed so it is assumed that the court has already declared that there is no need to exercise its powers. Beryl should be advised that the courts are not likely to interfere with what the parents agree amongst themselves unless there is concern that such arrangements will harm the children. The courts will not make any order concerning the children unless making that order would be better for the child than making no order at all: s1(5) CA 1989. The only matter which is not clear is whether Beryl has fully recovered from her depression. Even if the arrangements for the children were such as to cause the court to consider using its powers the decree could still be made absolute if there are exceptional circumstances which make it desirable to so direct. If there was a dispute about the children's residence then the court could make a residence order determining where the children should live. If there was a dispute about Abe having contact with the children the court make a contact order determining when the children should have contact with their father. In determining any such dispute the court would consider that the welfare of the children was its paramount consideration: s1(1) CA 1989. It would also consider that any delay in resolving the dispute would be likely to be harmful to the children: s1(2) CA 1989. If an application to the court was opposed it would consider a checklist of matters in deciding how to resolve the dispute: s1(3), (4) CA 1989. In the absence of any specific disputes or problems concerning the children being identified it is not possible to give any more specific advice.

QUESTION FIVE

Ann and Bill began living together three years ago in a house they bought in joint names. Last year Ann's sister died and since then she and Bill have looked after her sister's two orphaned children. Bill had only reluctantly agreed to look after them, and their presence caused a rift between Ann and Bill. Their relationship deteriorated to the point where there was very little contact between them other than during day-to-day necessities. Bill developed a mental condition, one symptom of which was agoraphobia. His behaviour became very unpredictable. Ann showed no sympathy for or understanding of his condition and on one occasion, after accusing him of giving no help in running the home, she started to push him out into the street, telling him to go to the shops. He struck her several times, observed by the children, who became very upset by what they saw.

Bill entered hospital for treatment for his condition two weeks ago. He made frequent telephone calls to Ann to apologise for his behaviour. On some occasions the telephone was answered by one of the children, who became very distressed on hearing Bill's voice.

Bill is due to leave hospital in one week's time. Ann now feels that she needs breathing space to allow her and the children to recover, but if Bill's condition does not improve, she would not want him to return to the house.

Advise Ann.

University of London LLB Examination
(for External Students) Family Law June 1997 Q5

General Comment

On 1 October 1997 Part IV of the Family Law Act 1996 came into force. It codified and revised the law dealing with occupation of the family home. In particular, it laid down the framework for occupation and non-molestation orders. This question invites the student to apply the new law to its particular facts. The difficulties of mental illness and how this affects the 'balance of harm' are added ingredients.

Skeleton Solution

- Application for a non-molestation order – s42 FLA 1996.
- Application for an occupation order under s33 FLA 1996 – consideration of:
    - housing needs and resources of each of the parties and the children;
    - financial resources of each of parties;
    - effect of order or not making order on health, safety or well-being of the parties and the children;
    - the conduct of the parties;
    - balance of harm test.
- The special circumstances of mental illness.
- Whether an application can be made ex parte and attaching a power of arrest.
- Long term solutions for Ann.

Suggested Solution

Ann seeks advice about not allowing Bill back should his condition not have improved. Generally she would like 'breathing space' and any advice should explain how she can achieve this.

Ann can be advised that she can apply to the High Court, county court or magistrates' court for a non-molestation order prohibiting Bill from molesting either her or the children: see s42 Family Law Act (FLA) 1996. She is able to apply for such an order since she and Bill are 'associated persons' (because they are former cohabitants: s62(3)(b) FLA 1996). Ann can be advised that 'molestation' has been given a wide meaning and includes pestering or harassing behaviour: see *Vaughan* v *Vaughan* (1973). It can include annoying telephone calls: see *Horner* v *Horner* (1983). It can include involuntary behaviour: see *Wooton* v *Wooton* (1984). In deciding whether to make a non-molestation order and, if so, in what terms, Ann can be advised that the court will have regard to all the circumstances, including the need to secure the health, safety and well-being of both Ann and the children. The children, though not the natural children of either Ann or Bill, are 'relevant children' because they are living with Ann: see ss62(2) and 63(1) FLA 1996. Bill's unpredictable behaviour, his assault on Ann in sight of the children and his phone calls which upset the children, are likely to amount to molestation of both Ann and the children. As a result, the court is likely to grant an order prohibiting him from molesting both Ann and the children in order to secure their health, safety and well-being. The order can prevent molestation in general or refer to particular acts of molestation or to both (eg be directed specifically at the telephone calls). It is likely that the court will limit the term of any non-molestation order. In the past a period of three months was the starting point: see *Practice Direction (injunction: domestic violence)* (1978).

Such an order may provide Ann with the protection and breathing space she needs. However, if she wishes to prevent Bill from returning to the home she should make application for an occupation order at the same time as applying for the non-molestation order. Since she is the joint owner of the property she has a legal right to occupy and can apply for a non-molestation order: see s33 FLA 1996. She can make application against Bill since he is an 'associated person' (as already outlined). Such an occupation order could exclude Bill from the home and from a defined area in which the home is included: see s33(3) FLA 1996. In deciding whether to make such an order the court will have regard to all the circumstances including particular matters: see s33(6) FLA 1996. The court will consider Ann's and the children's housing needs and resources and take into account Ann's financial resources. It will compare these with Bill's housing needs and resources. There is no information about either Ann's or Bill's finances. Bill's finances may be limited as a result of his illness and hospital admission. It is assumed that Ann has greater housing needs compared to Bill since she has the children to look after. However, Bill may find it difficult to find alternative accommodation due to his mental illness. The availability of local authority or housing association accommodation may be important: see *Thurley* v *Smith* (1985). The court will then look at the likely effect of an occupation order on the health, safety and well-being of Bill, and will compare it with the likely effect on the health, safety and well-being of Ann and the children if an order is not made. The court will also look at the conduct of Bill and Ann in relation to each other and otherwise. The court may have to make a value judgment on how reasonably or unreasonably the parties have acted. Bill's behaviour appears to be upsetting the children. His assault on Ann is likely to be viewed as a serious matter. His telephone calls may be unreasonable if they are both too frequent and clearly unwelcome. However, Ann's behaviour may not escape criticism if the court finds that she has been unsympathetic or lacking in understanding. In another context the courts have said a spouse would be expected to share the burden imposed upon the family as a result of mental illness but that there was a limit to what was reasonable for a spouse to put up with: see *Katz* v *Katz* (1972) and *Thurlow* v *Thurlow* (1975). Though Ann and Bill are not married the court may apply a similar test. Ann should be advised that the needs of the children are not paramount when the court is considering making an occupation order. The fact that an occupation order is in their interests does not oblige the court to make the order: see *Richards* v *Richards* (1983). However the interests of the children and the affect on them of Bill's behaviour is likely to be important in balancing the above considerations: see *Phillips* v *Phillips* (1973).

The court will apply a 'balance of harm' test: see s33(7) FLA 1996. If it appears to the court that either Ann or the children is likely to suffer significant harm as a result of Bill's behaviour if an occupation order is not made then the court must make the occupation order, unless Bill is likely to suffer significant harm if the order is made and the harm he is likely to suffer is as great or greater than the harm Ann or the children are likely to suffer as a result of Bill's conduct. 'Harm' is given a wide meaning and includes in the case of Ann ill-treatment or impairment of health and in the case of the children (assuming they are under 18) ill-treatment or impairment of health or development: see s63(1) FLA 1996. 'Significant harm' has been defined as any harm which the court should take into account in considering the injured party's future: see *Humberside County Council* v *B* (1993). In this case the court will have to balance the likely harm caused if Bill returns home 'uncured' against the harm which could be caused to Bill if he has no other suitable address to go to. It is difficult to advise Ann on how the court will apply the balance of harm test without more information on Bill's behaviour while he has been in hospital and his prognosis on release from hospital. If the balance of harm test is resolved in Ann's and the children's favour the occupation order must be made. If it is not, then the court could still make the order but is not obliged to do so.

If the occupation order is made the court could make orders against Bill to pay any mortgage or any other outgoings affecting the home or be responsible for its repair and maintenance: see s40 FLA 1996. In the absence of more information it is difficult to advise further on this point.

It is possible for Ann to apply for both the non-molestation and occupation order ex parte (ie without notifying Bill): see s45 FLA 1996. The court will only allow this if it considers it just and convenient to do so having regard to all the circumstances and in particular certain matters: see s45(2) FLA 1996. The court will assess any risk of significant harm to Ann or the children attributable to Bill's conduct if the order is not made immediately, whether Ann will be deterred or prevented from pursuing the application if an order is not made immediately or whether Bill would deliberately evade service. The court is unlikely to allow an application to be made ex parte since Bill is presently in hospital. He can be served with an application while he is in hospital for a hearing either while he is still in hospital or just after his release. Ann and the children do not appear to be in immediate risk from Bill, with the exception of the telephone calls. This could be dealt with by a change of telephone number if Ann so wished.

If an occupation or non-molestation order is made and it appears to the court that Bill has used or threatened violence against Ann or the children then it must attach a power of arrest unless satisfied that in all the circumstances Ann or the children will be adequately protected without a power of arrest: see s47 FLA 1996. Since Bill has used violence against Ann the court will be obliged to attach a power of arrest unless it is so satisfied. Since Bill has mental health problems this may increase the need for Ann to be protected by a power of arrest. If a power of arrest is attached, then any breach of an occupation or non-molestation order can be dealt with by a police officer arresting Bill forthwith and bringing him before a court within 24 hours. The court can then deal with Bill for breaching the court order by way of contempt.

As an alternative to an order the court can accept an undertaking from Bill that he will not molest Ann or the children and/or will leave the home: see s46 FLA 1996. This will depend on whether Bill would give such an undertaking and whether Bill is in a mental state to provide such an undertaking. In addition, the court cannot accept an undertaking where a power of arrest would be attached to an order. No power of arrest can be attached to any undertaking. As a result the court would have to be satisfied that Ann and the children would be adequately safeguarded by such an undertaking without an order with a power of arrest.

Ann should be advised that any occupation or non-molestation order is likely to be granted only for a limited period since the court will be concerned to provide a 'first aid' solution. Ann will need to look for a long term solution. This could include Ann applying to the county court or High Court for an order transferring the home to her sole name for the benefit of the children. She could only so apply if she is a guardian of the children or has a residence order for them in her favour: see s15 and Sch 1 CA 1989. Otherwise she could seek to buy out Bill's interest in the house so that she and the children can remain in the house and Bill would have to find alternative accommodation.

QUESTION SIX

Linda and Matt have lived together for 16 years but they never married. They have two children: Nat who is 15 and Olivia who is 14.

Nat has been unhappy at home for two years because he thinks his parents are too strict with him (Linda believes in corporal punishment but Matt does not). Nat has read that children can 'divorce' their parents and wishes to know how he can divorce Linda and Matt. He wants to live with his 15-year-old girlfriend Kate and her parents, who have agreed that he can share Kate's self-contained apartment built on to their house. Nat knows that his parents will object.

Olivia has recently become pregnant. She wishes to have an abortion but Matt, who is an active member of a pro-life movement, refuses to allow an abortion. Linda thinks that Olivia should decide.

Advise Nat and Olivia.

University of London LLB Examination
(for External Students) Family Law June 1997 Q6

General Comment

This question approaches private law applications under the Children Act 1989 from the interesting perspective of children seeking orders. First, the considerations involved in a child applying for a residence order need to be outlined, and second the difficult area of the medical treatment of a child against the wishes of a parent needs to be discussed.

Skeleton Solution

- A child applying for a residence order – s8 CA 1989 – requirement of leave – s10 CA 1989 – likely approach of the High Court.
- Application by third parent for a residence order on behalf of a child – requirement of leave – s10 CA 1989.
- No order principle, delay principle and application of welfare checklist, in particular:
    - wishes and feelings of child;
    - likely effect on child of a change in his circumstances;
    - any harm the child has suffered or is at risk of suffering;
    - the capabilities of the child's parents and of his girlfriend's parents.
- The medical treatment of a child – child's capacity to consent to medical treatment – *Gillick* competency – the extent of the parental veto – application for a specific issue order/prohibited steps order – no order principle, delay principle and application of welfare checklist.

Suggested Solution

Nat requires advice on his wish to 'divorce' his parents, Linda and Matt, and his wish to live with his girlfriend and her parents. Olivia requires advice on whether she can have an abortion.

Nat's situation will be dealt with firstly. He should be advised that it is not accurate to say that he can 'divorce' his parents. More accurately he can apply to the court for an order allowing him to live apart from his parents, namely he seek to apply for a residence order under s8 Children Act (CA) 1989. Nat should be advised that he cannot apply for a residence order as of right. He must obtain the leave of the court: see s10(1)(a)(ii) CA 1989. The court may only grant Nat leave to make such an application if it is satisfied that he has sufficient understanding to make an application for a residence order: see s10(8) CA 1989. The court will have to make an assessment of Nat's maturity and degree of understanding. For these purposes Nat should be advised that his welfare is not paramount (as it is if the application proceeds to a full hearing). If it considers that Nat is not sufficiently mature and lacks an appropriate degree of understanding of the application and its consequences the court will refuse leave. If it is so satisfied it has a discretion whether or not to grant leave. It will balance the need to give Nat's wishes serious attention against any harm which may befall him should his application be contested. For example, he could have to listen to his parents opposing his application and he could be cross-examined on their behalf: see *Re C (residence: child's application for leave)* (1995). As a result of the difficult issues in such an application he would have to apply to the High Court: see *Practice Direction* (1993).

Alternatively, he could ask Kate's parents to ask for leave to apply for a residence order on his behalf. They could only apply for an order as of right with the consent of each person who has parental responsibility for Nat: see s10(5)(c)(iii) CA 1989. Linda appears to have sole parental responsibility for Nat: see s4(2)(a) CA 1989. Matt, as an unmarried father, will not have parental responsibility for Nat unless he has made a parental responsibility agreement with Linda or has obtained a parental responsibility order from the court: see s4(1) CA 1989. It is assumed that in any event Linda would not consent to Kate's parents applying for a residence order. They could also apply as of right if Nat had been living with them for three years: see s10(5)(b) CA 1989. This does not appear to be the case. As a result Kate's parents would have to obtain the court's leave to make the application. In deciding whether to grant them leave to make the application the court would consider the nature of the proposed application, their connection with Nat and any risk there might be that the proposed application would disrupt Nat's life to such an extent that he would be harmed by it: see s10(9) CA 1989. Again Nat's welfare would not be the paramount consideration: see *Re A and Others (minors) (residence order)* (1992).

The court could consider the question of leave ex parte (ie without informing Nat's parents), but is more likely to direct that they have the opportunity to make representations as to whether leave should be granted.

Assuming that leave was granted to either Nat or to Kate's parents to apply for a residence order on his behalf then the court would consider the circumstances of his application. Nat's welfare would be the paramount consideration: see s1(1) CA 1989. The court would also endeavour to determine the application without delay since it has to assume that any delay is likely to prejudice Nat's welfare: see s1(2) CA 1989. To this end it is likely to lay down a timetable which the parties must comply with in order to prepare for the hearing. It will not make any order unless it considers that doing so would be better for Nat than making no order at all: see s1(5) CA 1989. In other words it must be satisfied that any order it makes would have some positive benefit for him. If the application is contested, as seems likely, the court must have regard to particular matters: see s1(3),(4) CA 1989. It will consider Nat's wishes and feelings considered in the light of his age and understanding: see s1(3)(a) CA 1989. Since Nat is aged 15 his wishes and feelings are likely to carry considerable weight. Nat should be advised that once he reaches the age of 16 the court would not normally be allowed to make any order since a child of that age can 'vote with his feet': see s9(7) CA 1989. Indeed if the court does make an order then that order cannot extend beyond his 16th birthday, unless there are exceptional circumstances: see s9(6) CA 1989. The court will consider Nat's physical, emotional and educational needs and the likely affect on him of any change in his circumstances: see s1(3)(b) and (c) CA 1989. The court will have to assess how any move to live with Kate and her parents would affect him. The court will consider his age, sex, background and any relevant characteristics: see s1(3)(d) CA 1989. The court will also consider any harm which he has suffered or is at risk of suffering and the capabilities of his parents and of Kate's parents in meeting his needs: see s1(3)(e) and (f) CA 1989. These two considerations are likely to crucial to Nat's case. If the court finds that his parents have harmed his welfare and have demonstrated that they are not capable of meeting his needs, while Kate's parents can meet his needs, then his application is likely to be a strong one. However, if the court finds that his parents are capable and have not harmed Nat or are unlikely to do so then it may decide that his wishes to live with Kate and her parents lack sufficient substance. At present English law allows parents to reasonably chastise their children. Without more specific information about how strict Nat's parents are it is difficult to advise in more detail.

One difficulty is that both Nat and his girlfriend are 15 years of age, below the age of consent for sexual intercourse. If they have sexual intercourse then Nat may fall foul of the criminal law: see s6 Sexual Offences Act 1956. Though prosecutions in these circumstances are rare the court may not feel able to sanction a situation in which Nat shares Kate's self-contained apartment. However, even if Nat's case is not a strong one, whether on this ground or another, once he reaches the age of 16 he can 'vote with his feet'. As already outlined the court is unlikely to grant any application by his parents to prevent him living where he wishes.

Olivia wishes to be advised on whether she can have an abortion given Matt's refusal to consent to this. As already outlined Matt, as an unmarried father, does not have parental responsibility for Olivia. This may limit his ability to prevent Olivia from having an abortion. If Linda has sole parental responsibility for Olivia then she can consent to the abortion. It is also possible for Olivia to determine her own treatment. Generally once a child reaches the age of 16 she can effectively consent to medical treatment without parental consent: see s8 Family Law Reform Act 1969. Where a child is under 16 the question of whether a child's consent would be effective to protect a doctor against legal action for infringement of parental rights will depend on the child's maturity and understanding and the nature of the treatment: see *Gillick v West Norfolk and Wisbech Area Health Authority* (1985). If the court determines that Olivia has the maturity and understanding to make an informed decision about having an abortion then it could allow the operation without parental consent. The objection of Matt could be considered but would not prevent an abortion which the court considered was in her best interests: see *Re P (a minor)* (1986).

As Olivia's father Matt could apply for a prohibited steps order to prevent the abortion even though he lacks parental responsibility: see ss8 and 10(4) CA 1989. If he did make such an application and it was opposed by Linda and Olivia then the court would apply similar considerations as with the residence application concerning Nat. Olivia's welfare would be paramount. Her wishes and feelings would be likely to carry considerable weight because of her age, assuming she is mature and understanding. Any likely harm to her of having a baby she does not want would be considered. Having a baby against her will may in particular harm her education and other aspects of her development. In all these circumstances it is likely that any application by Matt for a prohibited steps order is unlikely to succeed.

Matt could endeavour to obtain parental responsibility, either by agreement with Linda or by court order. If he applies for a court order under s4(1)(a) CA 1989 the court is likely to grant his application since he is likely to have shown commitment towards his children, have a relationship with them and be motivated in their interests: see *Re P (a minor)(parental responsibility order)* (1994). However, even with this status if Linda gives her consent and/or Olivia is *Gillick* competent then the abortion can take place without his consent. Where more than one parent has parental responsibility for a child each of them may act alone in meeting that responsibility: see s2(7) CA 1989. This further strengthens the case for Olivia.

QUESTION SEVEN

To what extent, in your opinion, has the Children Act 1989 achieved the aim of diminishing the powers of the state while asserting the autonomy of the family? What is the right balance? What part have the courts played in striking the appropriate balance?

University of London LLB Examination
(for External Students) Family Law June 1997 Q7

General Comment

This essay-style question invites a discussion about the 'public law' parts of the Children Act 1989. The Act laid down a code for local authorities to respond to requests for help for parents in difficulties with their children, to deal with the emergency protection of children and the taking of children into the care or their supervision. The Act tried create a balance between family autonomy and the powers of the local authority to protect. Has the Act created the right balance? This requires an outline of the relevant parts of the Act and how the courts have played their role in striking the appropriate balance, particularly *Re H and R (child sexual abuse: standard of proof)*.

Skeleton Solution

- Part III of the Children Act 1989 – provision of accommodation for children with the consent of the children (ss20–22 CA 1989).
- Part V CA 1989 – protection of children – emergency protection orders (s44) – child assessment orders (s43) – police protection (s46) – ex parte applications.
- Part IV CA 1989 – application for care/supervision orders (s31) – interim care/supervision orders (s38) – application of 'threshold criteria' criteria (*Re M* (1994) and *Re H and R* (1996)).
- The state intervening in private law applications (s37 CA 1989).

Suggested Solution

The Children Act 1989 which came into force in 1991 codified many areas of family law, particularly the law concerning the powers of the local authority in relation to protecting children. It endeavoured to strike a balance between the autonomy of the family and the power of the 'state' (invariably the social services department of the local authority) in protecting children from harm. Has the Act achieved that balance? What is the right balance? Since 1991 how have the courts interpreted the relevant provisions of the Children Act 1989 in striking the appropriate balance?

Part III of the Children Act 1989 lays down a duty on every local authority to provide accommodation for any child in need within its area who appears to them to require accommodation as a result of there being no person with parental responsibility for that child, or the child being lost or abandoned, or the person caring the child being prevented for providing the child with suitable accommodation or care: see s20(1) CA 1989. This is very much a voluntary arrangement in that the local authority cannot accommodate a child if any person with parental responsibility for the child and who is able and willing to provide accommodation for the child objects: see s20(7) CA 1989. Furthermore, any person with parental responsibility for the child may remove the child from local authority accommodation without notice: see s20(8) CA 1989. This Part of the Act replaced the parental rights resolution procedure under the Child Care Act 1980, whereby the local authority could prevent the return of children voluntarily accommodated with them by parents. This procedure was criticised for being unfair to parents who asked the local authority for help in looking after their children only to find they could not have their children returned to them – a form of care proceedings by the back door. The reform of the law in this area appears to have been welcomed in redressing the balance between the role of the state in providing help and the rights of the family to decide the extent of that help.

Part V of the Children Act (CA) 1989 lays down the procedures for the protection of children in emergencies. The most commonly used forms of protection appear to be emergency protection orders (under s44 CA 1989) and police protection (under s46 CA 1989). In order to obtain an emergency protection order any person (usually a local authority social worker) must satisfy the court that there is reasonable cause to believe that the child concerned is likely to suffer significant harm if the child is not removed to local authority accommodation or does not remain where s/he is then being accommodated (eg a hospital): see s44(1) CA 1989. There are two other grounds for applying for an emergency protection order but this first ground is the most commonly used. The application is made to the family proceedings court with at least one day's notice to the child's parents: see Sch 1 Family Proceedings Courts (Children Act 1989) Rules 1989. Application can be made to the justices' clerk for leave to make the application ex parte (ie without informing the parents): r4(4) FPC(CA 1989)R 1991. In deciding whether to grant leave the justices' clerk will balance the need to safeguard a child from any immediate danger or risk of harm against the right of a parent to put his/her point of view across to the court considering the application. Many applications for emergency protection orders are made ex parte. If the order is granted, then a copy of the order and a copy of the application must be served on any parent with parental responsibility within 48 hours after the making of the emergency protection order: r4(4) 1991 Rules. The order may only be made for up to eight days, though it may be renewed on application with notice to the parents for a further seven days: see s45 CA 1989 and Sch 1 1991 Rules. Once 72 hours have elapsed from the making of the order the parents can apply to discharge the order on the basis that there were no grounds for making the order in the first place: see s45(8)–(9) CA 1989. While an emergency protection order is in force the applicant has a duty to allow the parents to have reasonable contact with their child subject to any direction to the contrary from the court: see s44(13) CA 1989. This emergency procedure replaced the place of safety order procedure under the Children and Young Persons Act (CYPA) 1969 whereby the equivalent of the emergency protection order could be made for up to 28 days. There was no right of appeal against a 28-day place of safety order, so the parents could only take action to recover their child once the order had expired. The Children Act 1989 has therefore significantly increased the rights of parents to take action to recover a child taken away from them by court order in an emergency.

A second form of removing children in emergencies is by police protection. This allows a police constable who has reasonable cause to believe that a child would otherwise be likely to suffer significant harm to remove the child to suitable accommodation or prevent the child's removal from hospital or other place: see s46(1) CA 1989. The limit to police protection is 72 hours: s46(6). There are safeguards to inform parents that a child is in police protection and to allow reasonable contact between the child and his/her parents. This replaced a police protection procedure which allowed a child to be removed from his/her parents for up to eight days: see s28 CYPA 1969.

A further response to an emergency is an application for a child assessment order: see s43 CA

1989. This order, if granted, obliges a parent to produce a child for an assessment as to the child's health or development, and does not involve the child being removed from the parents' care (save for the purpose of the assessment). This order appears to be rarely used. It was intended to allow a local authority to examine a child where there was reasonable suspicion of significant harm before making any decision to remove a child under an emergency protection order or using care proceedings.

Part IV of the Children Act 1989 allows a local authority to apply for a care or supervision order with respect to a child: see s31 CA 1989. Such an application must be made to the family proceedings court with at least three days' notice to the child's parents: see Sch 1 1991 Rules. Since applications for care or supervision orders normally take a number of months to be finalised, the initial application for the court to consider is normally an interim care or supervision order: see s38 CA 1989. A court can only make an interim care order (which allows a local authority to remove a child from his/her parents for up to eight weeks on the first order) if it is satisfied that there are reasonable grounds for believing that the circumstances with respect to the child meet the threshold criteria. The court can only make a care order if it is satisfied that that the child is suffering or is likely to suffer significant harm, and that the harm, or likelihood of harm, is attributable to a lack of reasonable parental care or the child being beyond parental control: see s31(2) CA 1989. The key to removing a child from his/her parents is the threshold criteria. This one criteria replaced a series of grounds for the making of care orders under s1(2) CYPA 1969 which were not entirely consistent. For example, the commission of a single criminal offence by a child could lead to a care order being made: see s1(2)(f) CYPA 1969. The threshold criteria was designed to provide a single criterion which would promote a more consistent and fairer approach, particularly from the parents' point of view. It appears that the Children Act 1989 has succeeded to a large extent in this respect. The Act provides a wide definition of harm: see s31(9) CA 1989. The word 'significant' is not defined except to the extent of comparing a child's development with that of a similar child: see s31(10) CA 1989 and *Re O (a minor) (care proceedings: education)* (1992). The courts have attempted various definitions of varying degrees of usefulness. One attempt was to liken 'significant harm' to an elephant, difficult to describe but one knew it when one saw it! This appears to reflect how courts have applied the phrase. There have been some difficulties in defining the phrase 'is suffering significant harm' until the House of Lords resolved the matter in *Re M (a minor) (care order: threshold conditions)* (1994). That decision appears to have resolved that particular difficulty so that both the local authority and parents know how the courts will interpret the phrase. More controversially, the House of Lords has given guidance on the phrase 'is likely to suffer significant harm' in *Re H and R (child sexual abuse: standard of proof)* (1996). This phrase involves an assessment of risk. The majority decision was that s31(2) marked the boundary line between the interests of the parents in caring for their own children and the interests of the child, particularly where it was in the child's interests to be cared for by others. The word 'likely' meant a real possibility, namely a possibility which could not be ignored having regard to the nature and gravity of the feared harm in the particular case. A court had to make findings on disputed facts and then evaluate the risks of significant harm befalling the child. It was held that parents were not to be at risk of having their children taken away on the basis only of suspicions. This decision swung a delicate balance in favour of the parents. It may make the threshold criteria more difficult to satisfy in cases of suspected sexual abuse in which suspicions are many but hard proof thin on the ground. Even if the threshold criteria is satisfied the court has a discretion as to which kind of order to make. It must consider the welfare checklist: see s1(3),(4) CA 1989. This includes considering a full range of orders including a supervision order or a residence order:

see *Humberside County Council* v *B* (1993). This contrasts with the previous situation when either a care order could be made or no order at all.

If a care order is made then the local authority shares parental responsibility with the child's parents, though the exercise of the parents' parental responsibility can be limited by the local authority, particularly in terms of with whom the child lives: see s33(3) CA 1989. There is a presumption of reasonable contact in favour of the parents which can only be limited by court order: see s34 CA 1989. The courts have emphasised that any local authority plans which involves limiting or ending parental contact do not bind the court: see *Re B (minors) (termination of contact: paramount consideration)* (1993). The court can require the local authority to justify its plans to the extent that they limit or exclude contact between a child and his/her parents. In that particular case a local authority wished to terminate contact between two children in care and their mother. The court refused to allow this since it recognised that the mother's potential to improve and care for her children needed to be investigated. Both the courts and local authorities recognise the importance of a child's parents continuing to play a part in the child's life even after the making of a care order. Their right to withhold consent to an adoption remains as under the pre-existing law.

The Children Act 1989 also restricted the use of wardship, particularly as an alternative to care proceedings: see s100(2) CA 1989. This again reflects the need for consistency in deciding when a child should be removed from parents.

The Children Act 1989 removed a whole series of powers to make care orders in the context of private law applications. These powers were seen to be inconsistent and arbitrary. There is now no power to make a care order as a result of concerns raised during a private law application. The only power is to ask the local authority to investigate the circumstances with a view to deciding whether to bring care proceedings: see s37 CA 1989. This reform of the law has been most welcome since it again promotes consistency and removes powers which could be exercised unfairly and arbitrarily.

In general terms the Children Act 1989 has encouraged local authorities to work with parents rather than against them. This is reflected in the no order principle in s1(2) CA 1989, whereby a court cannot make an order unless it is satisfied that it would provide some positive benefit for the child. Applications for emergency orders or for care orders are seen as something of a last resort, eg when agreement between the parents and the local authority has broken down or where the nature of the harm or risk of harm to the child is too great and immediate to allow the local authority to wait to work with the parents. In conclusion, the Children Act 1989 appears to have achieved a much better balance between the powers of the state and the autonomy of the family. When compared with the law under the Child Care Act 1980 (particularly parental rights resolutions) and the Children and Young Persons Act 1969, the Children Act 1989 provides a much fairer and coherent code for child protection. The courts appear to have recognised the importance of this balance and have laid guidelines to protect parental autonomy (particularly in *Re H and R*).

QUESTION EIGHT

Peter and Ruth, who are husband and wife, separated when Peter left England eight months ago to work abroad. He returned after Ruth wrote to him to say that she had given birth to a son, Simon, although she told Peter that he was not the father. Recently Ruth was badly injured when, after drinking alcohol, she crashed her car. She had experienced problems with alcohol in the past. Ruth's mother tried to care for Simon after the accident but had difficulties coping with him. Neighbours informed the local authority that they thought the child was being neglected. The local authority took over the care of Simon and placed him with foster-parents. Peter has tried to discover Simon's whereabouts and, if he succeeds, intends to take Simon abroad with him.

The local authority now has told the foster-parents to return Simon as it is concerned that Peter may discover Simon's whereabouts and take him away.

Consider the steps Peter may take to achieve what he thinks is best for Simon, and what steps the local authority may take to secure what it thinks is best for the child.

University of London LLB Examination
(for External Students) Family Law June 1997 Q8

General Comment

This questions mixes issues of paternity, the rights of parents in relation to an accommodated child and what steps a local authority can take to protect a child without parental consent. The candidate has to demonstrate an under-standing of the status of a child in terms of the presumption of legitimacy and how it can be rebutted. This will include a discussion of blood tests. The law relating to the local authority accommodating a child needs to be explained. Finally, an outline of the powers of the local authority to intervene compulsorily needs to be given.

Skeleton Solution

• Status of the child – presumption of legitimacy and how this can be rebutted – sterility, non-access and blood tests.
• Accommodation of child by local authority and right of parent to ask for child's return (s20 CA 1989).
• Application by local authority for compulsory powers to protect a child – emergency protection order (s44) – interim care order (s38) – care order (s31 CA 1989) – grounds and evidence for obtaining such orders.
• Wardship and restrictions on its use by a local authority (s100 CA 1989).
• Application by mother for residence/prohibited steps order or application for leave by grandmother for same orders (ss8 and 10 CA 1989).

Suggested Solution

Peter asks for advice on what steps he may take to discover Simon's whereabouts and to take Simon abroad with him. The local authority asks for advice on what steps it can take to secure what it considers best for the child.

First, Peter should be advised that his status in relation to Simon needs to be established. Ruth has said that Peter is not Simon's father. Peter should be advised that since he and Ruth were married when Simon was born there is a common law presumption that Simon is the legitimate child of them both (the presumption of legitimacy). This presumption may be rebutted on a balance of probabilities: see s26 Family Law Reform Act 1969. However, Peter should be advised that the courts have considered the status of a child to be a grave matter so that the burden of rebutting the presumption is more than a narrow balance of probabilities: see *W* v *K* *(proof of paternity)* (1988) and *Serio* v *Serio* (1983). The presumption can be rebutted if Peter is sterile or if Peter was away during the time when Simon must have been conceived. The court will apply the present-day standards of medical science in deciding the possible dates of conception, taking into account the nature of the pregnancy and when the child was born: see *Preston-Jones* v *Preston-Jones* (1951). The question does not give sufficient details to be able to advise in more detail. Assuming that Peter is not sterile and that he was present with Ruth during the probable date(s) of conception then the presumption of legitimacy will apply. It is also possible to rebut the presumption of legitimacy through the use of blood tests. In any civil proceedings in which the paternity of a child falls to be determined the court may on the application of any party to the proceedings direct that blood tests be carried out to ascertain the paternity of the child: see s20 FLRA 1969. If blood tests are directed it is probable that they will use the DNA method. This method is invariably treated as being conclusive in determining the issue of paternity: see *Re A (a minor)(paternity: refusal of blood test)* (1994). Blood samples would have to be taken from Peter, Ruth and Simon (with the consent of whoever has care and control of Simon). The taking of samples is voluntary so cannot be taken without consent. However, any failure to comply with the tests can lead to the court drawing such inferences as it considers proper: see s23(1) FLRA 1969. If, for example, Ruth objects to the taking of blood samples Peter can be advised that the court can infer that she knows the truth, namely that Peter is Simon's father, but is not prepared for the DNA tests to conclusively prove this. Ruth is unlikely to be able to argue that blood tests are not in Simon's best interests. The courts generally consider that establishing the truth of a child's parents is important so that the adult relationships with the child can be settled for the future: see *Re G (a minor) (blood tests)* (1994) and *Re H (a minor) (blood tests: parental rights)* (1996).

Assuming that Peter is presumed to be Simon's father, or it is proved that he is, he can ask the local authority to disclose Simon's whereabouts. The facts in the question suggest that Simon has been accommodated by the local authority at the request of Simon's mother or grandmother (pursuant to s20 Children Act 1989). This is a voluntary arrangement, presumably on the basis that the person caring for him (the grandmother) is prevented from providing Simon with suitable accommodation or care (whether or not permanently): see s20(1)(c) CA 1989. Peter, as the married father of Simon, has parental responsibility for Simon, which he shares with Ruth: see 2(1) CA 1989. The local authority will cease to be able to accommodate Simon if Peter is willing and able to provide him with accommodation: see s20(7) CA 1989. Furthermore, Peter may at any time remove Simon from the foster parents: see s20(8) CA 1989. This is presumably why the local authority has told the foster parents to return Simon either to his mother or grandmother. The local authority has a duty to consult Peter about what any decision taken with regard to Simon if it accepted or established that Peter is Simon's father (see s22(4) CA 1989), which indirectly includes an obligation to disclose his whereabouts. If Peter is able to remove Simon then he is free to make arrangements to take Simon abroad. Either the local authority or Ruth would have to apply to the court to prevent this if they considered it was not in Simon's best interests. Peter could apply for a residence order whereby a court orders that Simon reside with him. This would strengthen his position with regard to Simon. However, as a parent with parental responsibility he can act alone in meeting that parental responsibility: see s2(7) CA 1989. As a result he may consider it more appropriate to do what he considers best for Simon and leave it to the local authority or Ruth to apply to the court.

If it is established that Peter is not Simon's father then he lacks any parental responsibility for Simon and lacks the status to remove Simon or be involved in any local authority decision concerning him. In addition, he would lose any right to apply for a residence order. He would have to apply for leave to make such an application. Since he has no connection with Simon and he would be attempting to remove a child who was not his child, it would seem highly unlikely that leave would be granted: see s10(9) CA 1989.

The local authority asks for advice on what steps it may take to secure what it thinks is best for Simon. As already outlined above, it appears that the local authority are accommodating Simon in circumstances whereby Peter can remove him. The local authority would have to apply for a court order to acquire rights over Simon if it wished to prevent Peter from removing him. In an emergency the local authority could apply for an emergency protection order. It would have to satisfy the local family proceedings court that there is reasonable cause to believe that Simon is likely to suffer significant harm if he is not removed to local authority accommodation or kept in the place he is living (whether with foster parents, his grandmother or mother or otherwise): see s44(1) CA 1989. Harm is given a wide meaning and covers ill-treatment or the impairment of health or development. 'Development' means physical, intellectual, emotional, social or behavioural development and 'health' means physical or mental health. 'Ill-treatment' includes sexual abuse and forms of ill-treatment which are not physical: see s31(9) CA 1989. The court can compare Simon's health or development with that which could be reasonably expected of a similar child in order to decide if he has suffered significant harm: see s31(10) CA 1989. The local authority would have to provide sufficient material to the court to demonstrate a reasonable risk of actual or likely significant harm. If the local authority is able to so satisfy the court, the court can make the emergency protection order for up to eight days. Peter would be able to apply to discharge the order once 72 hours had elapsed from when it was made: see s45(9) CA 1989. The local authority could apply to extend the order for a further seven days: see s45(5) CA 1989.

During the period of the emergency protection order the local authority would have to decide whether to take the long-term step of applying for a care order in order to acquire parental responsibility for Simon and so secure what it thinks is best for his future even if either Peter or Ruth do not agree. If no application is made then the emergency protection order will lapse and Peter will be able to remove Simon, unless either Ruth or Simon's grandmother apply to the court for an order preventing this. If the local authority does decide to apply for a care order it is likely to ask the court to make an interim care order to cover the period needed to prepare the case for a final hearing. In order to obtain an interim care order it must satisfy the court that there are reasonable grounds for believing that the circumstances with respect to Simon are such that the 'threshold criteria' are made out: see s38(2) CA 1989. The 'threshold criteria' have to be satisfied before a court can consider making a care order. In Simon's case the court would have to be satisfied that Simon is suffering significant harm or is likely to suffer significant harm and that the harm, or likelihood of harm, is attributable to a lack of reasonable parental care or Simon being beyond parental control: see s31(2) CA 1989. There are insufficient details in the question to indicate what harm Simon has suffered or is at risk of suffering. It is said that Ruth has been badly injured in a car crash but not to what extent this has limited her abilities as a parent. It is also said that Simon's grandmother had difficulties in coping with him and that neighbours thought that he was being neglected. The local authority should be advised that clear evidence of harm or likelihood of harm will be required if they pursue an application for a care order. Mere suspicions would not be sufficient to satisfy the threshold criteria: see *Re H and R (child sexual abuse: standard of proof)* (1996).

The local authority may choose to work with Ruth or Simon's grandmother. If it does so and considers that Ruth can reasonably care for Simon, it could advise Ruth to apply to the court for a residence order and/or a prohibited steps order. The residence order would mean that Simon would live with her and the prohibited steps order could prevent Peter from removing Simon: see s8(1) CA 1989. If a residence order was made in Ruth's favour it would operate to prevent Simon's removal from the UK without Ruth's written consent or the leave of the court: see s13(1) CA 1989. This possibility does not seem likely in light of Simon having to be cared for by his grandmother. Simon's grandmother cannot apply for either a residence order or prohibited steps order as of right. She could, however, apply to the court for leave to make such applications: see s10(1)(a)(ii) CA 1989. The court would consider the nature of the applications, her connection with Simon and any risk there might be that the proposed application would disrupt Simon's life to such an extent that he would be harmed by it: see s10(9) CA 1989. If Simon was still being looked after by the local authority the court would also consider its plans for Simon's future and the wishes and feelings of Peter and Ruth. Again this possibility does not seem likely, since Simon's grandmother had sufficient problems in coping with him that she agreed to him being accommodated by the local authority.

One other possibility is for the local authority to apply to make Simon a ward of the High Court. This would have the effect of preventing any major decisions from being taken without the consent of the High Court. However, a local authority is not allowed to use wardship as an alternative to care proceedings (see s100(2) CA 1989). The local authority would have to persuade the High Court that the result which it wished to achieve could not be achieved in any other way open to it, and that there was reasonable cause to believe that the child was likely to suffer significant harm if not made a ward of court: see s100(4), (5) CA 1989. It is difficult to see how the local authority could satisfy the High Court of these factors. The circumstances point to the local authority taking care proceedings rather than trying to use wardship.

Studying the Law:
The Law Student's Handbook

Second edition

Elizabeth Cassell, MA (Cantab), LLM, Solicitor,
Principal Teaching Fellow of the University of Essex

This book is primarily intended for students who are new to the study of law or new to an LLB programme. Many students are intimidated when taking their first steps in law – the language of the subject can be obscure and different rules apply to its assessment. This is an attempt to dispel the mystique which surrounds the study and practice of law and to enable the student to make a confident start.

The book is divided into separate parts for ease of reference. So that students know where to begin when everybody else around them seems to be making a confident start, an introduction is included to the law department, the scheme of study of law and the basic study skills, including use of the law library. There is a brief introduction to the legal process – the common law and equity, the court system, doctrine of precedent and principles of statutory interpretation – and also an introduction to European law, with a new chapter on the Human Rights Act 1998 being added to this edition.

Finally, some guidance is given on the academic skills of research, the writing and presentation to be applied to all aspects of the course, including examinations, and an introduction to the legal professions. There is also a considerably expanded chapter on legal ethics, as well as advice on a career in law and alternative careers with law.

For further information on contents or to place an order, please contact:

Mail Order
Old Bailey Press
200 Greyhound Road
London
W14 9RY

Telephone No: 020 7381 7407
Fax No: 020 7386 0952
Website: www.oldbaileypress.co.uk

ISBN 1 85836 431 0
Soft cover 246 x 175 mm
276 pages approx   £11.95
Publication date September 2001

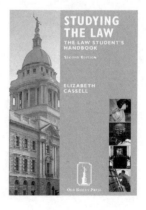

Studying the Law: The Law Student's Handbook

Second edition

Elizabeth Cassell, MA (Cantab), LLM, Solicitor,
Principal Teaching Fellow of the University of Essex

Suggested Solutions to Past Examination Questions 1998–1999

The Suggested Solutions series provides examples of full answers to the questions regularly set by examiners. Each suggested solution has been broken down into three stages: general comment, skeleton solution and suggested solution. The examination questions included within the text are taken from past examination papers set by the London University. The full opinion answers will undoubtedly assist you with your research and further your understanding and appreciation of the subject in question.

Only £6.95 Published January 2001

Constitutional Law
ISBN: 1 85836 389 6

Jurisprudence and Legal Theory
ISBN: 1 85836 393 4

Contract Law
ISBN: 1 85836 390 X

Land Law
ISBN: 1 85836 394 2

Criminal Law
ISBN: 1 85836 391 8

Law of Tort
ISBN: 1 85836 395 0

English Legal System
ISBN: 1 85836 392 6

Law of Trusts
ISBN: 1 85836 396 9

Forthcoming titles of Suggested Solutions 1999–2000 due early December 2001

Company Law
ISBN: 1 85836 442 6

Family Law
ISBN: 1 85836 445 0

European Union Law
ISBN: 1 85836 443 4

Public International Law
ISBN: 1 85836 446 9

Evidence
ISBN: 1 85836 444 2

For further information on contents or to place an order, please contact:
Mail Order
Old Bailey Press
200 Greyhound Road
London
W14 9RY

Telephone No: 020 7381 7407
Fax No: 020 7386 0952
Website: www.oldbaileypress.co.uk

Law Update 2001

Law Update 2002 edition – due February 2002

An annual review of the most recent developments in specific legal subject areas, useful for law students at degree and professional levels, others with law elements in their courses and also practitioners seeking a quick update.

Published around February every year, the Law Update summarises the major legal developments during the course of the previous year. In conjunction with Old Bailey Press textbooks it gives the student a significant advantage when revising for examinations.

Contents
Administrative Law • Civil and Criminal Procedure • Company Law • Conflict of Laws • Constitutional Law • Contract Law • Conveyancing • Criminal Law • Criminology • English Legal System • Equity and Trusts • European Union Law • Evidence • Family Law • Jurisprudence • Land Law • Law of International Trade • Public International Law • Revenue Law • Succession • Tort

For further information on contents or to place an order, please contact:

Mail Order
Old Bailey Press
200 Greyhound Road
London
W14 9RY

Telephone No: 020 7381 7407
Fax No: 020 7386 0952
Website: www.oldbaileypress.co.uk

ISBN 1 85836 385 3
Soft cover 246 x 175 mm
408 pages £9.95
Published March 2001

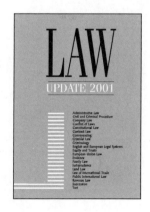

Old Bailey Press

The Old Bailey Press integrated student law library is tailor-made to help you at every stage of your studies from the preliminaries of each subject through to the final examination. The series of Textbooks, Revision WorkBooks, 150 Leading Cases/Casebooks and Cracknell's Statutes are interrelated to provide you with a comprehensive set of study materials.

You can buy Old Bailey Press books from your University Bookshop, your local Bookshop, direct using this form, or you can order a free catalogue of our titles from the address shown overleaf.

The following subjects each have a Textbook, 150 Leading Cases/Casebook, Revision WorkBook and Cracknell's Statutes unless otherwise stated.

Administrative Law
Commercial Law
Company Law
Conflict of Laws
Constitutional Law
Conveyancing (Textbook and Casebook)
Criminal Law
Criminology (Textbook and Sourcebook)
English and European Legal Systems
Equity and Trusts
Evidence
Family Law
Jurisprudence: The Philosophy of Law (Textbook, Sourcebook and
    Revision WorkBook)
Land: The Law of Real Property
Law of International Trade
Law of the European Union
Legal Skills and System
Obligations: Contract Law
Obligations: The Law of Tort
Public International Law
Revenue Law (Textbook,
    Sourcebook and Revision
    WorkBook)
Succession

Mail order prices:	
Textbook	£14.95
150 Leading Cases/Casebook	£9.95
Revision WorkBook	£7.95
Cracknell's Statutes	£9.95
Suggested Solutions 1998–1999	£6.95
Law Update 2001	£9.95

To complete your order, please fill in the form below:

Module	Books required	Quantity	Price	Cost
		Postage		
		TOTAL		

For Europe, add 15% postage and packing (£20 maximum).
For the rest of the world, add 40% for airmail.

ORDERING

By telephone to Mail Order at 020 7381 7407, with your credit card to hand.

By fax to 020 7386 0952 (giving your credit card details).

Website: www.oldbaileypress.co.uk

By post to: Mail Order, Old Bailey Press, 200 Greyhound Road, London W14 9RY.

When ordering by post, please enclose full payment by cheque or banker's draft, or complete the credit card details below. You may also order a free catalogue of our complete range of titles from this address.

We aim to despatch your books within 3 working days of receiving your order.

Name

Address

Postcode   Telephone

Total value of order, including postage: £

I enclose a cheque/banker's draft for the above sum, or

charge my   ☐ Access/Mastercard   ☐ Visa   ☐ American Express
Card number

☐☐☐☐ ☐☐☐☐ ☐☐☐☐ ☐☐☐☐

Expiry date   ☐☐☐☐

Signature: ....Date: ....